ILLINOIS STATE PARKS

*A Complete Outdoor
Recreation Guide
for
Campers, Boaters, Anglers
Skiers, Hikers and Outdoor Lovers*

Bill Bailey

Glovebox Guidebooks of America

To our readers: Travel outdoors entails some unavoidable risks. Know your limitations, be prepared, be alert, use good judgment, think safety and enjoy Illinois' terrific outdoors. Be bold!

Copyright ©1995; editorial revisions 1998 by *Glovebox Guidebooks of America/Bill Bailey*

Cover design by Dan Jacalone, cover photo by Willard Clay
Editor, Bill Cornish
Managing Editor, Penny Bailey

Published by   *Glovebox Guidebooks of America*
                          1112 Washburn Place East
                          Saginaw, Michigan 48602-2977
                          (800) 289-4843 or (517) 792-8363

Library of Congress, CIP

Bailey, William L., 1952-

Illinois State Parks Guidebook
(A Glovebox Guidebook of America publication)
ISBN 1-881139-11-5

Printed in the United States of America

Illinois State Parks

A Complete Recreation Guide

by Bill Bailey

Author's note

Much inspiration for the additional historical research for this book came from the *Lincoln-Douglas Debate* reenactments organized by *C-SPAN* and Brian Lamb during the summer and fall of my research. Illinois is blessed with great natural beauty and a fascinating political history.

In many ways, Illinois' state parks are the keepers of the state's history.

Thanks *C-SPAN* and *all* of the wonderful host communities and dedicated volunteers for the added inspiration and terrific history lesson.

And if this mention doesn't get me on *C-SPAN's Booknotes,* Mr. Lamb should know that I write in the evening; on a computer; it took nearly one year; my favorite state park is Starved Rock; I was born in Bay City, Michigan in 1952; I have two sons; and, Brian, if you want to know more you'll just need to schedule a taping.

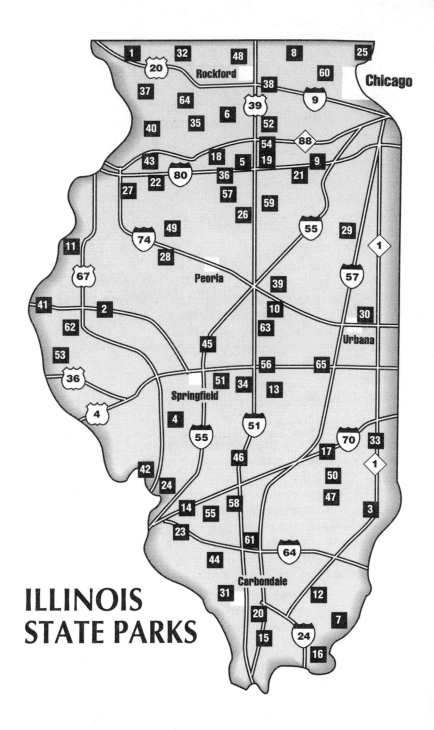

ILLINOIS
STATE PARKS

Contents

Introduction

Camping, Boating,
Fishing, Hiking,
Skiing and Hunting 7

State Parks and Recreation Areas

Introduction

Welcome to a guidebook that is just a beginning and to a state park system that's never exactly what you think it is. Welcome to sprawling parks and natural areas that never stop growing and improving. Welcome to unique places to rest—or play—where you can stay in wonderful modern lodges or in shady campgrounds, enjoy regional history, fish, hunt, go pleasure boating, canoe, cycle, sightsee, picnicking or hike. Welcome to Illinois' terrific state parks!

These one-of-a-kind open spaces and wonderful family places of the Illinois State Parks system are charming and rustic, sometimes modern, often wild—always friendly and exciting places—for unlimited recreation activities for every family member.

With all of its Midwestern charm and sparkling vitality, Illinois' state parks are a wonderland of diversity from the sandy beaches of Lake Michigan in the north, to the grassy prairies of its middle to the rolling hills and rugged cliffs of Southern Illinois. You can rough it in a primitive backpack campground, bring along a tent or RV and set up in a Class A campground, or pamper yourself in a resort lodge or soothing woodland cabin.

Almost anything you're looking for in the great outdoors is in Illinois. In addition to the scenic beauty are opportunities for enjoying dozens of outdoor pursuits including rock climbing, Jet Skiing, renting a paddle boat, slow walking along shady footpaths, water and cross-country skiing, nature photography, or perhaps jogging, bird watching, sky watching or just people watching. At rest or at play, "park it" in Illinois state parks.

The Illinois State Parks system has it all. This book is your comprehensive guide offering incredible detail about each great park, every campground, fishing tips and places to go. Descriptions of hundreds of miles of hiking and equestrian trails, water resources and waterfalls, swimming, boat launches, natural areas, wildlife watching and nature notes, lodges and cabins, day-use areas, game courts, nearby attractions and much more about the many facilities of the state parks and natural areas in Illinois.

From the fertile rolling farmlands of central Illinois to the palisades of the northwest corner, to the Mississippi bottomlands and rock outcropping of the southern tip, Illinois has diversity, which is why each year more and more visitors are traveling to the parks, camping, or fishing, picnicking or hiking the rugged and varied terrain's of Illinois.

Hours: Almost all of the parks are open sunrise to 10 p.m., but the hours do vary. Most park offices are open 8 a.m. to 4 p.m., but the busy staff in some parks can also be found in the park working and patrolling.

Pets: They must be on a leash at all times.

Campgrounds: Statewide, including state forest and conservation areas, there are 70 campgrounds, 12 state parks campgrounds that take advance registrations for a small fee. Call (217) 782-7454 or (312) 814-2070. You will find descriptions of the many fine campgrounds and recommendations on particular camping sites. All campgrounds are well-maintained and clean, but vary in services and facilities offered. All have drinking water, either flush or vault-type toilets, picnic tables and fire rings or grills. Some have park stores, camping equipment, rent-a-camps and electricity. Call ahead for group camping. Facilities for the disabled are being rapidly improved in camping areas and all facilities in the parks system. It is the goal of the department to eventually have most facilities accessible.

A camping permit must be obtained upon arrival at the site from parks personnel or campground host. If staff is available, you can usually pick a site, set up your camp and register on the spot.

Both group camping and family camping are limited to 14 nights in a 30-day period. Check out time is 3 p.m. Rent-A-Camps are available at a number of parks for a nominal fee for use of a wall tent and camping gear.

Class A sites are the most developed sites, they typically include nearby showers, electricity and vehicular access; Class B/E sites have electricity and vehicular access; Class B/S sites have showers and vehicular access; Class C, vehicular access; Class D, tent or primitive (walk-in or back-pack); and Class E sites, group youth camping. Some discounts of camping fees are available to senior citizens and disabled persons.

Lodges: Lodges, cabins and dining rooms are important features of Illinois Beach, Starved Rock, Pere Marquette, Giant City, Rend Lake and Eagle Creek. White Pines and Cave-In-Rock have cabins and dining rooms only. For further information call (217) 782-6752 or (217) 782-7454. Reservations for lodging should be made with lodge managers, as these facilities are leased to private concessionaires. Nature trails, scenic views and a wonderful atmosphere for meetings are featured at these parks.

Swimming: Only at designated areas in the following parks: Clinton Lake, Illinois Beach, Lake Le-Aqua-Na, Moraine View, Sam Dale, Stephen Forbes, Wolf Creek and at the swimming pool and small water slide at Dixon Springs.

Interpretive programs: Many state parks offer informal or seasonal educational programs designed to provide park users with a better understanding and appreciation of public lands and their resources. Year-round interpretive programs are available at Illinois Beach State Park (708) 662-4811; Fort Massac State Park (618) 524-4712; Starved Rock State Park (815) 667-4906; Volo Bog Natural Area (815) 344-1294; Goose Lake Prairie State Natural Area (815) 942-2899; I & M Canal (815) 942-9501; Kankakee State Park (815) 933-1383; Pere Marquette State

Park (618) 786-3323; and Buffalo Rock State Park (815) 433-2220.

Hiking: There are more than 200 trails totaling hundreds of miles in the state parks from the rugged bluffs at Mississippi Palisades in the northwest to the wooded ravines at Fox Ridge to the soaring canyons at Starved Rock State Park.

Bike touring: Roadways in the state parks are great places to bike. Some parks have dedicated bike paths—like the great bike trails at Moraine Hill or along the I & M Canal—while many parks restrict bike traffic to certain roadways only. For more information about bicycling in Illinois call (217) 782-7454.

Winter sports: Generally speaking, the state parks are open and encourage winter activities that typically include ice fishing, cross-country skiing, hiking, camping and snowmobiling.

Fishing: Anglers 16 years and older should have an Illinois license or a combined sportsman's license to fish on state sites. Illinois residents who are 65 years old or older, or who are physically disabled, are exempted from the licensing requirement. A handy fishing booklet is given to you that details rules and regulations when you purchase your license. The state also offers several fine fishing guides for certain geographical areas around the state; check at the office to see if there is a fishing guide for your park or area.

Snowmobiling: 21 state parks and recreation or natural areas maintain trails. For machine registration information call (217) 782-2138.

Hunting: Hunters using state property must hold a state hunting license or combined sportsman's license, as well as all applicable permits and stamps. Shooting times, dates and other specifics often change. It's best to call ahead for details.

For more information about Illinois State Parks, call (217) 782-7454

Resort Lodges / Conference Centers

Tucked into Illinois' finest natural environs, the resort lodges range from elegant contemporary to stately and majestic.

Most are open year-round, complete with modern meeting facilities, fine dining, golf, tennis, swimming pools, game rooms, exercise rooms, whirlpools, cocktail lounges, views of parks, rivers and lakes, playgrounds, marinas with courtesy docks, gift shops, horse rentals, coffee shops, air-conditioning and much more for every type of group or family.

Reservations may be made by calling the individual resorts.

Cave-In-Rock Restaurant and Lodging: (618) 289-4545

Eagle Creek Resort: 128 rooms, 10 suites, (800) 876-3245

Giant City Lodge: 34 cabins, Bald Knob Dining Room, (618) 457-4921

Illinois Beach Resort: (217) 782-7454

Pere Marquette Lodge: 50 lodge cabins and 22 natural stone cabins, (618) 786-2331

Rend Lake Resort: Boatel, marina, (618) 629-2211

Starved Rock Lodge: 72 guest rooms, 18 cabins, (815) 667-4211

White Pines Inn: 25 one-room cabins, main lodge, (815) 946-3817

1 Apple River Canyon State Park

Land: 297 acres   Water: Apple River

If you have been lucky enough to have spent some time at Mississippi Palisades State Park, less than an hour south of Apple River, and have a chance to make the drive up to Apple River from there, take Route 78, a scenic rolling, winding road that takes you by some wonderful farms, woodlots and vistas. This may be one of the most scenic drives in the state. The Apple Valley area looks like the label on a jelly jar or a wine bottle. You'll like it.

You turn the corner into the park, and there's a huge bluff and a gentle meandering stream and tiny park store with a 1950s lunch counter that has tongue and groove pine paneling and great food. This may be the prettiest entrance to any state park in the state. Off the beaten path, near the

Wisconsin border, the small 297 acre park is genuinely pleasant. This is no tourist trap. This corner of Jo Daviess County is carved in stone, large limestone bluffs, deep ravines, springs, stream, and wildlife characterize this area which was once a part of a vast sea bottom that stretched from the Alleghenies to the Rockies. In many ways, not much has changed, and I especially hope the little lunch counter never changes.

The park is centered around the cool and clear Apple River and the sheer walled cliffs of the canyon, which has been cut through the ages. Geologists are attracted to the area because it is part of the driftless area, untouched by glaciers. The Apple River enters the park from the northwest and promptly changes its course by a nearly right-angle turn. The turn is in the center of the park where a village called Millville once stood and was established in the 1830s. A grist mill also once stood in the area.

More than 330 people lived there by 1838. The east-west Elfrink stage coach ran from Chicago to Galena, on which passengers traveled the 160-mile distance through Millville. Much of this area was dotted with lead mines that were first mined by Indians. They exchanged the lead with traders, and later the lead was used to make bullets and sheet metal.

Apple River Canyon was acquired by the state in 1933, and was dedicated in October of that year.

Information and Activities

Apple River Canyon State Park
8763 E. Canyon
Apple River, IL 61001
(815) 745-3302

Directions: From Route 78 (which travels north and south), take East Canyon Road west to the park entrance. The park is about three miles south of the Wisconsin border and almost directly west of Waukegan.

Information: The park office is in the middle of the park, north of the Apple River and open weekdays 8 a.m. - 4 p.m. or by chance. Staffers are often working in the park when the office is closed.

Campground: The small, very private Canyon Ridge camping area has 50 primitive campsites. There are no electrical hookups or showers. Water is available for camping use. They do not accept reservations. Call ahead on Friday evenings, holidays or weekends to check availability. There are two small loops, sites 1-24 and 25-50. Organized youth group camping is available in the Walnut Grove area.

Almost all of the campsites are separated by vegetation, and many have gravel pads and picnic tables.

Sites 1-3 have tall staghorn sumac plants that act as a canopy for shade. Sites 10 and 11 are shady and grassy and have a view of a small valley. Sites 1-23 are grass covered with no gravel, but the area seems like it would dry quickly after rainfall.

Boating: Boating is not permitted in the Apple River.

Fishing: There are some smallmouth bass. They must be at least 14-inches in length with a one fish per day limit in the tiny Apple River. Fly fishermen often cast small poppers at the smallmouth; others use small spinners in the clear waters.

Hiking: The Tower Rock River Trail head at the concession stand near the entrance to the park is difficult and one mile long. This trail has a panoramic view of the day-use areas of the park. The four other trails at the park are easy walking and include Pine Ridge Trail, River Route, Sunset and Primrose Lane. Most of the trails are wooded and lightly used.

Day-use areas: No swimming or wading are allowed, although they are tempting in the almost gin-clear Apple River on a hot day. With sheer-walled cliffs as a backdrop, many picnic areas, complete with nearby toilets, make for terrific day use. Devil's Hollow is a very nice picnicking area on the west end of the small park. There is limited playground equipment in the main picnic area and near youth camping.

Nature: Extremely sharp, sheer vertical cliffs along the Apple River may rise to 250 feet above the stream. Most of the glacial rock is known as Galena dolomite, which is hard, and massive and usually rich in lead and ore. Fossils can often be seen in the dolomite, usually of sponge-like animals. The surface view of fossils looks like a sunflower head after the seed has been removed; in fact, they are often called Sunflower Coral.

Several types of habitat account for the abundance of trees and wildflowers. The stream community has many black willow, hackberry, silver maple and sycamore along its banks. Shrubs include meadow sweet spirea and heart-faced willow. Several kinds of smartweed also grow in the wetlands.

The richest areas plants are in the lowland communities just above the shoreline. Here, handsome species of basswood, sugar maple, black walnut, shagbark hickory, white ash and burr oak can be found. These forest denizens form such a heavy canopy that only isolated rays from the springtime sun reach the plants to urge blossoming. Sharp-lobed hepatica, bloodroot, bellwort, purple wake robin, white trillium, wild ginger, false Solomon's seal, wild lily of the valley and cicely bloom there.

Steep, shaded north-facing wooded slopes provide the habitat for white pine, which are usually found more northerly. The rare paper birch is also seen in this area. On drier wooded slope areas are aspen, red cedar, wild black cherry, black, white and yellow chestnut and others. The understory is more open than the understory in the lowlands, with the result that wildflowers bloom later in the spring. They include yellow golden rod, Alexander's, fringed loosestrife, round fruited St. Johnswort and bergamot.

It's not necessary to leave your car to enjoy many colorful wildflowers, since many of the showy plants appear as roadside weeds. Yellow rockets, of the mustard family, abound in the spring; tall cinquefoil, wild parsley and even primrose continue the yellow theme. The small white flowered verbena flowers from July until frost. During autumn the purple iron weed glows along the roadside. Perhaps the most interesting aspect of the state park is the presence of several distinctive plants which apparently survived as glacial relics. The driftless area seemingly served as a refuge for those plants during glacial times. Birdseye primrose and Moschatel are two tiny wildflowers that grow on dolomite ledges known at no other locality in Illinois. Nearly as rare are the jeweled shooting star, round leafed sullivantia, American stickseed and woodland white violet.

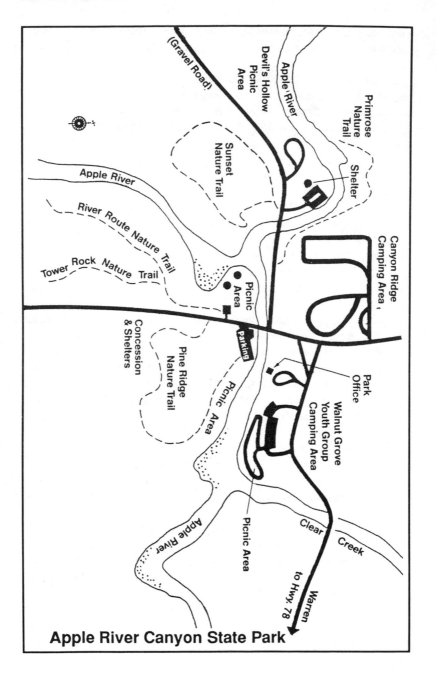

Apple River Canyon State Park

Ferns are plentiful, particularily in the canyon. Commonly seen are maidenhair, walking ferns, fragile ferns, rattlesnake ferns, lady fern, and others.

Most of the common mammals (whitetail deer, rabbits, etc.) make their home in the park. Less obvious, however, are the stripped skunk, long-tail weasel, red and gray fox, muskrat and gray squirrel. Nocturnal critters include mink, coyote, short-tailed and least shrews, eastern mole, 13-lined ground squirrel, white footed and meadow jumping mouse, and vole. Beavers are also seen at the park.

Only the timber rattler is poisonous among snakes occasionally seen in the park. You might encounter the blue racer, black pilot or garter snake. The eastern milk snake may also be seen.

Special notes: The most interesting thing about Apple River is the occasional use by a group of Chicago-based amateur astronomers that travel to the park at dark. There are no electrical lights at the campground, which makes it one of the few places within a two-hour drive of Chicago where serious night sky watchers can be in lightless condition.

Hardy astronomers relish the primitive campground with its lack of electricity and dark skies. They've even nicknamed the campground "Mt. Jennings Observatory," which is taken from the H.G. Wells "War of the World" radio show, and was the fictional mountaintop observatory in Chicago often mentioned during the famous show.

Their wonderful enthusiasm and nocturnal hobby certainly underline the fact that state parks are versatile places that can be used for much more than fishing, camping and eating way too much from the grills.

Winter: Sledding is a popular activity.

Nearby attractions: Grant's home in Galena; Long Hollow Scenic Tower near Elizabeth; Galena Water Park; and Silver Eagle Casino cruiser near East Dubuque.

2 *Argyle Lake State Park*

Land: 1,500 acres Water: 93-acre lake

The gobbles of captive turkeys and gentle cooing of doves in the distance greet visitors to the log cabin day-use area, where two log cabins are often used for picnicking and educational programs. The fowl, which include a variety of birds and watefowl, are displayed near the park office and are donations of a local townsmen.

Argyle Hollow, now Argyle Lake, once was the tract that high-wheeled stage coaches rumbled along crossing forested hills and distant valleys between Galena and Beardstown. The region has long been a source of coal, clay and limestone. In fact, often when a fella needed extra cash, he might dig his own "drift mine" to supplement his personal income. In the park you can see some remnants of this early entrepreneurship.

In 1948, the state bought the lands from homesteaders and farmers and erected a dam which flooded the hollow and created the fishing lake and was dedicated to the citizens of Illinois. The dam was completed in 1948 on a tributary of the east fork of the LaMoine River.

Recent renovations to the camping and day-use areas offer evidence of the state's commitment to Argyle Lake State Park and the well-being and positive experience of its visitors. The improvements make this park a great family outdoor destination.

Information and Activities

Argyle Lake State Park
R.R. 2
Colchester, IL 62326
(309) 776-3422

Directions: In Colchester, turn on Cole St. at the Food Mart. Take it north to the park entrance.

Information: The park closes at 10 p.m., and the park office is open weekdays. Staff is often in the park, if the office is closed.

Campground: The 86 site, Class A camping area is comprised of three loops, A, B and C. The Class B area has 54 sites and all campers have access to the showers.

The concession stand, built above the scenic watery cove at the boat ramp offers camping supplies, sandwiches, ice cream, boat rental, bait and firewood, and is open Memorial Day - Labor Day, Friday-Sunday, 7 a.m. - 8 p.m. and Monday - Thursday, 7 a.m. - 6 p.m.

You may register for camping at the little blue building near the entrance. It has a drop box for your camping registration form, maps of the park and other posted information.

Renovations to the campground in the recent past have improved the shower building, individual camping sites, a road and upgraded services to all size camping rigs.

In the A loop (Class A), the Twisted Oak Nature Trailhead can be accessed at site 7A, while the first camping site in this loop is for disabled campers. There are three such sites in the park. Sites 16A and 17A have a view of a shallow wooded valley and plenty of shade near a vault toilet. Sites 11A, 13A and 15A also have plenty of shade and would be considered the best spots in this loop. All other sites have young trees planted and will someday be shady, very nice camping sites.

In the B loop (Class A), sites 8B, 10B, 12B and 13B, and near the water and under shade. Site 22B, is near a jumbo poison ivy vine that makes its way up a tree; 24B is a bit more open, overlooking a tiny meadow, while a foot trail starts near site 29B. At the end of the loop is 37B-39B backed up against a wooded area, private and near a vault toilet.

In the C Loop (Class A), sites 27C-28C are heavily shaded. Other sites in the 20s are fairly open; sites in the teens are very open, lacking much shade.

Boating: A number of courtesy docks float in front of the concession stand, and the lake has a 10 hp limit on boat engines. Rental boats (flat bottom Johnboats and eight canoes), firewood, bait and other supplies are available at the elevated concession stand. Because of the quiet waters, many families rent boats and explore the lake; some even catch a few bluegill. Campers may leave their boat at the courtesy dock while staying in the park, or dock space can be rented seasonally. The launch is a one-lane hard-surfaced ramp with parking for about 30 cars and trailers.

Fishing: Right below the concession stand/tackle shop is very good bluegill fishing in the evening. Children can stand along the gently sloping bank and hook up many bluegills on summer evenings. Simple bobber and live bait (wax or red worms) rigs work well here.

The best bluegill fishing spot is in front of the dam, about four feet out and two feet deep. Bluegill anglers should also try to find the old Christmas trees that have been sunken in a variety of locations around the lake for fish cover. The bait shopkeeper says muskies are usually picked up by bass anglers, or buck tails and large minnows may produce muskies,

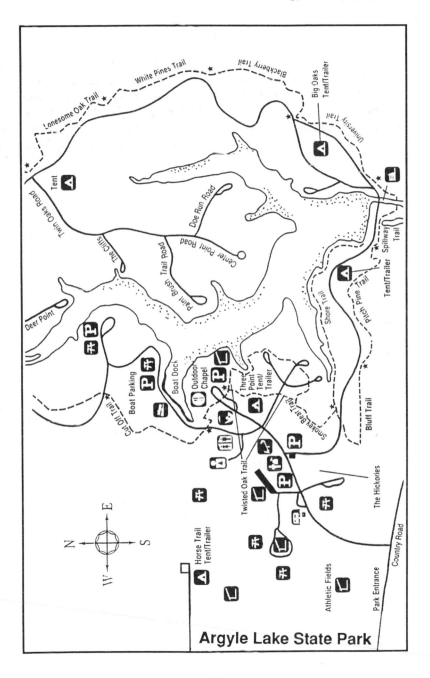

Argyle Lake State Park

but they are few and far between. Bass anglers use rubber worms in the weeds, and chartreuse-colored spinners. Try brightly colored lures; the water is not typically clear in the small lake.

Creel limits: Bass, one per day over 15 inches. Bass between 12-15 inches should be returned. Channel catfish, six daily.

Hiking: A new self-guided trail has been developed featuring a tour through the wooded park lands and offering natural history information. The interconnecting trails at the park wind around the park's main road for about six miles. Trailheads are scattered through the park and many of the hiking trails are moderately difficult, taking walkers up and down steep hills and some steep banks and stairways close to the lake.

In some places, horse trails join the hiking trails. One trail takes you near the dam and spillway, over small wooden bridges, and through bottomlands. During wet periods, some trails may not be passable or are muddy.

Day-use areas: The grove of white pine is terrific for all types of day-users. A quality playground, ball fields, volleyball courts, plenty of open spaces, 300 picnic tables, two reservable shelters, and more than 120 acres offers plenty of space and amenities for visitors.

Originally just a fishing lake state park, the day-use amenities, upgraded camping and general improvements are making Argyle Lake increasingly attractive for family vacations and weekend getaways. There is no beach or swimming at the lake.

Nature: The oak/hickory forest and outdoor education programming during the summers are welcome additions to the park. Seasonal naturalists offer guided hikes, birdwalks, natural history lessons, campside theater and more. There is a flier that details weekly programs available at the park office.

Hunting: 800 acres are used for seasonal hunting of archery and shotgun deer and turkey. Doves are also hunted at the unit; call the site superintendent for more information.

3   *Beall Woods State Park*

**Land: 635 acres   Water: Beall Woods Lake
and Wabash River**

As you turn into the entrance drive of Beall Woods, you might hear the balling of cattle, the whinny of an old saddle horse, or the flapping of an America flag straining against the wind. The rich agricultural soils spawn lush croplands that give way to one of Illinois' finest natural areas and hiker's heaven.

Owned by the Beall family for 102 years, the property was allegedly sold to be cleared of trees and farmed, but the interest and efforts of a variety of groups and individuals helped create the original acquisition. The heavily wooded area was purchased by the state of Illinois in 1965, invoking the law of eminent domain against an unwilling seller to preserve the virgin woodlands for recreational use for generations to come.

Today, the park is mainly used for environmental education activities and hiking. There are four walking loops that total 10 miles that pass by bottomlands, along creeks and a river, upland forests to a rocky ford.

The park is coming back from economic hard times. Some of the play equipment needs upgrading and the trails need grooming, but also for those reasons, solitary hikers can enjoy a quiet experience. The site is open year-round.

Information and Activities

Beall Woods State Park
R.R. 2
Mt. Carmel, IL 62863
(618) 298-2442

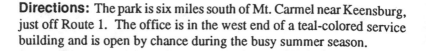

Directions: The park is six miles south of Mt. Carmel near Keensburg, just off Route 1. The office is in the west end of a teal-colored service building and is open by chance during the busy summer season.

Camping: There is no campground at the unit.

Boating: The first road on the right takes you to the single-land concrete ramp with a small wooded dock that points out into the tiny lake. There is parking for about 20 vehicles in the asphalt parking lot. Small boats with trolling motors are allowed. There is a nice day-use area with tables and shelter near the tiny ramp area.

Fishing: Fishing is typically good at the tiny 14-acre Beall Woods Lake that has less than a half-mile of shoreline and is getting shallower by the year. Many shoreline areas are weedy, making fishing from the shore sometimes difficult. Some fishing piers on the lake get you out over the water so that you can cast past the weeds and shallows.

There are populations of largemouth bass, sunfish, crappie and channel catfish. There is a catchable trout program for the small lake where you

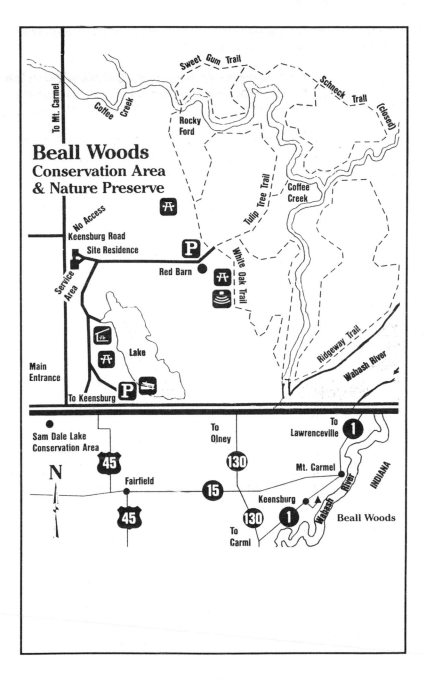

Beall Woods
Conservation Area
& Nature Preserve

Sweet Gum Trail

Schneck Trail (closed)

Coffee Creek

To Mt. Carmel

Rocky Ford

Tulip Tree Trail

Coffee Creek

No Access
Keensburg Road
Site Residence

Red Barn

White Oak Trail

Service Area

Ridgeway Trail

Wabash River

Lake

Main Entrance

To Keensburg

Sam Dale Lake
Conservation Area

N

To Olney

To Lawrenceville

To 1

130

Mt. Carmel

INDIANA

45

Fairfield

15

Keensburg

Wabash River

45

130

1

Beall Woods

To Carmi

may keep five per day and must have a salmon stamp. The season is closed from March 15 to the first Saturday in April.

Hiking: If you are hiking during the spring, summer or early fall, wear long pants, long-sleeved shirts, a hat and plenty of bug repellent. Early May is the worst time for mosquitoes.

Beall Woods has four very interesting trails with a unique character that help celebrate the Woods' registration as a national landmark in the U.S. Registry of Natural Landmarks. The site is referred to as the "University of Trees," where 64 species have been identified and about 300 trees have 30-inch trunks at breast height. State champion-sized species at the unit include Shumard red oak, green ash, sugarberry and sweet gum.

White Oak Trail: The trail has a terrific variety of vegetation and interesting forest conditions that wander along both an upland and through a moist bottomland along a creek. Some of the largest trees you'll discover in the entire state are along this trail that also takes you to the confluence of the Coffee Creek and Wabash River. You are in the middle of one of the largest virgin timber stands in the Midwest. The trail is less than two miles in length.

Ridgeway Trail: This 1.75-mile long trail is a memorial to Robert Ridgeway, one of America's foremost ornithologists, who spent his boyhood here. If the creek is low, you can access the trail, which takes you through a pecan grove and an opening with Kentucky coffee trees.

Sweet Gum Trail: This 1.5-mile long trail fords a creek, which you should try during low water times only, and meanders along shady, damp bottomlands and along a creek.

Tulip Tree Trail: Dry and easy, this 1.5-mile long loop traces the Coffee Creek along a tiny bluff. Some signage is in place, but bring your wildflower and tree finder guides.

Red Barn: A refurbished gable-roofed barn serves as a focal point for nature center activities at the park featuring seed displays, native woods of Illinois, and lots of other small interpretive exhibits. All of the trails can be accessed from the Red barn, which has day-use amenities nearby.

4   *Beaver Dam State Park*

Land: 744 acres   Water: 59-acre lake

Beaver Dam's bait shop owners call the trout that are planted in the main lake each October "rich man's carp." Then, in the next breath, they'll tell you everything you need to know to find and catch the tasty denizens. Per surface acre, the small lake has one of the highest fishing pressures in the entire state. Largemouth bass and bluegill are very popular, abundant and, according to local anglers, "the best eatin' in the Midwest."

The lake became well-known as a quality fishing spot in the early 1890s when 18 men from the Carlinville area formed the Beaver Dam Lake Club and spent $2,500 to build a dam at each end of the lake, doubling its size. Then the forested area became the property of the family of Sarah Rhodes, who for some time operated a small hotel at the present site of the superintendent's residence.

Only one-half mile north of the site is Macoupin Station. At one time there had been a cluster of houses and a small railway station where guests were met by a prancing horse-drawn coach and returned to the lodge for a quiet evening. When people took to cars, the little railroad and hotel disappeared and in 1947 the state acquired the original 425 acres for park use.

Information and Activities

Beaver Dam State Park
P. O. Box 127
Plainview, IL 62676
(217) 854-8020

Directions: The park is seven miles south of Carlinville. Watch carefully for directional signs.

Campground: Usually full on holiday weekends and surprisingly busy on other summer weekends, the small shady camping area is often lodging for avid fishermen and typical families at play. The Class A area has 59 sites, and there are 18 primitive tent camping locations in the park.

All of the sites in the Class A area have gravel pads, picnic tables and concrete fire pits. One newer shower building serves all of the campers and there are four vault toilets in the main campground. Reservations are not taken at the park.

With most of the sites about the same in size and other common factors, the parks staff says that the most popular sites are near the shower building, sites 13, 17, 18, 25, 27, 28, 30 and 39.

Firewood is sold at the concession stand, or you may collect dead and down wood (no cutting) or visit the nearby sawmill for a box of dried wood for a couple of bucks.

Fishing: The tiny concession stand is a terrific place for a bite to eat, lots of fish talk, fishing stories, maybe even some fishing lies, and a warm spot to pick up some additional angling supplies and bait. There are only

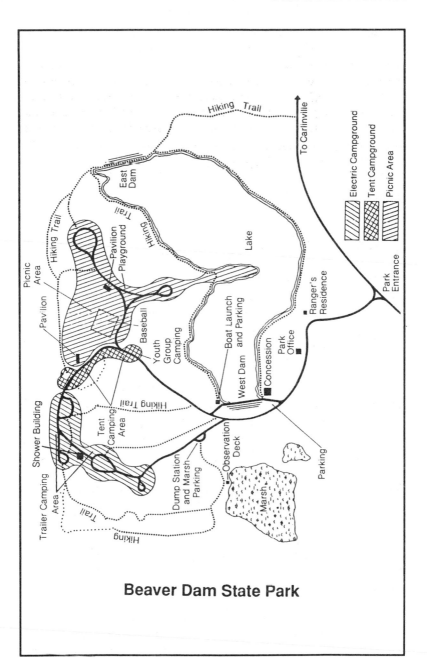

Beaver Dam State Park

two tables and five counter seats at the stand, but it is clean and the smells of home cooking waft their way into the parking lot. The concession is open weekdays, 7 a.m. - 7 p.m. and weekends 6 a.m. - 8 p.m. April - October.

Bluegills are tops in the lake, with largemouth bass a close second. In the early spring, bluegill action can be the best anywhere if fishermen use waxworms, small meal worms, and red wigglers and crickets as the season goes on. The lake has a maximum depth of nine feet, and an average depth of about seven feet with 1.7 miles of shoreline. A small fishing map is available at the concession stand that details depth and locations.

Trout can be taken on mini-marshmallows tipped with a meal worm, roaster-tails, and a teardrop with a waxworm through the ice. Some anglers use corn, but many chatty local anglers said that isn't productive.

The lake is a good top-water bassing lake where buzz baits, crankbaits and crawdad-colored topwater lures work well near either dam and along any structure.

Crappies are abundant along the south bank, along treetops and wood. Use live bait in early season for the best of big crappies. There are a number of flat handicapped accessible areas along the lake for fishing.

Creel regulations: Bass, 15 inches mininum, 3 daily; bluegill and redear 25 daily; crappies, 9 inches in length 10 daily; channel catfish, 6 fish per day limit. No swimming or wading are alowed in the lake.

Boating: Beaver Dam has a one-lane boat launching ramp at the west end of the lake near the concession stand. No gas motors are allowed on the lake. Paddle boats, rowboats and electric motors are rented.

Hiking: Seven miles of easy trails are laid out on five systems. The Lake Trail circumnavigates the lake and offers excellent shoreline fishing opportunities. The trail south from the camping area takes hikers by a small wetland and observation deck. Pileated woodpeckers, the largest of the species, are commonly seen and heard at the park. Look for triangular-shaped holes in tree and loud jack-hammer-like rapping sounds on hollow trees in the distance. The huge woodpeckers look, and are the general size of, crows.

Hikers might also see some gray squirrels that are almost white in color in the second-growth woodlands. The "white" squirrels are actually a color phase of the gray squirrel, like the ones in Olney, IL. There are some limited first-growth forest areas in the park.

Day-use areas: Astronomy is an interesting activity that takes place in the "dark" off-the-beaten-path state park. Due to the limited amount of light pollution, some amateur astronomers, like the ones at Apple Canyon State Park, use the park for nighttime recreation.

The park maintains three reservable picnic shelters. About 100 picnic tables are strategically placed in many day-use areas that also have play equipment, grills, toilets and drinking water.

Hunting: Limited archery deer and shotgun turkey by draw are available. Call the site superintendent for details on the seasons and local regulations.

Nearby attractions: A casino riverboat is 45 minutes away. Centerville has Christmas and apple festivals and Shipman Farm Museum.

5   *Buffalo Rock State Park*

**Land: 43 acres day-use area; 1,600 acres in managed
canal area.   Water: Illinois River frontage**

More than 100,000 people annually visit the 43-acre day-use part of the park. Most stop in to see Tatonka and Serenity, the two American bison, commonly known as buffalo, that are housed in a pen about 100 yards from the park office, behind the baseball backstop. Serenity, who was born in 1981, generally stands around and watches the much younger Tatonka cruise the fence line, gently snort and smack her grass-stained lips, and swat at flies as visitors file by.

Aside from the fun of watching the big buffalo, they do represent their magnificent cousins that once roamed the hilly prairies of Illinois by the millions. Don't feed the two female buffalo; frankly, they look pretty spoiled and well cared for by the parks staff.

Buffalo Rock State Park is five miles from the Fox River Aqueduct on the north bank of the Illinois River. From atop the sandstone bluff at the summit of Buffalo Rock, you'll have a wonderful view up and down the mighty river. You are also just south of the Illinois and Michigan Canal State Trail. In the Buffalo Rock section of the canal trail, there are 26.3 miles of canal, towpath trail, finished bike trail from LaSalle to Ottawa, other state parks, shelters, day-use areas and more. You can fish at Lock 14, with some of the best fishing between Lock 13 and LaSalle.

Buffalo Rock is part of the Illinois & Michigan Canal National Heritage Corridor, the nation's first heritage corridor. As the canal builders long ago foresaw its cultural and economic benefits, preservationists today envision the waterway as a centerpiece for tourism, recreation and historical interpretation.

The corridor became a reality in 1984 when Congress enacted legislation that recognized the area's unique contribution to the nation's development. Lucky for state park and other visitors the law specifies that the canal corridor's cultural, historic, natural, recreational and economic resources will be retained, enhanced and interpreted for the benefit and inspiration of present and future generations.

The corridor features many attractions and points of interest. Here are some that are nearby the corridor: Starved Rock State Park, Matthiessen State Park, Illinois Waterway Visitors Center, Illini State Park, Gebhard Woods, W.G. Stratton Park, Goose Lake Prairie State Natural Area, Des Plaines Conservation Area, McKinley Woods, I & M Canal State Trail access, I & M Canal Visitor Center, Black Partridge Woods, Old Illinois State Penitentiary, Pitcher Nature Park, Sagawau Canyon Nature Preserve and many more. A four-color brochure is available at these and other points of interest that details the fascinating history of the canal and places to visit along the linear corridor.

Buffalo Rock State Park
I & M Canal State Access
P. O. Box 39
Ottawa, IL 61350
(815) 433-2220

I & M Canal Access at Buffalo Rock.

Directions: On the north bank of the Illinois River, two miles east of Ottawa, on Dee Bennett Co. Road, the park entrance is five miles east of Rt. 178.

Information: The park is open year-round, and the ranger's office is the first road on the right inside the park entrance.

Campground: There are only three primitive campsites in the park and you must hike or bike into them. Talk to the staff about location, rules and fees.

Fishing: The canal is stocked with channel catfish, and also has populations of largemouth bass and northern pike. The depth of the canal is only 3-4 feet and warms up quickly in the early summer which slows any sport fishing action. Rough fish can be caught with doughballs, gobs of worms and stink baits for the channel cats.

Day-use areas: Two baseball diamonds, play equipment and a 43-acre day-use area offers picnicking, two shelters (that can be reserved), grills,

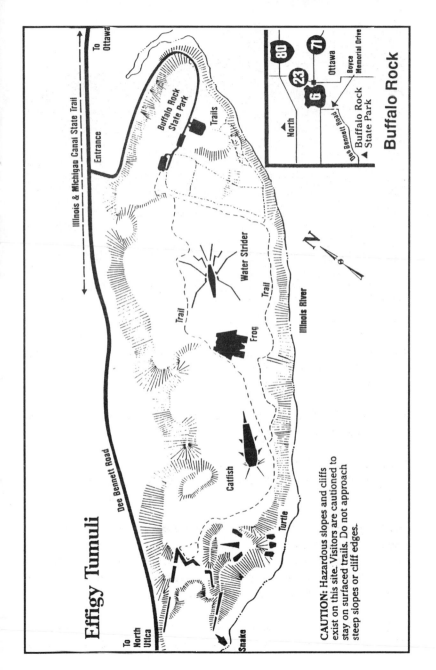

Effigy Tumuli

Buffalo Rock

To North Utica

Dee Bennett Road

Illinois & Michigan Canal State Trail

To Ottawa

Entrance

Buffalo Rock State Park

Trails

Water Strider

Trail

Trail

Frog

Illinois River

Catfish

Turtle

Snake

CAUTION: Hazardous slopes and cliffs exist on this site. Visitors are cautioned to stay on surfaced trails. Do not approach steep slopes or cliff edges.

North

80

71

23

Ottawa

6

Boyce Memorial Drive

Dee Bennett Road

Buffalo Rock State Park

hiking trails along the canal through the Effigy Tumuli Sculpture, and a fairly rough hike up and down some bluffs along the Illinois River. The park has a naturalist who offers public programs and coordinates special events that include Pioneer Days, a fishing program, music festival, bike rides, tours of the Blackball Mines, school programs and a program about the canals called Canal Capers. Snowmobiling and ice fishing are allowed on the canal during the winter. The sandstone bluffs are the most interesting natural areas in the park.

Effigy Tumuli Sculpture: The trailhead is located by the main parking lot and loops the 250-acre former mine that was once a major source of land and water pollution. It has been transformed into a unique Illinois landmark offering history buffs and outdoor enthusiasts a great hike.

The area now contains five large earthen figures, or effigies, of aquatic animals native to the areas. Represented in geometric form are a water strider, frog, catfish, turtle and snake. The earth-art was made possible by cooperation with a number of volunteers and a donation by the Ottawa Silica Company.

Inspiration for the Effigy Tumuli Sculpture was drawn from the mound building practices of prehistoric Indians in central and eastern North America that began 3,000 years ago and were often built to represent animals, man or other shapes in nature. As one of the largest earth sculptures ever built and the largest since Mt. Rushmore, the Effigy Tumuli Sculpture is a significant artwork in terms of its size, subject and use of huge heavy construction equipment.

The effort not only created artwork, it also healed scars on the landscape from the mining days. The project began in 1985 and included neutralizing 6.3 million gallons of acidic water, regrading 463,000 cubic yards of spoil material, seeding the area, establishing erosion controls, and developing a walking and viewing trail.

The earthen sculptures are probably best viewed from the air, but their size and scope from a ground-level hike is inspiring. This is a rare and wonderful example of site remediation that was ultimately an artwork— earthen art.

6 Castle Rock State Park

Land: 2,000 acres

Castle Rock, located along the quiet west banks of the Rock River in Ogle County, is a 2,000-acre day-use unit. Located across the river is the recently expanded low-impact natural area known as Lowden-Miller State Forest, a former tree and agricultural farm.

Castle Rock was set aside by the state to protect the natural resources of the area. A thin layer of glacial till covers this region and several distinctive plant species, remnants of the native forest and prairie, still exist. In one valley, 27 types of ferns have been identified and the park is one of the largest significant natural areas in northern Illinois.

The most outstanding natural features are in the dedicated (and generally off-limits!) nature preserve. Only scientific and limited educational activities are conducted in these 710 acres. The fine silt loams and sandy loam soils of the area are easily eroded and must be protected from heavy use.

The state is planning additional low-impact recreational programs consistent with state forest use at the Lowden-Miller State Forest that include additional hiking trails, hunting, nature study and management. There is a map available from the site superintendent that details the current trails, park boundary and hunting areas.

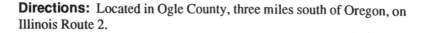

Information and Activities

Castle Rock State Park
R.R. 2
Oregon, IL 60161
(815) 732-7329

Directions: Located in Ogle County, three miles south of Oregon, on Illinois Route 2.

Campground: Canoe access only is available to 10 tent sites, which are equipped with tables and grills. The access point is at the south end of the park near the heads Oak Ridge, Lookout and Fox trails. More primitive camping is being planned; call ahead for details.

Boating: A small one-lane boat ramp offers access to the Rock River; during low water conditions only small boats can be launched from the ramp. There is no horsepower limitation on the Rock River. There is parking for about 30 cars and trailers at the launch, and toilets are nearby. The launch is across the street from the main park entrance.

Fishing: The Rock River is 34 miles long and can reach a depth of 25 feet, but it is generally slow moving and easy to navigate. The usual menu of fish species are present along the 1.5 miles of river that the park borders. Catfish are sometimes taken by shoreline anglers using stink baits, while an increasing number of bass and walleye are being taken during the spring. Drum, suckers, carp and other rough fish are also abundant. Fishing is considered only fair and seasonal in this stretch of the Rock

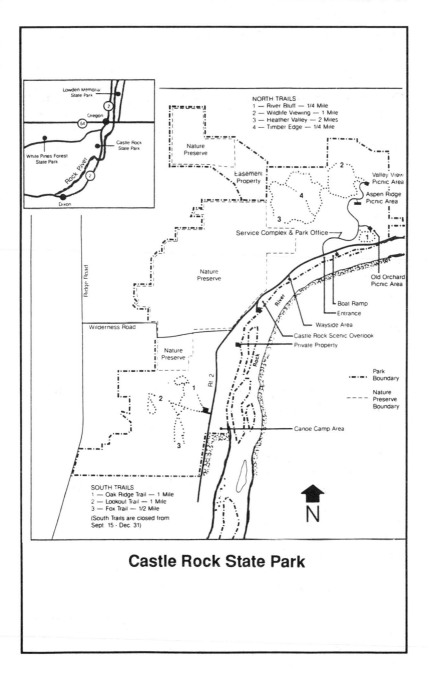

Castle Rock State Park

River.

You must release all smallmouth bass in this section of the river; you make keep six largemouth bass if they are 12 inches minimum size: six walleye with 14 inch size minimum; three northern pike with 24 inch size minimum.

Hiking: There are about six miles of hiking trails, with three short loops accessed off of Route 2 and five trails in the north part of the park. Hiking is closed in the nature preserve section of the unit in the central part of the park west of the office.

The Wildlife Viewing Trail is one mile long; the difficult to moderate trail starts near the Valley View Picnic Area and takes about 45 minutes to hike.

Castle Rock has an excellent self-guided nature trail that wanders through open fields that were once farmed, hillside prairies with steep sloping bluffs and ravines, and sandstone outcroppings which are a feature in this part of the Rock River valley.

The nature trail is about two miles long and consists of two loops. It takes about two hours to complete both loops. There are 28 trailside markers that begin at the wildlife viewing trail sign across the road from the Aspen Ridge Picnic Area. You will learn about vines, woody plants, fields of grass, twigs, leaves and bark, old stumps, shagbark hickory trees, wildflowers, wildlife, ferns, native hillside prairie, stream habitat, horsetail plants and enjoy s scenic view from atop a ridge looking down upon the lush valley floor. Birding is also good in this area; migrating warblers and waterfowl can be easily seen and heard both in spring and fall.

Self-guided trails are great for exposing youngsters to the world of nature. You don't need a live guide, just a booklet, maybe a pair of binoculars and a small hand lens or a field guide, and you can learn a ton of natural history in a pleasant family outing at Castle Rock.

Castle Rock: You will enter a small gravel parking lot off of Route 2 south of the park office. The Castle Rock'stairway disappears into the trees and takes walkers to the outcropping, which has a wonderful elevated view up and down the river corridor.

When taking the hike up to Castle Rock, please stay on the boardwalk. This is a fragile area. The rock is known as Castle Rock because it resembles a fort along the river and is comprised of St. Peter's sandstone, which underlines the entire state and only comes to the surface in a few places. It took millions of years to form this rock, but since the sandstone is so sensitive, just walking on it can damage it. There are two small observation decks, which give a great view of the tree-lined river in the foreground and the gently rolling valley and lands that stretch to the horizon. Visit at sunset for a windless and quiet experience.

Day-use areas: Across from the park office is a playground with a train-like play structure, shelter and ball field. The entire park is a day-use area, lacking regular camping. There are three picnic areas with tables, grills, toilets and drinking water. Two of the sites offer terrific views of the Rock River, and the Old Orchard area is very good for disabled park users. There are a number of turnouts along the river.

Hunting: 580 acres of wooded ridges and draws are interspersed with fields and former pastures growing up to a wooded succession. There are some tillable lands used for wildlife food plantings. There is also a spring turkey hunting season. Hunters should call ahead for hunting rules and opportunities.

Nature: On a fence rail in front of the main ranger office is a series of four feel-and-see boxes with natural objects for children to touch and learn about. See hiking for details about the self-guided nature trail. There are some limited weekend nature programs, occasional wildlife walks and other naturalist programs.

Nearby attractions: They include Jarrett Nature Center, John Deere Historical Site, Ogle County History Museum, White Pines Deer Park and Valley Kartway and Amusements. The city of Oregon has shopping and other services for visitors staying in any of the three area state parks-Lowden, White Pines or Castle Rock.

7 Cave-In-Rock State Park

Land: 200 acres Water: Ohio River

More than 90 percent of the fluorite produced in America comes from Hardin County, but more importantly some of the best catfish dinners come from the lovely restaurant that is perched above the beautiful Ohio River at sleepy little Cave-In-Rock State Park in the county. The outdoor seating--the best views of the Ohio River in the state--summer breezes, a historic cave and deluxe guest houses makes this small, neatly-trimmed park one of the best in the system. The tiny town of 400 residents is classic southern Illinois with a ferry and down-home cafe.

Today, the amenities of the park, tall bluff tops and gaping 55-foot-wide cave, tiny campground and nearby ferry that putters back and forth across the Ohio River connecting passengers to Kentucky barely reveal the area's intriguing, albeit morbid history.

Following the Revolutionary War the cave, which was carved out of limestone rock by thousands of years of water action, was home to bandits, outlaws and murderers who used the recess as a lair for all types of nasty doings that were as wild and provocative as you can imagine. The bad guys preyed upon river travelers. One of the most ambitious of these robbers was a former Revolutionary War officer, Samuel Mason, who discovered the site and lured river travelers in to the cave area with signs that read, "Liquor vault and house of entertainment."

As boats neared the cave, the Mason gang would disable them or force them toward the yawning hollow, where hapless crews and shaking travelers would be robbed and often killed. Even more notorious, the Harpe brothers joined the Mason gang for a time. The murderous duo grew up with a renegade Indian tribe, continuing to use the cave as a hideout and headquarters. The brothers Harpe were so nasty they once chased a woman and her mount off the edge of one of the huge bluff tops near the cave. Eventually they were forced to leave the Mason gang for being just a bit too rowdy.

In 1929, the state of Illinois acquired 64.5 acres and since then the park has increased to 200 acres. They are wooded and composed of 60-foot-high hills and rugged bluffs that frame the expansive views of the famous waterway. By the way, there haven't been any pirating or river rat robberies in more than 100 years!

Information and Activities

Cave-In-Rock State Park
P.O. Box 338, Cave-In-Rock, IL 62919
(618) 289-4325

Directions: The park is south of the intersection of Route 1 and SR 146 on the Ohio River. From I-24, take exit 16 east onto SR 146 at Vienna and drive about 50 miles to the Junction of SR 1.

Information: Open year-round, the small office is open daily and offers a brochure rack and a chance to see a large chunk of fluorite displayed on the countertop. The three-man staff is either in the office or on the park grounds weekends.

Camping: The hilly park operates 34 trail sites and 25 tent sites. The camp office is up the first road to the right upon entering the park. The trailer sites have asphalt pads and are all the same size. There are no showers or flush toilets.

A number of sites have views of valleys and hillsides, woodlots and small open spaces. Sites 1-4 have a scenic view down into a pleasant valley. There is a small playground between sites 3 and 4 that make these two sites perfect for families with small children. Sites 22, 23, 26 are perfect for a big RV rig, offering extra space between sites and plenty of room to back up your trailer or motor home. Near sites 28, 29 and 30 are a small play area and picnic shelter with a view of a pond. Children can fish in the quarter-acre pond. Sites 32, 33 and 34 have a perfect combination of shade, space and view.

The 25-space Hickory Ridge tent camping area is east up the gravel road from the trailer camping area past a picnic shelter, where tent campers park their cars in a small lot and walk into their shady sites. There are two small loops that comprise the area. Each site has a small grill, picnic table and a cleared flat spot for your tent. Site numbers 8 and 14 are the most private and shady in the tent camping area. The sites are marked, but there is plenty of room to shift your tent around and pick your own spot.

Boating: A new ramp at the park offers access to the Ohio River, as does the two-lane launching ramp at the town park. Boaters will also want to visit the Golconda Marina, located near Golconda at Lusk Creek on the Ohio River. With more than 100 slips, the marina has full services which include covered and open slips, overnight moorage, many ramps, boat sales and service, bait and tackle, gifts and snacks, and all sorts of marine supplies.

Unique to most state parks, Cave-In-Rock supplies 15-20 sticks of split and dried firewood to campers.

Lodge and restaurant: The cabins are along a bluff in front of the flagstone restaurant, which is open seven days and has a patio area and dining tables that overlook the river. The history of the golden age of

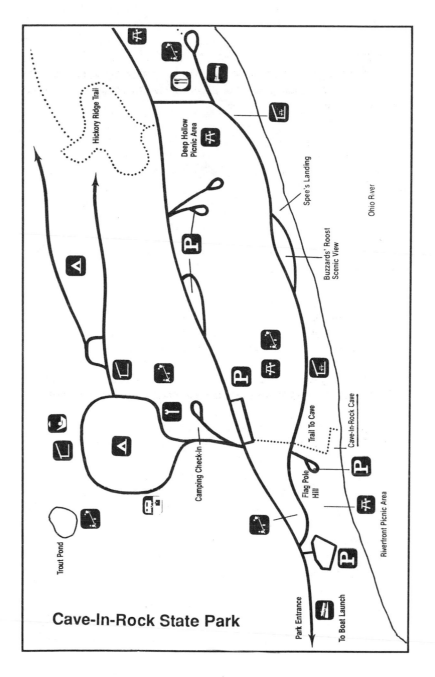

Cave-In-Rock State Park

The film "How the West was Won" was shot at the park. The cave is 160-feet deep.

steamboats, which once operated up and down the Ohio River, is depicted in photographs and other information on the walls of the attractive restaurant.

The five mile-long view each way along the mighty Ohio River greets guests to cabins that are furnished with a kitchenette (no cooking is allowed), bathroom, large bedroom/living room and a private deck overlooking the river. The kitchenette includes table, chairs, small refrigerator, sink and cabinets; there's no stove. The bathroom includes a closet, large sink, tub/shower unit and lavatory. The bedroom has two double beds, chairs, settee, color TV and clock radio. Parking is right at your door. Linens, blankets and pillows are provided. For reservations call (618) 289-4545. The lodge is closed December through February and you should call well in advance for reservations during the busy spring/summer/fall season.

Fishing: The river in this area offers good sauger angling. Bluegill, redear and catfish (simple cutbaits for cats) are also taken. Bass anglers need a boat and electronics to identify structure. Buzz baits, jerk baits and some rubber worms are used for bass angling. There are limited shoreline fishing opportunities. Mike's Guide Service, (618) 287-7465, offers fishing trips and considerable information about the area.

Hiking: The park maintains two trails, the Hickory Ridge (.75-mile long) and the nearly one-mile-long Pirates' Bluff Nature Trail at the east end of the park. Pirates' Bluff can be accessed at cabin No. 4 and follows a path downhill to a river ravine and sandy cove.

The cave: The famous cave, with its opening facing the flowing river is naturally lighted with about 60 steps down a stairway, then back up a few stairs to the wide entrance. Graffiti artists over the decades have scratched messages and symbols into the surfaces and will help your imagination run wild about all of the often terrible activity the 160-foot-long cave has seen.

The movies, *"How the West Was Won"* and Walt Disney's *"Davy Crockett and the River Pirates,"* featured many scenes of the Cave-In-Rock as well as Battery Rock. The cave is a short 200-yard walk from the main road parking area. You'll love the coolness of the cave and quiet lapping of the Ohio River at the stony cave entrance. The ledges and strata in the rock are easy seen once inside the cave, and the cooing of pigeons is now the welcome call of a cave that was once the notorious hideout for dozens of outlaws. Kids will love to hoot and howl, and listen to their echo inside the cave.

A scenic ridge tops the south side of the park. There are five parking lots, three playgrounds and four large shelters for group gathering. The Delta Queen, a tourist riverboat, passes by the park and can be seen from many locations.

Nearby attractions: The Shawnee National Forest (call (618) 287-2201) scenic highway and the Elizabethtown Ranger Station are nearby. So are Garden of the Gods, Pounds Hollow Recreation Area, Bell Smith Springs Recreation Area and Tower Rock. You are near several large Kentucky state parks, just a ferry ride away. The ferry is located in the town of Cave-In-Rock and near many Shawnee National Forest features.

8 Chain O' Lakes State Park

Water: nearly 6,400 acres of lakes

The Wisconsin glacier of 12,000 years ago carved out more than 6,400 acres of lakes, valleys and rivers in northwest Lake County, which is now often called the northeastern morainal division, 1.5 hours west of Chicago. From Al Capone's cottage in the area and legends of his exploits to Jet Skis and muskie anglers, the area bustles with activity that includes a Six Flags amusement park, Gurnee Mill Shopping Center and many small lakes, cottages, marinas, Lake Michigan, Waukegan and more.

The state park is a centerpiece in this region of high-energy activity, offering camping, boating, fishing, hunting, picnicking, horsback riding, natural areas and much more. The theme of this park is busy, especially the waterways, which some say are the busiest in North America. If you are looking for high-energy, this is the state park for you!

Information and Activities

Chain O' Lakes State Park
8916 Wilmot Rd.
Spring Grove, IL 60081
(708) 587-5512

Directions: Less than two hours from Chicago, take Route 173 west to Wilmot Road. Go south to the park entrance.

Information: The park is open in the summer (May 1- Oct. 31) from 6 a.m. - 9 p.m., winter from 8 a.m. - sunset.

Camping: You may reserve camping sites at Chain O' Lakes State Park by mail only for a non-refundable $5 fee. There are about 35 reservable sites in the northern part of the Honeysuckle Hollow camping loop.

The park operates one Class A area (Honeysuckle Hollow) with 106 sites and three Class B camping areas (Turner Lake South, Prairie View and Mud Lake East) with a combined total of 87 sites. The park also offers a youth group camping area near Mud Lake for up to 150 youth for $1 per person. Campers in all areas must have a permit and bring their own firewood. No one is allowed to pick up firewood in the park.

In Honeysuckle Hollow, sites are a bit tight with light shading. Sites number 97-102 have a view of a small wetland area and are reservable. Sites 76-98 are backed up against the lake, water is visible through the trees. Sites 17, 18, 80, 81, 84, 85, 88, 89, 92, 99,100, 101 and 103 also have a through-the-trees-type of view of the lake. Sites 15 and 16 are rent-a-camps that come complete with a tent and other amenities. Sites 9-12 are big and near lake and fishing access points. Sites in the 50s and 60s have a blacktop lane and gravel sites, but there's not a lot of shade in these sunny sites. Firewood is sold at the concession at the main boat ramp.

Emergency numbers: sheriff (708) 680-1111; state police and local 911.

Boating: A full-service concession called the Chain O' Lakes State Park

Concession is located at the huge launch offering good food, live bait and tackle, lake maps, rowboats, canoes, boat motors, electric trolling motors and bikes for rent. The store is open 6 a.m. - 6 p.m., weekends 6 a.m. - sunset. Call (708) 587-7165. There are lake maps and guide service information available at the lower level of the concession.

There is no charge to launch or horsepower limits on any boats in the Chain O' Lakes; however, no motors are allowed in 44-acre Turner Lake, which is located within the park boundaries. Boats, canoes and inflatable boats must comply with State of Illinois watercraft rules and regulations.

The launch at Chain O' Lakes is one of the largest in the state park system, offering only four lanes, but a huge amount of parking, staging lanes, prep lanes, five-minute docks and map that shows you where and how to park your trailer and vehicle. This is a very busy launch. From boaters to shoreline anglers, the area bustles with activity, complete with the smell of Polish dogs from the food stand and the presence of a U.S. Coast Guard Auxiliary Station trailer that offers boat checks, search and rescue, radio and other services. There also is a good kiddie play area and picnicking sites near the boat launch and lots of places to view the launching antics.

You can rent a canoe for two adults for a scenic 3-4 hour float trip where you can pack a lunch and enjoy the waters.

There is a small boat launch for campers and a two-lane launch on Route 173.

Fishing: The entire Chain O' Lakes area is highly used by fisherman, with many large marinas and lodging opportunities available. The lakes were connected during the 1920s by a man-made series of channels and now have heavy fishing and boating pressure.

Catfish and stripper can be taken from the bridges. Nightcrawlers with no bobber can take many species throughout the lake system. 480-acre Lake Marie is the best lake for walleye and bass and can reach depths of 30 feet. Like all of the lakes in the chain (Grass Lake at 1,360 acres, Fox Lake, Pistakee, Nippersink, Channel Lake, etc.) the shorelines are crowded with cottages. Bass fishing is sometimes fair to good around docks, pilings and other structures.

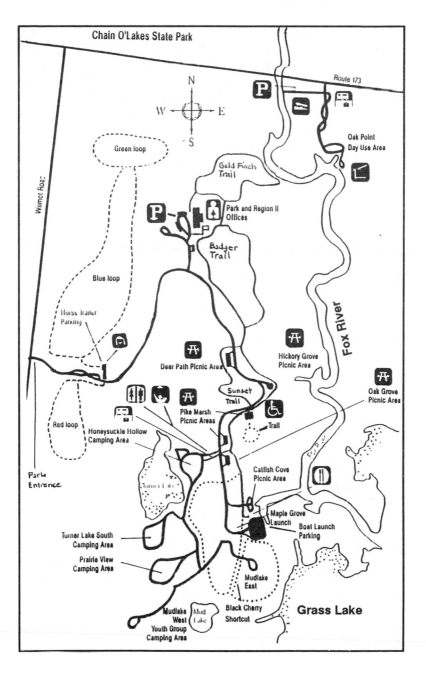

Chain O'Lakes State Park

Route 173

Green loop

N
W · E
S

Wilmot Road

Gold Finch Trail

P

Park and Region II Offices

Oak Point Day Use Area

Badger Trail

Blue loop

Horse Trailer Parking

Fox River

Deer Path Picnic Area

Hickory Grove Picnic Area

Oak Grove Picnic Area

Sunset Trail

Pike Marsh Picnic Areas

Trail

Red loop

Honeysuckle Hollow Camping Area

Turner Lake

Catfish Cove Picnic Area

Park Entrance

Maple Grove Launch

Boat Launch Parking

Turner Lake South Camping Area

Prairie View Camping Area

Mudlake East

Mudlake West Youth Group Camping Area

Mud Lake

Black Cherry Shortcut

Grass Lake

Generally, shoreline fishing is good for bass, catfish and stripper in the channels, and good offshore for crappie. Maybe the best shoreline, according to the bait shop and other locals, is near the large boat ramp where the water is calm, shallow and weedy. Muskie anglers usually concentrate their efforts in Lake Marie and Channel Lake where Mepp's Giant Killer, Golden Roaches and buck tails can bring them in. Try trolling in deeper waters for muskie also. There is a muskie guide that operates on the lakes and can be reached through the bait shop.

Turner Lake is only 8-9-feet deep and a good place for youth fishing. Bluegill, sunfish, bullhead and channel catfish can be taken on crawlers or other live baits. The lake has an aerator and the best action is around the lily pads at the west end.

Fishing regulations: Bass, 15 inch minimum size, one possession; muskie, 30 inch minimum, one possession; pike, 24 inch minimum, three daily total; catfish, six daily total possession. There is a small fishing pier near camping sites 15 and 16 in the Honeysuckle Hollow area.

All muskie must be reported.

Hiking/biking: There is a Chain O' Lakes Biking/Hiking Trail map available that features a series of routes. At the northern edge of the rail system, the Gold Finch Trail parallels the Fox River, which the park roadway serves as an excellent biking route. The Nature's Way trail is 2.25 miles long and starts at the Oak Grove Picnic area. There is also a handicapped accessible trail with a trailhead at the Pike March North area. Many trails can be accessed at picnic areas.

Horseback riding: The horse rental facility includes a large staging area, which includes a parking lot for riders who bring their own horse and trailer. There are about a dozen equines awaiting your arrival at this clean and well-maintained facility. The stable is open from May 1 through October 31; hours are 10:30 a.m. - 6 p.m. weekdays; 9 a.m. - 6 p.m. on weekends and holidays. The horse rental concession is inside the park one mile west of Deer Path picnic area, about one-half mile from the Wilmot Road entrance. The horse rental also offers hay rides; call (815) 675-6532. There are four equestrian trails that total more than seven miles that originate from the stable area. There is a map available of the trail system and all trails are marked.

Day-use areas: Chain O' Lakes has seven picnic areas with tables, water fountains, vault toilets and grills. Oak Grove, Maple Grove and Oak Point have playground equipment. Oak Point has a picnic shelter and groups of 25 or more must have advance written permission from the site superintendent. There is no swimming or wading allowed at the park. In the winter, skiers are welcome to use the trails and the office as a warming spot.

Nature: The unit offers a tempting self-guided interpretive trail called Nature's Way, which wanders by grassland, Grass Lake, near Mud Lake, by a meadow, along a cattail marsh and through upland woods. The trail has eight stations where you can learn about the forest floor, a changing marsh area, non-native plants, sedge meadow, lakeside lowlands, a small fen, a great view of Mud and Grass Lakes, moraines, view the remaining American Lotus beds (there are only a few places in the world where they blossom!), and the hand of man on the lakes, channels and park developments.

Hunting: Dove, waterfowl (duck blinds drawing is the last Saturday of July), pheasant (youth hunt first Sunday of permit season), and archery bow deer hunting are offered within the park boundaries. Hunters should request an up-to-date fact sheet for rules, regulations and dates.

Nearby attractions: Six Flags, Illinois Beach State Park, Lake County Forest Preserve, Volo Bog, shopping centers, Cuneo Museum and Gardens and much more. Call the Lake County CVB for more details at (800) 525-3669.

9   *Channahon State Park*

Land: 18 acres   Water: canal

Channahon (which means the "meetings of water") is one of the most pleasant access points along the 96-mile-long Illinois and Michigan Canal. Tucked away under a canopy of large shady trees, the canal access is used by canoeists, hikers, occasional fishermen and tent campers.

Two I & M locks and a restored locktender's house offer visitors a chance to learn about the canal history. Visitors can access the I & M Canal State Trail beginning at Channahon along the old towpath to LaSalle and experience 60 miles of scenic views of the canal and the Des Plaines and Illinois rivers.

This canal provided the first complete water route from the east coast to the Gulf of Mexico by connecting Lake Michigan to the Mississippi River through the Illinois River. Early French explorers like Jolliet and Marquette recognized the value of this water route for navigation in the 1600s. The water route from that time was heavily used by Native Americans and traders until 1823, when Illinois created a Canal Commission to oversee design and construction of the canal that was ultimately completed in 1848 at a cost of $6.5 million.

The linear waterway was built by men and mules, carving a path from the south branch of the Chicago River at Bridgeport to LaSalle. The canal was originally 60 feet wide and six feet deep, and there were 15 locks built to accommodate the difference in elevations.

Commercial traffic began immediately after completion and loaded barges were pulled by straining teams of mules or horses walking along the narrow towpath. In 1933, the Illinois Waterway was completed and the I & M Canal was closed to navigation and opened for recreational use. Facilities continue to be developed along the entire length of the canal.

Information and Activities

Channahon State Park
P.O. Box 636
Channahon, IL 60410
(815) 467-4271

Directions: West of I-55.

Campground: About 30 tents could occupy the open flat area near the little brown office building that is maintained as a camping area.

Boating: Canoe access only.

Fishing: Rough fish are a popular group of species many canal-side fisherman pursue, while many smallmouth bass anglers try their luck near the dam around the rocks.

Hiking/biking: There are eight miles of trails west of the park along the canal, and six miles east of the park along the canal. These trails connect to the canal trail system. Biking is encouraged, especially early in the morning.

Day-use areas: The park is primarily an access point to the canal, but there are many picnic tables and a shelter that is open year-round.

Nearby attractions: An active aquaduct is nearby, as are Goose Lake Prairie State Park, Des Plaines Natural Area, White Fence Farm, Joliet Area Historical Society Museum and Seneca Grain Elevator.

10   *Clinton Lake State Recreation Area*

Land: 9,907 acres   Water: 4,895 acres of Clinton Lake

Clinton Lake is big and brash, high energy and active, heavily used and a destination park that offers excellent fishing, recreational boating, water skiing, camping, hiking, picnicking and hunting. The park complex is a terrific blend of rustic areas, full service amenities, aquatic recreation with swimming areas, and many other modern facilities that will suit the entire family.

The cooling lake and surrounding 10,000 acres of land are operated under a lease agreement by the state with Illinois Power Company, which built a power generating facility in the late 1970s under a jointly created master management plan that guides development and general operation of the large recreational area. Clinton Lake is an impoundment of nearly 5,000 acres formed by a 2,900-foot-long earthen dam across Salt Creek. The lake has an average depth of 15 feet, with its deepest point being 40 feet. The heavily used lake has a watershed area of 296 square miles and about 130 miles of shoreline.

Long before the area was flooded to form a lake that supports the power needs of the region, historians believe that the area was the site of a small village and hunting camps of tribes of the Illini confederacy. Kickapoo also lived in the area until the 1820s, when the first European settlers began infiltrating the area and settling the areas significantly by the early 1830s.

The first settlers to the area were farmers from Kentucky and Tennessee who cleared portions of the land, created pastures and typically led a quiet agrarian life for decades. When the dam was built and the area flooded, it was primarily an area of open pastures, croplands and scatterings of woodlots and second growth forests.

Information and Activities

Clinton Lake State Recreation Area
R.R. 1, P.O. Box 4
DeWitt, IL 61735
(217) 935-8722

Directions: Located in central Illinois, three miles east of Clinton. Near the intersection of 74 and 54. The park office is open Monday - Friday, 7 a.m. - 3 p.m.

Camping: Clinton Lake has a huge campground that can accommodate about 300 Class B campers. Each site has a picnic table and grill. Many sites are completely shady and can be used by tent or large RV campers.

No reservations are taken. All sites are on a first-come, first-served basis, with the best sites being those near the lake shore. Group camping is also available by advanced registration.

Boating: The 4,895 surface acres of Clinton Lake is widely popular with all types of water craft including unlimited horsepower recreation boats, personal watercraft, and small fishing boats. With 130 miles of shoreline and a maximum lake depth of 40 feet, many larger boats also operate on the lake. Five 2-lane launching ramps and one small canoe launch are operated on the lake. Rental boat slips, boat rentals and marine supplies stores are nearby. Sailboating is popular on small catamarans and larger vessels.

The upper arms of the lake are no-wake areas and portions are restricted to electric motors only. Experienced local sailors warn about how fast the lake can get rough in windy conditions, urging small craft to stick to the north fork of Salt Creek on rough days. Water-skiing is permitted from the Route 54 bridge to the Route 48 bridge.

Fishing: The almost endless series of coves and small bays offer anglers excellent locations to fish for many species including largemouth and smallmouth bass, bluegill, sunfish, drum, walleye stripped bass, tiger muskie and rough fish varieties. Certain fishing restrictions apply on the lake.

Many local bait and tackle shops can provide details about where to go, lake maps, and the latest hot spots. Generally speaking, the lake can be fished using traditional techniques, with the upper arms offering excellent angling during the spring and the fall season. Catfish are also found in good numbers in the upper arms all year-around. In the spring, action can be good for walleye, strippers and cats near the dam spillway.

Shoreline anglers should fish near the bridges for panfish using small light-colored jigs tipped with live bait. A small full-service marina with bait, tackle, ice, snacks and so on is located one mile north of Route 10.

Day-use areas: Clinton Lake has a good mix of day-use areas scattered around the lake offering picnic tables, grill, water and safe playground equipment for the kids. Reservable picnic shelters are available at the Mascoutin, Weldon, Lane and West Side access areas. Mascoutin and Weldon have electricity. Weldon also has a softball field and plenty of shoreline access.

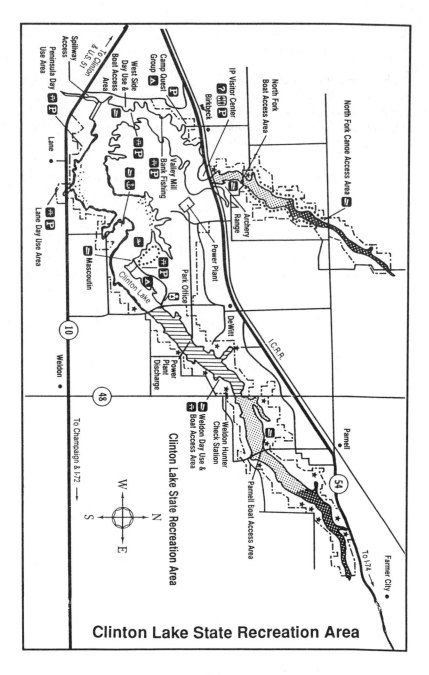

Clinton Lake State Recreation Area

If you are looking for a lake view for your family picnic, plan a visit to the West Side or Mascoutin day-use areas.

Hiking: For an easy two-hour hike try the 3.5 miles Houseboat Cove Trail, a loop north of the beach that follows the shoreline for one mile and through a wooded area. For more adventure, hike the 12 mile-long trail that follows the perimeter of Clinton Lake between North Fork Boat Access and the North Fork Canoe Access Area.

You may also access the moderately difficult pathway at the northern tip of the trail by the canoe access parking lot. The barely used trail is often overgrown and is steeply wooded along the banks of the lake. Underbrush, open fields and dense woods are also found along the trail. Stream crossings are via small footbridges that are usually accessible year-round. Bring your water bottle, camera and be ready for a hilly shoreline-type hiking experience. A 40-acre restored prairie is also in the North Fork area.

Hunting: Nearly 3,000 acres of the park are used for seasonal hunting of rabbit, pheasant, squirrel and dove. There is also an archery deer season and an archery range for pre-season practice sessions.

11   *Delabar State Park*

Land: 89 acres   Water: Mississippi River

The pine tree-lined park entrance road takes you into the park about one mile, where a mixed deciduous wooded area canopies the day-use area, small campgrounds and river's edge. The oak/hickory, along with some birch forest, serves as a natural habitat for a variety of wildlife species including quail, woodchuck, deer, raccoon, squirrels and more than 50 species of songbirds that fly up and down the Mississippi River corridor nesting, resting and migrating each spring and autumn.

The small park honors two brothers, Roy and Jack Delabar, who donated the site to the state in 1959 to be developed for use as a state park. The park was dedicated and opened in 1960 and has remained mostly unchanged since that time.

The neighboring Big River State Forest, which is in many ways an extension of the state park, offers many amenities for outdoor lovers and compliments the gateway-like state park. Big River State Forest lies in a linear shape along the east banks of the Mississippi River and features 62 miles of horse trails, horse camping, 90 camping sites, fishing access to Lock and Dam No. 18, boating, hunting and 3.5 miles of hiking trails.

The 2,671-acre state forest has many unique natural areas that include a vast prairie woodland border community, large-flowered perstemon and Patterson's bindweed, which were first found in this area in 1873 by N. H. Patterson. At that time, this was the only location in the world for it. Fifteen miles of scenic drives (auto trail, 2.5 miles), picnicking areas, hunting, Oquawka Refuge, timber stands and managed wildlife areas are also part of the state forest near Delabar.

Information and Activities

Delabar State Park/Big River State Forest
R. R. 2
Oquawka, IL 61469
(309) 867-3671

Directions: 1.5 miles north of Oquawka, near Illinois Route 164, Henderson County.

Information: The park closes at 10 p.m. and the park office is located at the Big River State Forest station on Route 164 about five miles north of the state park.

Campground: The Yellow Banks Camping Area (Class B) is located immediately upon entering the park past the road to the boat launch and trailer dump station. There are numbered sites, but low use and no marked gravel pad allows campers to place their rig near the general area of the indictated sites on flat, dry ground. The little campground road that loops around the area is really a two-tract lane, but is solid and wide enough for large rigs. With good shade and large trees, virtually any of the sites are fine places to set up. There is electricity in the camping area.

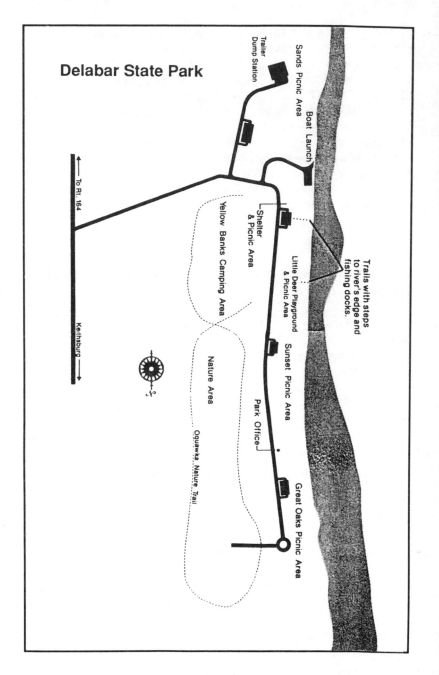

Delabar State Park

Sites 2, 18 and 20 are near the toilets. Near site 5 is the Mills Slough Hiking Trail, and all of the sites have grills and picnic tables.

Farther north along the main park road is some unstructured Class D camping in open areas. You can register for camping at the small unmanned timber-structure check-in building near the entrance.

Boating: The launch, at the south end of the park, has one lane. Nearby are two picnic tables, two grills and one small dock. About 10 cars and trailers could park in the small lot. 150 yards straight out from the boat ramp is a mud bar; otherwise, the river is very wide and along this area small craft would have long runs between fishing areas.

There are many boat ramps in the area, including at the Big River Forest north camping area, about six miles north of the state park. Boaters will find interesting mud flat areas, wide water expanses and many areas to explore in this underused stretch of the river. There are no motor or boat size limits in this stretch of the mighty river. There are no boat rental, bait sales or concession stand at the park.

Fishing: Fishing is poor in the area, but if you like water impoundment, where the action can be fair to good, head for the 27-acre Gladstone Lake that has camping and day-use areas also.

Hiking: Two marked trails travel two miles of wooded terrain near the river.

Day-use areas: The playground, complete with wooded play structures, is probably the most used element in the unit. There are three picnic areas, with the middle area in the linear park offering drinking water and toilets. Picnic tables are scattered in these areas and cooking is permitted only in the camp stoves. Open fires are prohibited.

Hunting: None. Try the Big River State Forest, (309) 374-2496.

12 Dixon Springs State Park

Land: 786 acres   Water: Dixon Springs

Like many of the fine natural areas and man-made attractions in southern Illinois, Dixon Springs State Park, in Pope County, is a little off-the-beaten-path, under promoted and more often than not, peaceful and quiet, away from the so-called "travel destinations" and "flatlands" of the central Prairie State.

This part of the state is beautiful and ear-plugging hilly; in fact, the Illinois Ozarks are among a very few mountain ranges that run east-west rather than north and south. The expanses of the Shawnee National Forest, fine parks, festivals, riverboat casinos, fishing, golf, cycling, history and much more make this entire area unique and underdeveloped.

Frankly, the area might have been more popular for 19th century travelers and Native Americans who sought out the "Great Medicine Waters" of Dixon Springs. The brown sulfur-smelling waters were said to cure your bones, but probably also kept the mosquitoes off. Pew phew. Today bathers can cool off and try the nearly 100-foot-long swimming pool and 10-foot-tall water slide under the watchful eye of lifeguards or, like the pioneers or Indians, hike back into the cool woods and squat under cliff overhangs for Mother Natures own air conditioning.

Dixon Springs takes it name from William Dixon, one of the first white settlers to build a home in this section. No one knows if he bathed in the "medicine waters," but it is said his livestock died off, so he might have!

He obtained a school land warrant in 1848 from Gov. Augustus C. French, built a cabin and worked the land alongside ailing travelers who were attracted to the seven mineral springs in the area. A small town grew up around the "medicine waters" to serve the needs of those looking for the healthful bath. Soon a bathhouse was erected and hot or cold, soft water baths were offered round-the-clock. By rail and river, from Paducah to Evansville and Cairo to Golconda, the park was a popular summer resort in those days.

Information and Activities

Dixon Springs State Park
R.R. #2
Golconda, IL 62938
(618) 949-3394

Directions: Ten miles west of Golconda on Illinois Route 146 near its junction with Illinois Route 145.

Campground: The campground in the middle of the park offers 40 sites with electricity and water, and 10 tent sites. Campers may shower at the pool for a fee.

Sites have gravel pads and most can easily accommodate medium-sized RVs. Sites 1-7 are open and sunny, while 9-11 are shady. Site 21 is private

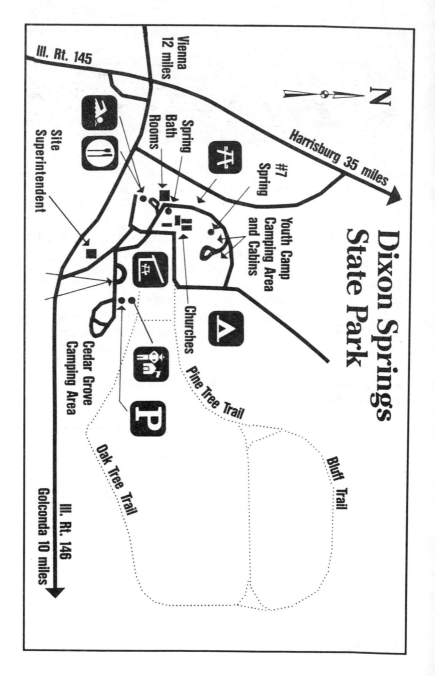

Spring house in the day-use area.

and shady. Some of the sites are separated by trees, but it's not dense vegetation. Site 26-33 are shady and private, while sites 37 and 38 are large enough for most any size camping rig. If you like open and sunny sites, try 12-18. The firewood pile is at site No. 10, where campers may help themselves.

The campground is compact, and many older campers like sites 11-19 because they are close to the office.

Hiking. Like lots of parks in southern Illinois, many rock outcroppings enhance the scenic value of the trail systems. A number of water rivulets of different sizes and shapes pour out of the rocks and are of interest during and after rains offering unusual patterns, trickling sounds and coolness.

The 1.7-mile-long, seven foot-wide self-guided nature trail takes walkers along the eastern portion of the property crossing hilly terrain by a short leaf pine plantation and near three white churches, along crags, cliff overhangs, outdrops and woodlands.

The Ghost Dance Trail is a one-mile-long loop that meanders down Hill

Branch and along the east canyon wall. This trail is scenic but considered difficult, especially when crossing the stream bed on slippery rocks.

Day-use areas: There is no swimming (except at a swimming pool), boating or fishing allowed at the park.

A baseball field, picnic sites, mowed areas, waterfall, foot bridges and a nice day-use area behind the pool are available. The outcropping of rock, walkways, one-lane wooded planked bridge and hiking offer plenty to do for the day-user.

Swimming: The 45-foot by 96-foot crystal-clear pool is open Memorial Day through Labor Day weekend, 11 a.m. - 6 p.m. There is a fee to enter the pool and a 10-foot tall, 40-foot-long water slide and small food concession that sells hot dogs, hamburgers, pizza and cold drinks. For more information about group outings or the pool complex, call (618) 949-3871. Two lifeguards are on duty. There is also a small "baby pool" for toddlers.

Nature: This is one of the few parks that rainy days will be of interest to visitors. When the rain pours, rivulets cascade down the hills in the park, forming waterfalls of varying sizes and heights. The springs will run full.

The water-flushing nature of the area offers interesting creek beds to explore, overgrown ferns, ivy and lichen, moss flats and thick growth blankets on each side of the hills. Giant century-old trees interlock above small creeks as cliffs rise on either side of huge boulders that are scattered about the unit. Also interesting are the intriguing names given to features and points of interest, including Album Rock, Red Man's Retreat, Lover's Leap, Alligator Rock, Ghost Dance, Pluto's Cave and many others you will want to find.

Wildflowers include lady's slippers, sweet William, Jack-in-the-pulpit, and many beautiful tree species that flower like the fragrant catalpa blossom.

Nearby attractions: Horseback riding, Glen Lake, riverboat casino and the Chocolate Factory.

13   Eagle Creek State Park

Land: 2,200 acres   Water: Lake Shelby, 11,000 acres

Eagle Creek State Park, which faces Wolf Creek State Park across the lopsided "Y"-shaped Lake Shelbyville, in central Illinois is just minutes from Decatur, Champaign, Effingham and surrounding communities. The park offers full amenities for all types of outdoor recreation. Sharing more than 250 miles of shoreline, large tracts of indigenous woodlands, and near the many U.S. Army Corps of Engineers recreation areas, the entire area is a high-energy region with complete services, golf, shopping, tourist attractions and neighboring communities that are actively catering to park users and travelers.

Either of the state parks is a great staging area for exploring the many resources of the area. And the resources and attractions in the general area are numerous: three beaches, scenic picnic areas, designed wildlife management areas, more than 500 campsites, Corps visitor's center (recreation areas off Route 16), boat rentals, hiking, guided fishing outings, special events, fish rearing ponds, history tours and much more (some Corps areas require a small fee).

Like the other large reservoir complexes in the state, Eagle Creek and Wolf Creek state parks are perfect examples of potential benefits of natural resources management as means of flood control, water supply, water quality and exciting outdoor recreation facilities and opportunities.

The Shelbyville Reservoir Project was a monumental undertaking. Before actual work on the dam at Shelbyville could begin, several old mines in the area had to be completely filled in, cemeteries were relocated, gas and oil pipelines were rerouted, a power plant was demolished and huge tracts of land were cleared and leveled on the west side channel, which hugs the bluff to the east of the river bottom. The $56 million project and began in May 1963. The dam towers 110 feet above the original stream bed and is 3,025 feet long with reinforced concrete and a gate-controlled spillway that manages water for more than 25,000 acres.

Most of the work was done by the Corps of Engineers, who also developed some great facilities that compliment the two area state parks and nearby communities.

Information and Activities

Eagle Creek State Park
R.R. 1, P.O. Box 6
Findlay, IL 62534
(217) 756-8260

Directions: Four miles southeast of Findlay.

Information: The park office is open weekdays, 7:30 a.m. - 3:30 p.m. The tan-colored building has a state flag flying and a helpful brochure rack and information service inside.

Campground: Eagle Creek has 160 vehicular sites (including 130

Class B sites with electricity, water, fire blocks and picnic tables), a tent camping area and an organized group camping area. The campground is rarely filled, even on holiday weekends, yet it is a very nice camping area.

There are no showers in the campgrounds, and the campground is divided into three loops. The first loop, Fire Drive, sites 1-19, is quite open, narrow and not very shady. The shadiest sites in this open loop are 8 and 9. At the end of this loop is the half-mile-long Camp Fire Trail. Vault toilets are near site 5.

Along Hickory Lane, the campground drive that connects the loops, site 20 is backed into a natural and private area. Sites 21 and 22 are good adjacent sites for two families to occupy for a long weekend.

Hawk Lane, sites 37-56, is more shady and private than the first loop. More mature trees offer a nicer camping feeling to this area. At the end of the loop are sites 47 and 48, which offer considerable privacy and are large enough for big families or big RV units. Site 46 is also a good site toward the end of this flat-terrain loop. The campground host in this loop has a small brochure rack that details area attractions and has park maps.

Quail Drive, sites 66-142, are open, with lots of room for large rigs. The backs of many camping sites are next to wooded areas, flat, dry and convenient. A small shelter for three picnic tables is located in the middle of the loop; there are also overflow parking areas for boat trailer parking about halfway into this large loop. Site 88 is near the toilets, while sites 91-97 are well-shaded. At the end of the loop is a half-mile walking trail called High Bluff Trail that takes you down by the lake. Site 131 is good for a big RV rig, but not sites 133, 134, or 138, which are very open with no shade at all.

If you take the gravel road to the left when you enter the campground, you'll end up at the Oak Ridge walk-in tent camping area, a pleasant 11-site area that is shady and private, away from all of the other park amenities. Sites 3, 5, 7, ,8, 9, 10 and 11, occupy a ridgeline and have a water view. The best site is No. 11. Backpacking camping is by permit only; call the park office for details and a permit. Adult and youth group camping are also available with advance registration.

Eagle Creek Resort has an 18 hole golf course.

The tent camping area, which is actually at the end of the campground road, is flat, dry and complete with picnic tables, Prairie View Hiking Trail (1.5 miles) and open space.

There is also an archery range, and Chief Illini Trailhead is near this small, very nice tent camping area.

Emergency numbers: sheriff, 774-3941; state police, 1-867-2211; ambulance, 756-3110; rescue squad, 774-3433; fire, 756-3110.

Resort: The inn sets on a peninsula with golf carts buzzing up and down the sidewalks shuttling golfers about as they prepare to take on the 18-hole, Ken Killian designed, 6,900-yard course. The championship course ratings from the gold (back) tees is 73.5, and slope rating is 132. Watered fairways, picturesque acres, mature trees, foursets of tees and expert greenskeeping got the the course rated the "Best Resort Course" by *Golf*

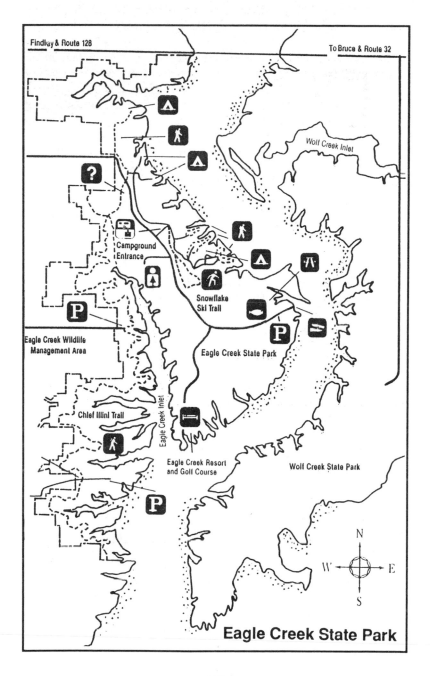

Findlay & Route 128

To Bruce & Route 32

Wolf Creek Inlet

Campground
Entrance

Snowflake
Ski Trail

Eagle Creek Wildlife
Management Area

Eagle Creek State Park

Eagle Creek Inlet

Chief Illini Trail

Eagle Creek Resort
and Golf Course

Wolf Creek State Park

N
W — E
S

Eagle Creek State Park

Digest magazine. The pro shop is in the lower level of the lodge.

If golf isn't your game, try fine dining at the Wildflower restaurant and restful lodging at the 138-room inn with executive suites, indoor pool, saunas, whirlpool and exercise room. Don't forget the nearby fishing in Illinois' second largest lake, water-skiing, windsurfing, hanging out in the terrific lobby, warming up by the fireplace, playing tennis at the nearby court complex, sunning at a nearby beach, horseback riding, biking and hiking. Comfortable and modern, the resort portion of the park is great. Meeting planners will love the facilities for their next conference.

Some of the second-floor inn rooms have a great view of the courtyard and lake, while many ground-level rooms have patio doors that open up on the grassy courtyard and are outfitted with outdoor seating.

Boating: The launch at the park, north of the resort, is one of many public ramps around the lake. It is about three boats wide, concrete, and has parking for 100 cars and trailers. There are no horsepower limits on the lake, and you see just about every type of watercraft cutting the waves. Even big houseboats are seen floating leisurely about the quiet waters. There is a temporary mooring dock next to the main ramp. A fish cleaning station gets heavy use after fishing tournaments held on the lake.

Fishing: Anglers in Illinois have the wonderful opportunity to fish many kinds of waters. From small artificial lakes to the Mississippi River, fast-flowing streams to jumbo reservoirs like Lake Shelbyville, one's choice of fish to catch is varied, ranging from carp, crappie, catfish and bass, to walleye, northern pike, trout and salmon.

With quality fishery management, improving water quality, rearing activities, soil and water conservation and the reduction of pollution, sport fishing is better than it's been for 50 years in Illinois.

Lake Shelbyville, a U.S. Army Corps of Engineers reservoir, was formed by damming the Kaskaskia River in 1970 and offers some of the finest tree-lined shore and structure fishing in the region. Along most of the shoreline in the lower two-thirds of the lake, the water depths quickly drop to 10-15 feet. Flooded ridges with good underwater cover are abundant throughout this portion of the lake. Extensive shallow flats, three to eight feet deep are found along Eagle Creek and Wolf Creek State Park, Sand and Skull creeks, the Finally Marina area, the junction of the Okaw-Kaskaskia Arms, northwest of the Wilborn Creek Recreation Area, Whitley Creek Recreation Area, and the upper portions of the Kaskaskia Arm east of Fox Harbor Marina.

Anglers should try the small tributaries that feed into the lake in addition to the West Okaw and Kaskaskia rivers, including: Sand, Wilborn, Lithia Springs, Skull, Whitley, Wolf and Coon creeks. The creeks offer some of the best crappie, bluegill, largemouth and bullhead fishing found in the region.

Flooded timber in many coves are also excellent areas to explore. Pick up a copy of the Lake Shelbyville Fishing Guide, and use the maps to find places where old Christmas trees have been sunken, old road beds and so on.

The most popular sport fishes in Lake Shelbyville are black and white crappie, white bass, largemouth bass, bluegill, black bullheads, channel catfish and walleye. White bass and walleye, not normally found in central Illinois, are increasingly popular in the lake. Northern pike, carp, sunfish, smallmouth bass, warmouth and muskie are also occasionally taken.

Crappies like cover, and are generally found in coves with stickup, bays, flooded timber, submerged fencerows and along rock riprap areas from mid-September to early June. Go deeper in the summer. Crappies at Lake Shelbyville are traditionally on the nest in May and early June that range in depth from 2-12 feet, depending on water clarity. They will bite best when the water temperature is 50-75 degrees.

8-12 pound line, a bobber and live bait are the tools needed after you find the crappies. You can also jig 4-6 inches with a lead headed jig or small spinner blade, maribou/minnow. Light jigs and twister tails cast toward stickup, steep banks, submerged brush or riprap are effective if you jerk back the retrieve.

During warm weather, when campers and vacationers want to catch tasty crappies, the fish will be in deep water, typically along steep dropoffs, river and creek channels, spring holes and old flooded ponds. They are hard to find in the summer. But, if located, beetlespin or small brightly colored twister tails can be twitched in the depth to gather their attention. Also try dawn and dusk. If the fish come to the shallows to feed, use poppers.

Nighttime lantern anglers are having luck. Tie a gas lantern to a stout stickup, wait for the insects and fish to gather, and jig and cast like crazy.

Largemouth bass fishing is generally best from early May to mid-June and again from early September to mid-October when the water temperature ranges between 55-75 degrees. Try shoreline stickups and rocky riprap. Largemouth bass are sight feeders, if you can find them on the reservoir, casting the heavy hardware often works. During the spring try wobbling or flashing spoons and pork. As the water clears, buzz baits and top-water lures--even plastic worms and diving baits--will work.

In the summer, you need to jig the bass out of cool hiding places in deeper waters of Lake Shelbyville. Fall largemouth fishing might be the best time frame to hit the productive waters. At this time of the year, depending on water turbidity and temperatures, just about any lure and technique can produce fish.

Bluegills are taken in big numbers from May- to mid-June in 2-5 feet of water. Ice fishermen also do well on bluegills along creeks. In the summer you need to probe the cover and fish at dusk with live baits or light spinning lures. Crickets, roaches, grasshoppers, grubs, small lively minnows, and redworms also tempt the denizens.

White bass were introduced to the lake in 1971 and today, thousands are taken annually. During the long and early (late April) spawning runs (up the Kaskaskia and West Okaw Rivers), just about any colorful spinning lure or jig and minnow drifted will produce fish. After the spawning run the fish return to the lake in May and June, and are often caught in the shallow flats when they are feeding. Fish early and late, or on cloudy days during this time of the year. In the fall anglers should look for jumping schools of shad, and cast and retrieve in the direction of the jumping bait fish.

The resort has 138 luxurious guest rooms and 10 suites with fireplaces.

Walleye have been stocked for many years in the lake. They do some spawning in the lake and streams and may run up the Kaskaskia River and to a lesser degree in the West Okaw River. The run begins in mid-March and lasts until mid-April, and presents the best opportunity to catch them on jigs and minnows, diving lures and small spinners. White and yellows are the preferred colors according to several bait shopkeepers.

Muskies in excess of 20 pounds have been captured by biologists during routine population surveys, and it's said fishermen that have seen have never been the same again. Muskie are the lone wolf of the fish world, lurking in dense vegetation or along rocks and other structures waiting for prey. Try trolling deep with muskie plugs and spoons in the summer, or time your visits in spring and fall when they move to spawn and feed and sometimes chase large minnows, large spinners and jerk baits.

Creel limits: largemouth bass, 14 inch minimum, six daily; crappie, 10 inch minimum, 10 daily; walleye, 14 inch minimum, six daily; muskie, 36 inch minimum, one daily.

Hiking: Eagle Creek, an area with generally flat terrain, has four nature

79

trails and the three-mile Snowflake cross-country ski trail that begins at the campground check station and travels through a natural prairie and wooded area. There are also opportunities for snowmobiles and horseback riders.

The Campfire Trail (.5-mile) begins and ends at the end of the Campfire Drive and is a moderate loop along the lakeshore and along two coves with one bench about halfway out. The Windy Point Trail (1-mile) begins on the north side of Hawk Lane and traverses three wooden bridges and borders part of the lakeshore. The High Bluff Trail (.5-mile) is ideal for family ventures to the high banks of Lake Shelbyville and begins and ends on Quail Drive. There is a bench along the way. The Prairie View Trail (1.5-miles) leads from the campground to the boat ramp and takes you through a variety of flora communities.

But the biggest and best trail, which I only completed half of before being rained out by drops the size of walnuts, is the Chief Illini Trail, an 11-mile scenic journey along the edge of Lake Shelbyville. The trail was originally going to be highly developed trail, but over the years funding and momentum were lost and the trail is now partly maintained by the Corps and the state's Department of Conservation.

The trail was developed in the early 1980s and ranges from Lone Point to Eagle Creek along the east shore of the lake. It is marked with white, diamond-shaped blazes and post markings, and in parts is somewhat difficult to follow. The trail traces some up-and-down ridges along the lake, through fields, even near some residential areas. Although I hiked only part of the Eagle Creek section, park staff say the section near Lone Point Recreation Area is the nicest and has the best vistas of the lake. You be the judge.

Day-use areas: Basketball, volleyball, a golf course, tennis courts, shoreline fishing and several fully developed picnic areas with grills, water, tables and toilets are scattered along the western edge of the lake in Eagle Creek State Park.

Hunting: About 800 acres are hunted in the Eagle Creek Wildlife Management Area west of the park. Also in the area is the 3,000-acre Shelbyville Fish and Wildlife Area.

14   *Eldon Hazlet State Park*

Land: 3,000 acres   Water: Lake Carlyle

The Illinois state park system's largest campground and most modern sailboat harbor (it has hosted Olympic trials) is along the west banks of the state's largest man-made lake, where campers, sailors and fishermen swell the park to capacity during warm weather months enjoying the huge lake and the many facilities around its shoreline.

The oval-shaped, 26,000-acre lake was built by the Army Corps of Engineers in the late 1950s and was named for a Carlyle attorney who organized the development of two of Illinois' three largest reservoir/ recreational complexes, Carlyle and Lake Shelbyville, plus improvements along the Kaskaskia River during the 1960s.

Recent improvements to the state park include a campground renovation, nearby Corps visitor's center, a "smell-less" fish cleaning station, improvement at the sailing association, biking trails and reasonable fees. They have helped balloon annual attendance to nearly one million at the state park, and more than 4.5 million visitors to the lake area. Significant infrastructure improvement throughout the region is rapidly making Carlyle Lake a destination for visitors, special events, golfers, tournament fishermen, Jet Ski events, meetings and much more.

In 1972 there were a rash of UFO sightings that occurred in the great lake area, about the same time American bald eagles began their comeback in the area. Nearby Salem, Illinois, is the birthplace of Miracle Whip salad dressing and the birthplace of William Jennings Bryan.

The Lake Carlyle area is consistently one of the top two visitor designations in the state. It's no wonder. The area has the state's largest lake, 85 miles of shoreline, sailboats on the horizon, four marinas, 15,000 acres of waterfowl hunting area, 1,000 picnic tables and grills, two state parks, and thousands of acres to roam. Some pretty good restaurants, too!

Information and Activities

Eldon Hazlet State Park
1351 Ridge Street
Carlyle, IL 62231
(618) 594-3015

Information: The park office is just inside the entrance of the park and is open 8 a.m. - 3:30 p.m. The Corps Visitor Center is in the Dam West area (618-594-LAKE). The park closes at 11 p.m. and quiet hours are 10 p.m. to 7 a.m.

Campground: Illini Campground at Hazlet is the largest of the state-owned camping facilities and has undergone significant renovations and upgrading in the past few years. There are 328 gravel camping pads for Class A campers, and 36 tent sites. There are some pull-through sites, and many sites along the cove where you can bring your boat up to your shoreline camping site. The north end loop is the most private area, and group leaders must call for reservations and information about the youth and group camping areas. The tent camping is a walk-in area that is shady and complete with picnic tables and grills.

Hazlet operates three shower buildings with flush toilets, 12 drinking water fountains and one water fillup station. All camping sites have a picnic table and fire grill. More than 75 percent of all camping sites are accessible by the disabled. Big RVs won't have any problem maneuvering in this spacious campground.

Generally, the campground is 75 percent shady, moderately private, busy during the warm weather months, and great for large camping rigs or tiny tents.

Other nearby privately operated camping includes Green Acres, Harbor Lights, Lakeside Camping (618-749-5381), Shady Oak and Hide-Away (618-749-5369) campgrounds. The Corps operates other camping, including Dam West Recreation Area (618-594-4410), Coles Creek Recreation Area (618-226-3211), Dam East Recreation Area, and Boulder Recreation Area (618-226-3586).

Emergency numbers: State police, (618) 345-1212; Clinton County Sheriff, (618) 594-4555; other emergencies, dial 911.

Fishing: You may receive a 24-page *"Carlyle Lake Fishing Guide"* (free) at the visitor center or park office, or by writing the Illinois Department of Conservation, Division of Fish and Wildlife Resources, Lincoln Plaza Tower, 524 S. Second St., Springfield, IL 62706. Also call the toll free *(800) ASK-FISH* for up-to-date fishing information that details conditions, regulations, lodging, camping and other pieces of information on many major Illinois lakes, rivers and streams.

Carlyle Lake offers good fishing for crappie, white bass, largemouth bass, channel and flathead catfish, drum and carp. Other species commonly caught are green sunfish, yellow bass and yellow and black bullhead. The tailwater area directly below the spillway has had 32 species taken from that area.

Crappies are typically found in good numbers in bays with stickups, river and creek channels, bottomland lakes, rock riprap, and areas with just

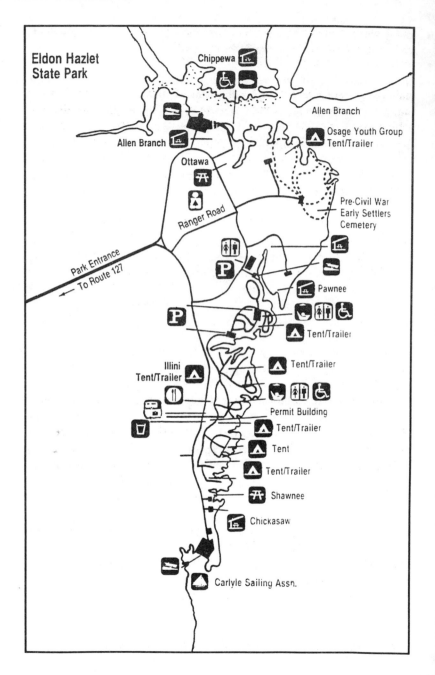

Eldon Hazlet
State Park

Chippewa

Allen Branch

Osage Youth Group
Tent/Trailer

Allen Branch

Ottawa

Ranger Road

Pre-Civil War
Early Settlers
Cemetery

Park Entrance
To Route 127

Pawnee

Tent/Trailer

Tent/Trailer

Illini
Tent/Trailer

Permit Building

Tent/Trailer

Tent

Tent/Trailer

Shawnee

Chickasaw

Carlyle Sailing Assn.

about any type of cover. April and May are the best months for crappies; go deep and pray during the hot summer months. Minnows and jigs tipped with a live bait are practiced rigs.

Fishing is best for largemouth bass from May to mid-October in Lake Carlyle, and areas with cover or an abundant food supply are the best fishing spots. Bass like the water temperature between 58-75 degrees. Pre- and post-spawn are good fishing periods; during the summer, move to deep holes, cooler waters of river and creek channel ridge dropoffs, spring holes and submerged brush. Bass angling is also very good in the fall as the fish begin to roam before freeze-up.

Fortunately, largemouths can be caught on a wider variety of lures and baits than practically any other species. Spinnerbaits, wobbling or flashing spoons with pork rinds, spinning lures and light colored surface lures work well in spring or murky waters. In early summer and as the water clears, try buzz baits, sub-surface lures, plastic worms and diving baits. Live baits, crayfish, crawlers and minnows can also get the attention of old bucketmouth.

Many locals use their expensive flyrods to simply cast small poppers or dry flys for bluegills. The action can be fast, producing many eating-size gills. Traditional bluegill methods also work for pre- and post-spawn bluegills. Use live bait for the fastest action from May- to mid-June.

The most popular fish on the lake is channel catfish---they are most easily caught in May, June, September and October. Preferred baits include shiners, gizzard shad, crayfish and leeches, or cut baits of carp, bowfin, white carp and shad. In the summer season catfishing is best in the tailwater with stink baits, cheese, soured clams or liver.

Boating: West Access Marina, (618) 594-2461; Boulder Marina, 226-3223; Keyesport Marina, 749-5222; Carlyle Sailing Association, 594-3622; or the state park office, 594-3015. There are three launching ramps in the park: Allen Branch (concession stand) has three-lanes; the day-use launch has two-lanes; and Peppen Hoist has a one-lane ramp. Sailboat launching is available for a small fee at the sailing association facility.

There is no horsepower limit, but the lake is a very controlled body of water and all boating regulations and safety rules should be closely followed. Many Jet Skis operate on the lake alongside of sailboats and water skiers. Lake Carlyle is a busy body of water.

Sailboats: One of the state's few specially designed sailboat marinas is here, offering overnight mooring, supplies, lessons, rentals and excellent wind conditions from its unique prairie setting. There are two regattas annually, a festival, races and even Olympic trials are held.

Hiking: Four miles of hiking trails wander across five wooden bridges, through bottomlands, and past black cherry, sassafras and oak trees. All of the trails can be accessed from one trailhead, Cherokee Hiking trails. The easy trails pass by an old family cemetery. If you are quiet and visit at the right times of the year and day, you may see osprey, bald eagles, many varieties of herons, and some of more than 155 avian species spotted in recent years (birding lists are available from the Corps visitor center). There are also two trails south of the Cherokee Trail that meander through field areas, with no lake views. Bike trails are also maintained by the park.

Day-use areas: There are abundant day-use opportunities that include five reservable picnic shelters, hundreds of picnic tables, a basketball court, shuffleboard, horseshoes and bike trails. The attractive picnic shelters are some of the nicest in the entire park system. The concession stand at the Allen Branch boat ramp offers grocery items and cold drinks for park users. In many ways, this is a destination park for day use.

Nature: A small interpretive staff at the park offers a variety of natural history programs for school groups and park users. Check with the office for an up-to-date schedule. Most programs are one hour in length and might include group tours, evening programs, off-site presentations, guided hikes and special events.

Hunting: Disabled hunters and fishermen can shoot and catch their limits at specially-designed hunting and fishing facilities at the lake. The Army Corps of Engineers has a 150-foot pier for disabled anglers at the east end of the dam, and a duck blind accessible for the disabled is near the Cole Creek recreation area. Call for information and reservations at 594-2484. For the put-and-take pheasant season and waterfowl hunting, call the site superintendent for information.

15   Ferne Clyffe State Park

Land: 1,100 acres Water: 16-acre lake

Can you imagine what it must have been like to be a hunter or a family group from the Late Woodland Indian culture of as long ago as 500 B.C. to use the many rock overhangs at Ferne Clyffe State Park as shelter? Home? The rich lands around you, not polluted, pristine, teaming with wildlife and lush forests must have been wonderful. Luckily, you can still experience many of those feelings while walking some of the park's 10 nature trails that visit rock shelters, canyons, brooks and meadows and a nature preserve that is mostly like it was thousands of years ago.

More recently, George Rogers Clark and his famous Kentucky "Long Knives" used the area in the late 1830s as they moved westward. In 1899, the Dennison bothers purchased a portion of the park that had a large shelter bluff known today as Hawk's Cave/Rocky Hollow and named the area Ferne Clyffe.

The area became increasingly well-known for its quiet natural beauty and was eventually sold to Emma Rebman, an area teacher and ardent conservationist, who opened the park to the public on Sundays for a 10-cent admission (today it's free!). It didn't take long for the hilly and wooded terrain to become even more popular. Soon train service was initiated, and in 1929, Miss Rebman sold the park to the state for posterity. Thanks to her untiring efforts, the park was preserved.

Today, about 250,000 people annually visit the majestic Shawnee Hills to enjoy the dells, cascades and scenic vistas.

Information and Activities

Ferne Clyffe State Park
P.O. Box 120
Goreville, IL 62939
(618) 995-2411

Directions: Between I-24 and I-57 in Johnson County, south of Goreville, take exit 7 from I-24 then west to I-37 to the park entrance. From I-57, take exit 40, then east to I-37 and south to the lush park. The park is open year-round.

Campground: Deer Ridge has two Class A loops with a total of 66 camping sites. Turkey Ridge (near the parking lot) offers 20 tent camping areas, and there is a backpacking campground that requires about a half-mile hike down the Happy Hollow trail to five shady sites at the west side of the park.

Deer Ridge is well shaded and has gravel parking pads, electricity, picnic tables and cooking grills. The showers are open seasonally (late April-late November) and in the shower building there are flush toilets and other comforts. Loop 1-23 is mixed shady with lots of mature maples towering overhead, with odd-numbered sites backing up to a wooded view. The Blackjack Oak Trail starts behind site No. 2 and is considered difficult.

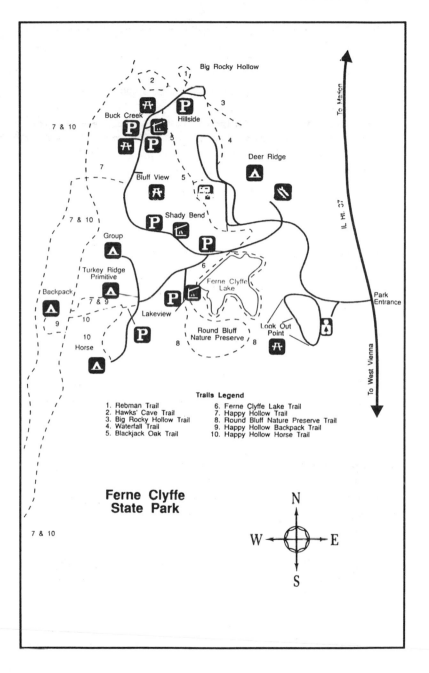

Big Rocky Hollow

7 & 10

Buck Creek

Hillside

Deer Ridge

Bluff View

7

7 & 10

Shady Bend

Group

Turkey Ridge
Primitive

Backpack

7 & 9

9

Lakeview

10

10
Horse

Ferne Clyffe
Lake

Park
Entrance

Look Out
Point

Round Bluff
Nature Preserve

8

8

To Macon

IL Ht. 37

To West Vienna

Trails Legend

1. Rebman Trail
2. Hawks' Cave Trail
3. Big Rocky Hollow Trail
4. Waterfall Trail
5. Blackjack Oak Trail

6. Ferne Clyffe Lake Trail
7. Happy Hollow Trail
8. Round Bluff Nature Preserve Trail
9. Happy Hollow Backpack Trail
10. Happy Hollow Horse Trail

7 & 10

Ferne Clyffe
State Park

N

W — E

S

In the loop with sites 24-55, most of the sites are not very private. Generally speaking, the campground is of medium quality, clean and well-clipped. This is a hikers' park!

Boating: Not allowed on the small lake, nor is swimming.

Fishing: Shoreline angling is allowed on the 16-acre lake and fishermen have some pretty good luck using corn to lure trout that are stocked most alternate years. Use crickets for bluegill and smelly livers for channel cats, say the locals. A trout stamp is required for trout fishing and the season is closed May 15 to the first Saturday in April.

Built in 1960, the lake has a maximum depth of 21 feet, and nearly one mile of shoreline.

Creel limits: channel catfish, six per day, no size limit; bass, six daily, no size limit; bluegill, crappie and redear, no limit; trout, five daily. Funds for stocking trout come from the inland trout stamp program.

Hiking: Hiking is very popular at the park. Ten diverse trails are well-marked and easy to difficult, taking hikers by unique natural and often rare flora communities and great rock formations, cliffs, rock shelters, brooks, meadows, canyons and bluffs.

In many ways, this state park lives up to its name with many types of wispy ferns species, rocky cliffs and tall bluffs reaching out and up at many points along the maze of hiking trails. The views from the bluffs during the fall are dazzling, and many visitors use the park at this time of the year to view the small waterfall and streams (if it has rained recently) at the end of Big Rocky Hollow Trail or look for deer as they become increasingly active in the autumn along the edges areas of fields and trails.

There are both short and easy trails and long, challenging nature walkways at the park. Trail Nos. 1-6 ultimately connect and are on the north side of the lake, while Trail No. 8 circles the natural area south of the lake. The remaining trails, 7, 9 and 10, tour the Happy Hollow area. Isn't Happy Hollow a great name for a walking trail? There is some horse traffic on portions of trails 7 and 10.

Rebman Trail (Trail No. 1) is a 300-yard-long level loop that is dedicated to Miss Emma Rebman and passes by a small waterfall in Little Rocky Hollow at the northern tip of the park.

Hawk's Cave Trail (Trail No. 2) is just west of trail 1 and takes you to one of the largest shelter caves in the park. The trail is an easy one mile trek.

Big Rocky Hollow (Trail No. 3) starts at the Hillside picnic area and travels along a tiny stream to a 90-foot narrow waterfall at the end of a three-sided canyon. Large sandstone boulders, ferns and the cool wet canyon make this one of the best hikes at the park. It is an easy one-mile walk.

Waterfall Trail (Trail No. 4) is a moderately difficult three-quarter-mile hike that departs from the Deer Ridge Camping Area. This trail is great for campers to reach the water, as are trails 1, 2 and 3.

Blackjack Oak (Trail No. 5) is a one-mile hike that will steal some of your breath. It begins at the Hillside picnic area, offering beautiful vistas and a brief tour of the dry cliffs of Shawnee Hills and blackjack oak blufftops. There are two steep climbs, and the pathway is considered moderately difficult.

Ferne Clyffe Trail (Trail No. 6) is a gentle walk that fishermen can use to access most of the lakeshore. Bring a sandwich, rod and reel, and spend the morning sunning and fishing the boatless lake.

Happy Hollow Trail (Trail No. 7) has a trailhead in the primitive camping area and is a five-mile long spur that winds through forests and fields and joins trail 10.

Round Bluff Nature Preserve (Trail No. 8) has a trailhead at the Lakeview picnicking area and offers one of the best opportunities to see dry and wet plant communities, great rock formations and facing bluffs.

Happy Hollow Backpack Trail (Trail No. 9) take backpackers to the backpacking primitive camping area downhill to trail 7 and 10. The half-mile trail is a short, easy trail to the canyon. Backpackers should call the park office before they visit.

Happy Hollow Horse Trail (Trail No. 10) is an eight-mile-long equestrian delight. Hikers also use the trail along the west side of the park.

Day-use areas: The Lakeview picnic area is a terrific location for a family gathering complete with a large covered shelter, lake view, open spaces, parking and a private, wooded terrain next to the nature trail that accesses the Round Bluff Nature Preserve.

The seven picnic day-use areas are concentrated and usually near open spaces, equipped with grills, drinking water, trash barrels and vault toilets.

Nature: The Round Bluff Nature Preserve, formally dedicated as a sanctuary for native fauna and flora, is maintained in its natural condition for present and future generations to see Illinois land as it appeared to the pioneers. This living example of our natural heritage is also important for science studies in geology, soils science and natural history, and provides habitat for rare plants and animals. Visitors are welcome in the area, but please help preserve this natural area that is protected by law. The trail is a one-mile, difficult loop with wonderful rock formations along the shady pathway.

About 30 species of warblers are spotted during spring migration, according to Todd Fink, a well-known biologist and expert birder stationed at the park.

Hunting: Deer, squirrel, rabbits and some upland game are hunted. Call for details on open seasons and special rules.

Nearby attractions include Crab Orchard Wildlife Refuge (fishing, boating and hunting), Little Grassy Lake, a small fish hatchery and Illinois Centre Mall.

16　Fort Massac State Park

Land: 1,470 acres　Water: Ohio River

From tour bus visitors to history buffs and casino boat stowaways, Fort Massac in Massac County combines a historic fort, sunny camping, professional museum and scenic beauty to please every user. Overlooking the Ohio River, with Kentucky lying on the opposite shore, the splendid historic area was the first state park in Illinois, dedicated in 1908, and is typically the second most visited unit year after year.

Fort Massac is the perfect place to quietly relax and enjoy the soothing cool wooded sites and immerse yourself in a unique hands-on opportunity to explore our national heritage.　A well-stocked museum presents engrossing tales, artifacts, a videotape presentation, dioramas, photographs, period costumes and the wildly popular October encampment, an authentic re-enactment of the lifestyle of the 1700s and early 1800s that includes mock battles, Voyageur canoe races, fife and drum corps, traders and crafts persons and lots more. The park also has a number of smaller living history weekends throughout the year.

The area has seen at least two fortifications over the years, with both structures destroyed by Indians and earthquakes. The existing fort was built east of the 1757 original, whose outline is based on archeological digs, including a blockhouse.

The rich background of the region begins long before recorded history, when Native Americans used the area that was flush with game, fish and forests along the mighty Ohio River. Europeans recognized the same advantages of the area and occupied the site by 1540, when Spanish explorer Hernando DeSoto build a small fort. Years later, in 1757, the French built Fort De L'Ascension during the French and Indian War, and rebuilt it in 1759-1760. The fort was renamed Massiac (which was later simplified to Massac) after the then French minister of Marine.

The French abandoned the fort at the end of the war in 1763. It was burned by the Chickasaw tribe and rebuilt until President George Washington ordered it reconstructed. Ravaged by an earthquake in 1811, the fort was again rebuilt and played a minor role in the War of 1812, only to be abandoned in 1814. The site served the military briefly in the mid-1800s, but it wasn't until 1903, through the efforts of the Daughters of the American Revolution, that 24 acres surrounding the site were purchased by the state and the park was dedicated in November 1908.

Several archeological digs were conducted over the years, and modern reconstruction of the fort didn't begin until 1971. Today, the impressive fort offers visitors a personal experience of what life was like behind the timber walls, and the museum does a wonderful job of interpreting the history and lifestyle of the 1700s and 1880s. It is amazing to think about the three flags that have flown over the fort and the lives the area has touched since. Nearly two million visit the park and fort annually.

Fort Massac is a perfect place to bring the family for camping, education, nearby services—a Kentucky Fried Chicken restaurant is across the street—camping and exposure to a rich living history experience.

Information and Activities

Fort Massac State Park
1308 E. 5th Street
Metropolis, IL 62960
(618) 524-4712

Directions: Exit 37 off I-24 west to U.S. 45. The park is about 2.5 miles west of the interstate, near Metropolis at the southern tip of the state. The park is open daily 7 a.m.-10 p.m. The museum is open year-round, 10 a.m. - 5:30 p.m. and guided tours are available by advance request.

Campground: The campground is about 80 percent open and sunny. Fifty Class A sites have gravel pads, picnic tables and grills. A walk-in tent camping can accommodate many campers, many more than the advertised 10 tent camping sites. The showers for all campers are open April 15 to Dec. 15.

The campground host is located immediately upon entering the campground at the northeast side of the fort and museum complex. Sites 1-12 are very open, while sites 13 and 15 offer more shade and privacy. Site 16 is out in the open. All of the trailer camping sites are the same size, with some having mature trees. You may want to take a look around to find the best site for your rig. Sites 35, 38, 40, 42, 44, 45, 46, 47, 48 and 50 are shady. Medium- to large-sized RV rigs won't have any trouble navigating the camping area. Look for camping sites along the perimeter drive that back up against a wooded buffer area. There is one small playground area at the trailer campground.

The tent camping area is heavily wooded and shady, north of the trailer camping area. Sites are not marked, but have tables and grills nearby.

Emergency phone numbers: 911; ambulance, (618) 524-2176; police; 524-2310. Church services are offered at the small shelter in the camping area each Sunday morning.

Boating: A small, narrow and hard-surfaced boat ramp is open to the public with access to the Ohio River. It is located just east of the fort and

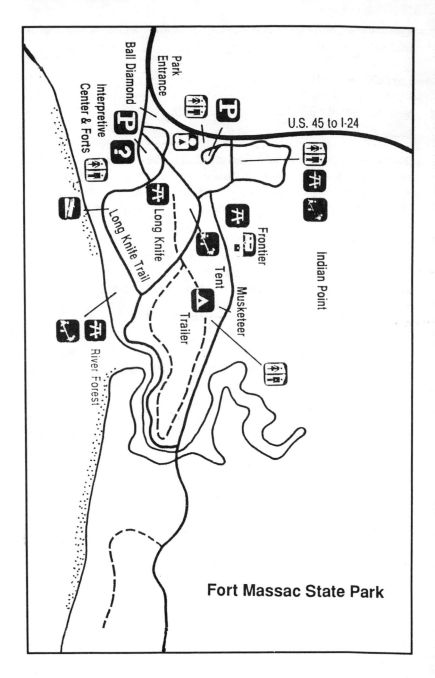

Fort Massac State Park

Fort Massac is one of the busiest and most educational parks in the state.

museum complex. The Ohio River at this location is more than a mile wide.

Fishing: You may bank fish the Ohio River or Massac Creek. Both places are only poor to fair locations, but youngsters may have luck catching some small rough fish.

Hiking: The easy 2.5-mile Hickory Nut Ridge trail traces the northern shoreline of the Ohio River east of the fort and museum complex. It's half road and half well-used trail, offering terrific views of the river, floodplain areas, mixed deciduous woods, and the occasional osprey, songbird and wading shorebird.

The Long Knife Trail starts near the fort and loops back to the picnic area on a half-mile route over grassy fields and sometimes wet wooded areas. Visitors may walk in the nature preserve, but there are no designated trails.

Day-use areas: There is a significant day-use area just inside the park entrance and across the street from some shopping and small restaurants. The shady, open space has plenty of parking, picnic tables, grills and drinking fountain and is along U.S. 45 north of the fort and museum complex. There are two picnic shelters (one is reservable) and three small playgrounds in the park.

Nature: The park is divided by roadway. East of the state park is Massac Forest Nature Preserve, a 245-acre forest that features bald cypress swamps, pin and white oak flats, pecan, American elm, endangered flora and a large floodplain area. A large flock of wild turkey and pileated woodpecker are often seen, while park staff have sighted a bobcat a few times in the preserve.

Hunting: Archery deer. Call for information.

Special notes: The museum is great and the living history activities are even better. At the fort and museum complex, learn about the Indians of Illinois, flintlock muskets, authentic clothing, military lifestyles, mess kits, legions of the U.S., how the fort was built, tools, river, fishing, archeological finds, arrowheads and other projectile points, George Rogers Clark and much more. Inquire about the many special events and activities at the popular and well-maintained park. Increased marketing of the area and planned improvements to the museum complex will make Fort Massac State Park one of the finest educational parks in the system.

Nearby attractions: The Merv Griffin's Players Riverboat Casino, in neighboring Paducah, Ky., steams up and down the mile-wide Ohio River daily, offering 35 gaming tables, 630 slot and video poker machines, big six wheel, bar and grill, all on the authentic 1,400-passenger side wheel riverboat. The Shawnee National Forest, Weeping Willow Arts and Crafts Mall, Superman statue, Ferry Street Station and Cash River and Huron Ponds natural areas are also close to the park.

17   *Fox Ridge State Park*

Land: 864 acres   Water: 14-acre lake

Unlike the billiard table-flat adjoining terrain, the Fox Ridge park enjoys rolling hills, thickly wooded ridges, herbaceous valleys and scenic footpaths interlaced by steep, broad wooded plots and rare openings along the bluffs of the Embarras (pronounced "Ambraw") River. In 1938 and 1939 the state of Illinois took over management and development of the small parcel which has grown and been preserved by an active volunteer foundation. More parks should have active foundations dedicated to park programming and improvement and fund-raising.

Much of the pioneer life of this area was centered around the Embarras River that provided food and transportation, and of course, water. Before the railroad, flat bottom boats weighed down by loads of livestock, barrels, and all types of merchandise traveled downstream to Wabash,

Ohio, and often to the Mississippi River and on to New Orleans.

The presence of prehistoric Indian cultures is also evident at the park, with the finding of many projectile points, a stone ax and pottery bits. The early historic tribes of the area include Piankeshaw and the Illinois, both of whom were pushed out of the rich region when the Kickapoo migrated into this area from Wisconsin in the late 1600s. Several battles are on record between the Kickapoo and early settlers of the Fox Ridge area.

Tiny Ridge Lake is man-made and used for limnological investigation designed to improve fishing in all Illinois lakes. Studies include the effects of drawdowns, supplemental feeding, pollution, aquatic communities and more, all located in the little red brick building built in 1941 that lies along the shoreline at the bottom of a long stairway. The dam is 385 feet long and 29 feet wide at the crest.

Information and Activities

Fox Ridge State Park
R.R.1, P.O. Box 234
Charleston, IL 61920
(217) 345-6416

Directions: In Coles County, eight miles south of Charleston in east-central Illinois, off Route 130.

Information: Open 6 a.m. - 10 p.m.

Campground: Wilderness Campground has several recent upgrades, including a new shower house and other infrastructure improvements around the campground and main park roadway.

The camping area is about 70 percent shaded, with walls of vegetation separating camping sites in many areas. Some of the most private sites are 3, 4, 5, 7, 9, 12, 14, 16 and 18. At sites 14-18 you will actually back your rig right into the woods, enjoying shade, and tons of privacy. Sites 19, 20, 21, 23, 24,28, 29 and 30 are also cut right into the forest. All of these sites have picnic tables and gravel pads, and are some of the best

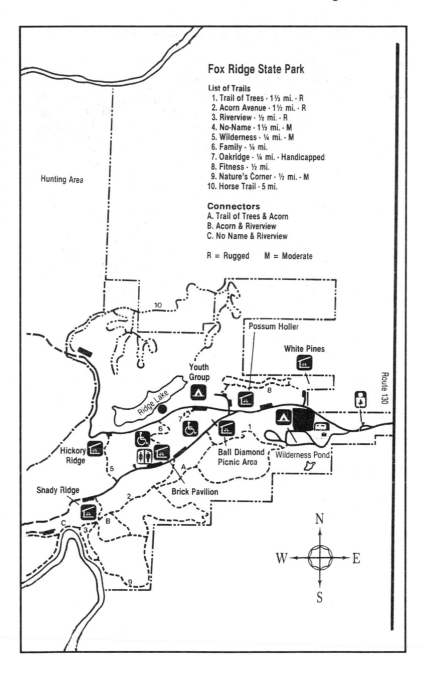

Fox Ridge State Park

List of Trails
1. Trail of Trees · 1⅓ mi. · R
2. Acorn Avenue · 1½ mi. · R
3. Riverview · ½ mi. · R
4. No-Name · 1½ mi. · M
5. Wilderness · ¼ mi. · M
6. Family · ¼ mi.
7. Oakridge · ¼ mi. · Handicapped
8. Fitness · ½ mi.
9. Nature's Corner · ½ mi. · M
10. Horse Trail · 5 mi.

Connectors
A. Trail of Trees & Acorn
B. Acorn & Riverview
C. No Name & Riverview

R = Rugged   M = Moderate

Hunting Area

Possum Holler

White Pines

Youth Group

Ridge Lake

Route 130

Hickory Ridge

Shady Ridge

Ball Diamond Picnic Area

Wilderness Pond

Brick Pavilion

N
W   E
S

camping sites in the entire state parks system.

Site 36 is a particularly cozy site that you can back your trailer into a carved-out portion of the forest with enough room for extra chairs, picnic space and children's toys.

The campground is rarely filled, even on holiday weekends, although it has a few of the best sites you will find in any public campground. Group camping is available.

Boating: There is no boating on the lake, other than boats offically checked out for fishing. Nearby Canoe Limited offers canoe and kayak rentals four miles west of the park entrance, offering water-based touring.

Fishing: Ridge Lake, a tree-lined experimental fishing lake, is fished by permission granted by the Illinois Natural History Survey, a division of the Department of Energy and Natural Resources. Ridge Lake was drained in 1985 and all fish were removed. The lake was restocked in 1986 with largemouth bass, bluegill, black crappie and channel catfish. In the early 1990s walleye and additional channel catfish were introduced. Slot limits are in effect on the lake for walleye and bass.

The lake is open to fishing from April to October. Fishing hours are 6 a.m. - 10 a.m. and 3 p.m.- 8 p.m. daily. The lake is closed to fishing on Monday and Tuesday. Only boat fishing is permitted and boats are provided free of charge. You must check in for boat assignments. Anglers can make reservations by writing the Illinois Natural History Survey, Fox Ridge State Park, R.R. 1, P.O. Box 233, Charleston, IL 61920, or call (217) 345-6490 during daily fishing hours. Because the lake is so highly controlled, fishing is good to very good. Shoreline fishing, ice fishing and ice skating are prohibited.

Take the 131 winding steps down the wooded stairway to the red brick and green roofed building where you can request a boat and talk with the fish biologists that work there. About 10 green flat-bottom johnboats are docked in front of the building waiting for registered anglers to row away and catch a big one.

Try fishing the Embarras River during the early spring.

Hiking: A fitness trail, near the White Pines day-use area and youth group camping, is a .5-mile trail with a reader board that tells you how to warm up and improve your cardiovascular fit and monitor your heart rate. Fitness/exercise stations are located along the course, where you can stop to do simple exercises. Check with your physician before trying this trail. If the doctor says no, try a game of volleyball on the court across the road.

Five trails total five miles and interconnect along the south side of the park roadway. There are some trails on the north side of the lake also.

The 1.3-mile-long Trail of Trees is considered rugged, wandering along steep valleys and wooded ridges; Acorn Avenue, 1.5-mile-long, is also considered rugged and very enjoyable as it treks through some towering mature hardwoods and down a lush valley to connect with the Trail of Trees. Riverview, No Name and Wilderness trails offer some fine overlooks and moderately difficult hiking.

The main park road is also terrific for leisurely walks in the evening. No bikes are allowed on hiking trails.

Trails in some areas are closed Nov. 1-April 15. A four-mile-long horse trail is located at the north side of the park.

Day-use areas: Unlike most parks, a big part of the clientele at Fox Ridge is corporate and business outings, using the quality picnic shelters, game areas and open spaces for company getaways and picnics. Five quality shelters and upgraded children's play equipment are complimented by tables, toilets, game courts and drinking water along the many day-use turnouts south of Ridge Lake. Many picnic shelters have soft drink machines, cooking grills, trash barrels, and even phones.

Other points of interest in the park are a couple of CCC timber and stone picnic structures that continue to stand strong and look wonderful.

Nature: A bird checklist is available at the park office.

Hunting: About 800 acres at the north end of the park are used for seasonal hunting activities. Call the site superintendent for details.

18   Franklin Creek State Park

Land: 520 acres Water: Franklin Creek

The linear day-use park extends along Franklin Creek as it meanders east and west, winding past rock outcroppings and bluffs, near farmlands, and bisects brushy fields now used for hunting, horseback riding and hiking.

Picnicking shelters in the park are busy, with many sporting a weekly schedule of users posted on wooden spans. One principal picnic shelter is the Hausen-Knox Day-use Shelter, located at the east end of the park near the widening of the creek called Black Bass Pond. This shelter and surrounding woodlands were donated by the Winifred Hausen-Knox Foundation and represents a living monument in honor of those that came to Lee County as settlers. The shelter and surrounding area now see plenty of uses and many families gather at the restful picnic sites weekly.

Pioneer families in the 1830s found the Franklin Creek area an inviting new home on the sometimes unfriendly and stark prairie. The large cool springs provided ample amounts of drinking water and early refrigeration. In addition the creek provided construction materials, fish and food. Franklin Creek also provided power for mills, much like the restored mill at the park. These settlers also benefited from the deep, pleasant valleys protected by limestone and sandstone bluffs that made ideal shelters from the bitter winter winds.

The park's 180-acre nature preserve has diverse natural areas in a uniquely beautiful setting framed by high, rocky bluffs, a wandering creek and rich areas where flora and fauna flourish. Geology lovers will remark about the three distinct rock strata that are exposed at the park.

New Richmond sandstone, a soft rock of the Lower Ordovician age, is exposed at the bottom of the gorge in the central part of the park. This is the oldest rock formation in the state, dating to 500 million years ago.

Information and Activities

Franklin Creek State Park
1872 Twist Road
Franklin Grove, IL 61031
(815) 456-2878

Directions: Eight miles east of Dixon, north of Route 38 in Lee County.

Campground: none

Boating: none

Fishing: The meandering Franklin Creek can be fished from adjoining state properties and a population of smallmouth bass, channel catfish and carp are sometimes taken. Fishing can be fair in the early spring for bass when they are on the beds. Youngsters will enjoy trying for rough fish in the typically slow-moving creek. Stay in the designated day-use areas and use live baits.

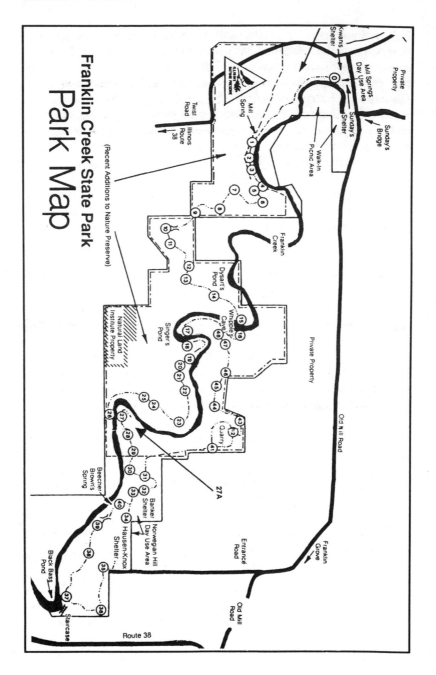

Franklin Creek State Park
Park Map

Hiking: Franklin Creek has 4.5 miles of hiking trails, one of which is the Mill Springs Handicapped Trail, a hard-surfaced trail suitable for wheelchairs or other mobility challenged visitors. A map is available at the park office that details the four other hiking trails, which includes the nearly two-mile-long Pioneer Pass that is moderate in difficulty and crosses the creek three times while taking hikes through woods, across fields, near outcroppings and along some great bottomlands. All of the hiking trails can be accessed from various day-use areas along the stretched-out park, and the trailhead marks offer maps in a nifty metal lift-up box.

Other trails include the Norwegian Hill Trail (1 mile), Black Bass Trail (1 mile) located at the east end of the park, and the Quarry Trail (1 mile). Snowmobiling and cross-country skiing are allowed on portions of the equestrian trails.

The park has six miles of equestrian trails, with a staging area directly behind the tan-colored park office building.

Day-use areas: Norwegian Hills and Mill Springs day-use areas have two and three picnic shelters respectively, and are complete with electricity, cooking grills, picnic tables, restrooms and drinking water. Facilities at Sunday's Shelter are handicapped accessible. The larger day-use shelters, Sunday's, Bartlett and Hausen-Knox, may be reserved in advance by calling the site superintendent.

Nature: A small glacial drift hill prairie remnant is present in the preserve where Indian grass and tall dropseed are seen. Other interesting plant species include false toadflax, flowering spurge and hoary puccoon. Nineteen species of fish have been recorded in the creek, while a variety of breeding birds populate the site.

Hunting: Archery deer hunting is allowed in the north section of the park that consists of about 180 acres of hardwoods and brushy fields. Call the site superintendent for additional information.

19 Gebhard Woods State Park
I & M Information Center

Land: 30 acres   Water: canal

The 30-acre Gebhard Woods is only two miles from the state's largest tree, adjacent to a restored aqueduct, and is one of the most informative and scenic access points to the I & M Canal along its 96-mile corridor.

The park closes at 9 p.m. and there is limited Class D camping in the Big Bend Youth Group area north of the ball diamond along Nettle Creek. The camping area is about one-third mile from the parking lot. You may set up if the park office is closed. Someone will be around to register you later. Gebhard

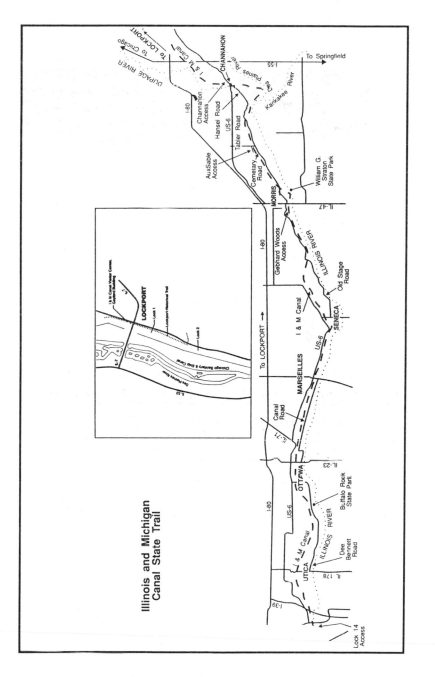

Illinois and Michigan
Canal State Trail

is located west of Morris; P.O. Box 272, Morris, IL. Call (815) 942-0796.

Access to the canal is the focal point of the small, shady park. The historic canal bisects a large portion of the state. Construction on the long canal began in 1836 and finished in 1848 helping the development of northern Illinois. It is now devoted to some interesting recreational opportunities along its linear path.

The arched bridge over the canal at Gebhard Woods takes you over the placid waters of the canal and is a perfect place to stop and look up and down the straight canal. The I & M Information Center is in the park office. A sign at the end of the bridge uses arrows and numbers to describe the distance to other parks and towns along the graveled canal trailway. The total length of the canal-side trail is 55 miles, linking parks and communities along its path. Buffalo Rock State Park is a 26-mile bike ride or hike from this access point.

The small information center has a wall-sized chart showing the canal's main access points, towns and parks along the entire length of the waterway, and an entire wall of brochures that include information about parks, attractions, history, archaeology, natural history, places to go and local interest. Small photographs, dioramas and expert staff can answer your questions about the canal, parks, lodging and much more.

Experts say this section of the canal that runs through Gebhard is one of the best preserved parts of the historic canal system that linked the East Coast with the Mississippi River and the Gulf of Mexico. Canal diggers took great pride in their work during construction. The canal traffic brought goods and business up and down the corridor, through locks and to the people along the way.

This portion of the canal is still navigable by canoe.

The quiet park is a good day-use facility with horseshoe courts, toilets, ball fields, playground structures, two CCC picnic shelters, two foot bridges, ponds and shady respites. This is a great park to access the trail and slowly walk for a couple of hours, vigorously bike to the next town or try your luck fishing the murky waters for rough fish.

20   *Giant City State Park*

Land: 3,694 acres   Water: Little Grassy Lake access

The towering sandstone structures found in the park will remind you of the canyon-like streets and lofty office buildings of downtown Chicago. Like solemn gray buildings along Michigan Avenue, the ancient craggy formations look like urban skyscrapers along the shady walking trail—or "streets," you might call them—that lie between the outcropping at Giant City State Park in Jackson County. The name of the park was indeed derived from this group of huge sandstone blocks in the park. These magical passageways must have seemed like streets of the city of giants to the early pioneers. They are impressive. See for yourself!

Giant City is a destination park with breathtaking beauty, a wonderful lodge and restaurant, nature trails, fishing, sandstone cliffs, boating, hunting, nearby swimming at Crab Orchard Refuge and rock climbing— if you dare. Outdoor lovers of all types will be captivated by the retreat and enjoy the majestic landscape, lush fern-covered cliffs, flowering mints, hundreds of species of wildflowers, 75 species of trees, or just the fresh air that is filled with the sounds of songbirds and the whispers of the wind.

The hand-of-man accomplishments at the park are nearly as impressive as those of nature. The stately lodge that was constructed in 1939 by the depression-era Civilian Conservation Corps of multi-hued sandstone and white oak is found in the heart of the park, and is a favorite place for equestrians to visit, anglers to trade stories, businesspeople to attend conferences, or campers to enjoy a dinner in the Bald Knob dining room.

Each year about 140,000 people are served in the family-oriented restaurant, and thousands stay in the 34 tasteful cabins. The lush woodlands and natural environs beautifully contrast the elegant, but somewhat rustic, lodge and conference facility. In 1981, the state park was recognized as a National Natural Landmark by the Department of Interior.

Historians believe that the area around the park was populated as early as 400 B.C. and evidence of these inhabitants has been found in artifacts discovered in the rock bluffs and the smoke blackened ceiling of the two rock shelters of the park. Documentation of later habitation is found in the 80-foot sandstone wall near the entrance to the park. Archaeologists claim this wall dates to the late woodland period between 600-800 A.D. The first white settlers reached the area in the early 1800s from Kentucky and Tennessee. Sadly, none of these former residents of the area had a chance to taste a family-style chicken dinner at the restaurant.

Information and Activities

Giant City State Park
P.O. Box 70
Makanda, IL 62958
(618) 457-4836

Directions: In the Shawnee National Forest, 12 miles south of Carbondale off U.S. 51.

Campground: The park operates a horse camping area—bring your own horse—89 trailer sites (Class A), and 14 tent sites, which are typically full on holiday weekends and some weekends. There is also backpacking camping by permit for 15 tents about eight miles out on the moderately difficult trail. The unit also maintains a group camping area; leaders should call ahead for details.

Sites 1-10 are backed up against a woodline and are good for pop-up campers. Sites 12 ,14, 16 and 18 are also shady and next to a woodlot, while sites 13, 15 and 17 are more open. All sites have gravel pads, picnic tables and fire pits. Site 27 is a pull-though site. Sites 48-87 are more shady and compact.

Sites 39 and 42   are excellent sites, while site 40 is handicapped accessible.

The camping area is on the west side of the park not too far from Little Grassy Lake in a wooded and hilly area made up of a mixture of open and shady camping sites. There is a convenient boat launch at the nearby fishing lake. A shower house, flush toilets, water and sanitary facilities are in the camping area.

There are some pull through sites and two handicapped sites with hard-surfaced pads. Most sites in the campground are large enough to park medium to large RV rigs. Take a quick drive around the campground to identify the type of site you like most. The campground is usually filled on holidays, but spaces are generally available on summer weekends.

Emergency numbers: sheriff, (618) 684-2177; state police, 542-2171; ambulance, 684-5678; fire, 457-4131; hospital, 549-0721.

Lodge/Cabins: Dining and conferencing are increasingly popular at the unit, while guest cabins have long required advance registration. The restored lodge features a huge lobby, gift shop and the best family-style chicken dinner money can buy. If you don't like chicken, try a tender steak, prime ribs, ribs, chops or seafood. The 150-seat restaurant is open

Some of the rock formations for which the park is named.

seven days a week, with the Sunday family-style chicken dinner offered from 11:30 a.m. - 4 p.m.

The cabins are open the first Friday in February to mid-December. For reservations call (618) 457-4921. Reservations should be made for one of the 34 modern units as soon as you know your plans. The bluff cabins have fireplaces, wet bar and refrigerator. Four people can stay in the top-of-the-line bluff cabins for under $100 per night. The Historic and Prairie cabins have slightly fewer amenities, but are modern and nice. There are no cooking or pets allowed.

Boating: There are many boat launches in the nearby Crab Orchard National Wildlife Refuge recreation area around Little Grassy Lake (and Devil's Kitchen and Crab Orchard Lake). Giant City's one-lane ramp is east of the park on the eastern shore of Little Grassy Lake. There are four launching ramps on this productive lake. Boats are limited to 10 horsepower or less motors, and the jagged tree-lined lake is ideal for quiet

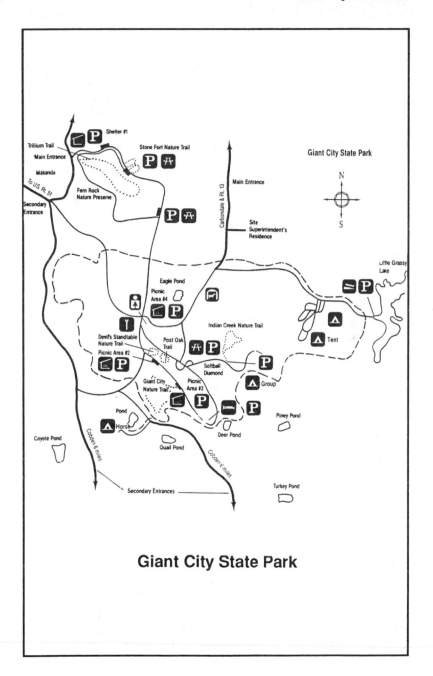

Giant City State Park

canoeing.

Fishing: Bluegill, bass and crappies are the species most sought after in Little Grassy Lake, while seven small ponds that average about 1.5 acres and about 10-feet deep are stocked within the park. Anglers often take good catfish catches using simple chicken liver drop rigs.

Serious anglers should visit the Devil's Kitchen Boat Dock off Grassy Road at the north end of the lake for daily updates on places to fish and what's biting.

Hiking: The overall facilities at the park are impressive, but they can't compare to the panoramic views from the trails, plunging valleys, lush ridgeline pathways, and cool trails that trace cliff faces and shady forested areas. The Post Oak Trail is handicapped accessible.

The featured hiking trail at the park is the 16-mile Red Cedar Hiking Trail (backcountry hiking/overnight campers will need a fee permit) that starts and ends at the camping area off the Giant City blacktop road and may also be accessed at other locations around the park. The trailhead starts at the tent camping area near a small parking lot, where a marker board indicates the layout and points of interest along the moderate to difficult trailway. The sometimes rugged trail is marked with white bands painted on trees with an orange spot in the middle. One white band indicates that the trail continues, while two white-colored bands means the trail changes direction. A small trail map is available that also matches 15 numbered markers that offer interpretive descriptions and trail information. An observation platform at a water tower is your reward for this long hike.

The initial part of the trail is heavily used, then it gets narrower as it passes an old cemetery, a wooded area and over an open field. Past the cemetery you'll cross a stream, pass by many rock outcroppings, hike a ridge top, and trek by narrow waterfalls, ponds, cliffs and more. Depending on the time of the year, crossing some of the stream beds might be difficult or impossible.

The most popular hike is the one-mile-long Giant City Nature Trail, a moderately rugged loop that encircles a bluff near the "city" of Makanda sandstone blocks that compose the area that looks like a city and streets,

A jolly "wired-for-sound mannequin"greets diners in the lodge.

and where the park gets it name. "Fatman's Squeeze" is at this trail, where occasionally a chubby hiker gets temporarily stuck in the narrow corridor of sandstone. Staff says once they poured vegetable oil over a guy to "unstick" him.

The Devil's Standtable is a bulging dollop of rock that makes an interesting foray from the main park road south of the park office. There is also a shelter cave at the creek along the half-mile walk that is shady and easy walking. Climbers often challenge their skills at the Standtable.

Other trails, all of which are very good, include the Post Oak Trail, a one-third mile paved looped with Braille signage; Indian Creek Shelter and Nature Trail, a one-mile difficult loop through virgin forest, stern rock ledges and shelter bluffs that served Late Woodland people; the two-mile long rugged Trillium Trail; and others. Take plenty of water, long-sleeved shirts and pants, and field guides.

Climbing: Climbing and repelling are allowed at the park; contact the park office for information. Most climbing takes place in the Devil's Standtable and near shelter No. 1, Makanda Bluff.

Day-use areas: From ball diamonds to riding stables, Giant City has four picnic shelters and lots of children's play structures along the main park road. The shady park is terrific for day-use and exploration by cabin guests or campers. The horseback riding stable is closed on Monday and Tuesday.

Nature: Fern Rock Preserve is a 110-acre area dedicated to low-impact use and preservation of a number of spectacular rare plants that include flowering mints and French's shooting star. The preserve is just south of the main entrance, and hiking is restricted to trails only. Groups of 25 or more must obtain permission to enter the preserve.

There are more than 75 species of trees, 800 types of ferns and plants, and many songbirds that include the easy to recognize whippoorwill and the chuck's-will-widow.

The park is in a belt of hills that crosses the narrow portion of southern Illinois. It was once a low plain. This area slowly emerged from the sea, which formed the northern edge of the present Gulf of Mexico. As this unique region slowly rose, rains and streams cut deep to form valleys and striking rock formations. Faulting and folds occurred, forming wonderful structures seen nowhere else in the state.

Bobcat have been sighted by some staff and hikers in the park.

Hunting: Upland game; call the site superintendent for details.

Nearby attractions: Crab Orchard National Wildlife Refuge, between Carbondale and Marion offers 43,500 acres of forest, wetlands and grassland. Public use areas include hunting, fishing, a full-service marina, camping and much more. Call (618) 997-3344 for additional details. Also are Little Grassy Fish Hatchery, Touch of Nature Environmental Learning Center, University Mall and canoe rental. Call (618) 845-3817.

VISITOR CENTER
HOURS
Weekdays 10 to 4
Weekends 10 to 4

OPEN COME IN

21 Goose Lake Prairie State Park

Land: 2,537 acres Water: Heidecke Lake

An unknown early settler to northern Illinois described this vast terrain as "a sea of grass and with pretty flowers." As the settlers came in the mid- to late 1800s, nearly 66 percent of the state was covered by prairie grass. Today Goose Lake Prairie is the largest tract of prairie left in the state, and efforts continue to restore and preserve what's left for study and appreciation by visitors. Other good remnants of native prairie exist near Romeoville and Lockport.

Displaying a profusion of color from early spring until fall, Goose Lake Prairie has eight varieties of prairie grass and numerous forbs. Buffalo, wolf and prairie chicken once inhabited the area that is now a state park, along with mound-building groups of Native Americans that lived just northwest of the area. The land was largely undisturbed by these gentle users, but in the early 1800s ambitious settlers began planting trees as wind breaks, coal mining started, clay was dug out and removed, and hundreds of acres of the area were drained for farming. Most of these scars are gone, but observant visitors may still see strip mine spoil mounds and the small marshes and ponds that are evidence of the land-draining activities of the 1890s.

Farming took place on about 600 acres of the land at Goose Lake Prairie. Plowing destroyed many of the native plants. Happily, prairie vegetation is now being restored in some of these areas. Areas that were grazed and not plowed have remnants of many native plants and are very much like the lands were 150 years ago.

To restore the prairie, native plant seeds are mixed 60 percent grass seed and 40 percent forbs or wildflowers worked into the soil. The area is then kept free of woody, non-native plants. Additional seeds are collected each year only for research. This type of quality restoration is labor intensive and expensive, and can be undertaken in small areas.

Fire is used as a management tool also. It is used as a means of restoring and managing prairies. When a prairie burns, fire releases nitrogen and other nutrients into the soils, clears dead vegetation to make way for new growth and burns off the non-native plants or weeds and invading trees. Prairie plants are adapted to the natural fires that once swept the open plains. Non-native plants are non-fire tolerant. Carefully controlled burns are conducted in the spring before birds and other animals have their young.

William Cullen Bryant once said, "These are the gardens of the desert, these the unshorn fields boundless and beautify for which the speech of English has no name...the prairies."

Information and Activities

Goose Lake Prairie State Park
5010 N. Jugtown Road
Morris, IL 60450
(815) 942-2899

Directions: In Grundy County, about 60 miles from Chicago and one mile southwest of the confluence of the Kankakee and Des Plaines rivers.

Boating: Neighboring Lake Heidecke, formerly called Collins Lake, is a Commonwealth Edison cooling lake that has been leased to the state and is operated as an Illinois state fish and wildlife area. Only boats for fishing and duck hunting are allowed on the lake. No water skiing, swimming, sailboarding or wading are allowed on the lake or from the three-lane asphalt ramp. All boats must have a gasoline powered motor as main propulsion unit. A small launching ramp is north of the state park, and on the south side of the lake at the end of Jugtown Road. Boating access is open 6 a.m. - sunset. Because water conditions can change so quickly on the lake, a system of weather warning flags have been established as a visual warning system. There are rental V-bottom boats and motors, live bait and food available at the concession stand on Lake Heidecke.

Fishing: There is no fishing at the state park, but angling is considered fair to good on nearby Heidecke Lake, the 1,400 acre cooling lake is stocked often and has special slot and catch limits on the 1,400 acres cooling lake. A lake map is available at the state park or the concession that details lake depths and structure. The bass populations in the lake are considered good, while anglers try for muskie, striped bass, crappies, bluegill, catfish and rough fish. The east end of the lake is reported to be the best place for fishing.

The lake is a designated walleye brood stock lake, and special regulations have been established to protect this population. Minimum length for walleye is 22 inches and three fish daily. You may take a total of 10 striped bass daily; smallmouth, three per day; largemouth, 18-inch minimum size, three per day; catfish, a limit of six per day; all other state fishing regulations apply. Bank fishermen may want to try the shore fishing day-use area at the end of Dresden Road at the east end of the lake.

Hiking: Just a short, flat, easy hike from the visitor center is the reconstructed Cragg Cabin that stands as a monument to pioneer spirit. The original cabin was the handwork of intrepid pioneers John and Agnes Cragg in the late 1830s near Mazon, IL., 10 miles southwest of the park. The cabin, according to park literature, was the "predecessor to a truck stop." The cabin served as a resting place along the old Chicago-

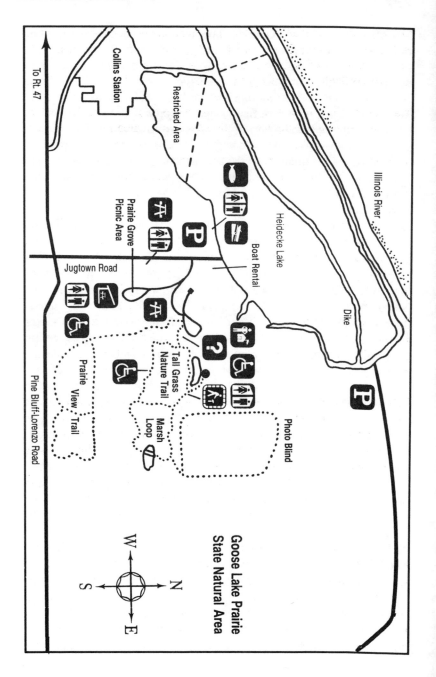

Goose Lake Prairie
State Natural Area

Bloomington Teamster Trail. The cabin was also the first two-story house in Grundy County after the fertile Craggs produced six children. The cabin will assist visitors in visualizing how pioneers lived, coped with, and viewed the surrounding prairie lands.

The Prairie View Trail, with 3.5 miles of easy hiking starts behind the visitor center and travels through intimate prairie areas, farmlands and groves of black ash and choke cherry trees. This is one of the best of the seven miles of trails to view the prairie, much the way pioneers did 150 years ago. Visible, also, are strip mine reclamation areas, low-lying marshes and timbered areas.

Goose Lake's self-guided interpretive trail offers trekkers a chance to see the trademark grass and open expanses of prairie that include big bluestem and Indian grass that can reach eight feet in height. Depending on your route, you can take a one-mile or 3.5-mile length of trail using the brochure to learn at 17 marked learning stations. The prairie at Goose Lake is fairly moist as prairies go, and offers excellent growth of switch grass, examples of prairie potholes, little bluesteam (the most widespread grass in North American prairies, except for Goose Lake), water on the prairie, bluejoint grass, cordgrass, and information about prairie soils and management science and the techniques in practice.

Day-use areas: Goose Lake has excellent playground equipment and lightly used picnicking areas. The Prairie Grove Picnic Area, south of the visitor center, has a shelter, grills, waters and toilets. Plan about 30 minutes for a visit to the visitor center that is complete with a 90-seat lecture theater, collections of fossils and minerals, a zebra mussel display, dioramas, "Why do we need prairies?" natural history displays, and plenty of information about the surrounding prairie. The center is open daily 10 a.m. - 4 p.m.

Nature: Visitors, especially during mid- to late summer, will find the 10-foot-tall cordgrass and the two-foot-tall delicious smelling northern prairie dropseed—it smells like buttered popcorn. Other interesting plant species include cream false indigo, shooting star and early violets. Autumn, when the grasses turn to golden strands and bronze nodding heads, is a favorite time for a hike along the miles of easy trails.

22 Hennepin Canal Parkway State Park

104.5-mile linear parkway

With linkages, cooperation and sharing the buzzwords in the business world for product development and global competition, it's great to see the state of Illinois many years ahead of the game. It has successfully developed a linear park that stretches more than 100 miles and incorporates dozens of day-use sites and many chances for visitors to have fun.

As you can learn at the Visitor Center in Sheffield, the canal linkage and long parkway are much more than just fun places, they also played an important role in the history of United States commerce and industry. Canals, especially those in Illinois, were the first major cooperative ventures spanned great distances, over many corporate jurisdictions, often with the cooperation of landowners, government and business.

Information and Activities

Hennepin Canal Parkway State Park
Visitor Center
R.R. 2, P.O. Box 201
Sheffield, IL 61361
(815) 454-2328

Directions: The park stretches for more than 104 miles from west of Milan (Route 67) to the Illinois River (Route 180). The feeder line runs north and south from I-80 roughly along Route 88 to Lake Sinnissippi. The Visitor Center is off of Route 88, south from I-80.

Information: The Visitor Center has a variety of displays that interpret canal history and its construction including a model lock. The center also features a half-acre wildflower patch, observation deck, brochure rack and day-use amenities. There are three picnic shelters at the Visitor Center.

Canal history: Innovators discussed building a canal in the early 1830s, but the dollar didn't catch up to the idea until about 1890. The canal was completed in 1907, reducing the distance from Chicago to Rock Island by more than 400 miles. Sadly, by the time the construction was funded and completed, the canal was virtually obsolete because railroads were growing cheaper and the size (capacity) of barges were growing too wide for the canal. The huge barges found the narrow canal far too small to hold their mighty loads.

So, since about 1930, the canal has been used primarily for recreational uses. Unlike the sister I & M Canal, which was used for 60 years before the demise of the Hennepin, it indeed did have a major role in building Chicago, but ultimately also fell victim to alternative transportation methods.

The canal was a genuine innovation, an engineering design that helped builders of the Panama Canal.

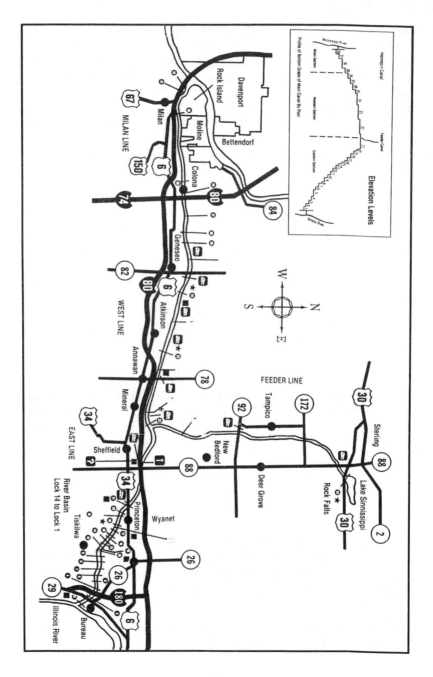

There are 32 locks still visible along the 104 miles of canal, with five of them restored to working condition. Most of the lock gates have been replaced with concrete walls. The canal is still a historic and innovative work of the hand of man, and is listed as a national historic place.

Boating: You can use unlimited horsepower on your boat between Lock 24 and bridge 37. Elsewhere, horsepower is restricted to 10 hp. There are 10, one-lane launch ramps along the parkway at Locks 21, 22 and 24, Route 82 north of Geneseo, Route 92, Route 78 north of Annawan, Bridge 39, Bridge 28 and Bridge 45.

Canoeists can enjoy any part of the canal, but be ready to paddle in either direction.

Fishing: Talk to the local bait shops about which pools are stocked and when. There are about 70 bridges or locks that you can fish from, and during the spring might be the best time for angling action. Bluegill, some walleye, bass and bluegills are taken.

Kids can have fun angling for rough fish. Gobs of crawlers can attract lots of action for small fisherpeople.

Day-use areas: I don't think anyone knows exactly how many picnic tables are along the parkway. I lost count as I visited a number of the access points, finding toilets at Locks 11, 17, 21, 22, 23 and 24 and Bridges 14, 15 and 23. About half of the picnicking sites have good shade; only two have drinking water at Locks 21 and 22, to be exact.

The old tow path, used by oxen and horses to tow barges, is great for walking or mountain biking. There are about 155 miles of easy trails; locals claim the trails are nicest in autumn.

Horseback riding is allowed along most of the parkway, but stay off the towpath between Bridges 43-46. No motorized vehicles, except snowmobiles, are allowed on the towpaths. The 4-mile-long trail at the main complex is hilly and can be cross-country skied during the winter.

Hunting: Waterfowl hunting at Sinnissippi Lake and limited dove hunting are allowed at the main complex.

23   Frank Holten State Park

Land: 1,125 acres   Water: 208 acres, two lakes

The Frank Holten unit is not your typical Illinois state park. It's urban. The park has 27 golf holes, a clubhouse with dining room, a small pro shop, a driving range, and has only recently developed a hiking trail that circumnavigates the lakes. You can even see the St. Louis Gateway Arch in the distance over the municipality of East St. Louis, Illinois. The park is very busy.

Established in 1964, the park originally was named Grand Marais State Park, but was changed in May 1967 to Frank Holten State Park in honor of the late distinguished legislator from East St. Louis who was first elected to office in 1916 and served 48 years in the General Assembly. Holten died in December 1966 at the age of 98.

Information and Activities

Frank Holten State Park
4500 Pocket Road.
East St. Louis, IL 62005
(618) 874-7920

The state park is one of the largest day-use areas in the area, capable of accommodating up to 2,000 patrons per day using barbecue pits or picnicking at tables or shelters near toilets, playgrounds, drinking fountains, adequate parking and shoreline fishing. The day-use area also features ball fields, an area for cross-country skiing, football-soccer field, and plenty of open spaces.

The urban setting has an assortment of scattered shade trees and wooded strips with such species as maple, oak, redbud, tulip, poplar and many other ornamentals. Wildlife watchers might also catch a glimpse of red fox, woodchuck, maybe a mink, raccoon and migratory songbirds and visiting waterfowl.

Take a picnic basket, golf clubs or a fishing rod to the park. The updated golf course features wide fairways, earth berming that has created rolling fairways, and plenty of golfers. The course is busy on all days, especially on the weekend.

Fishermen can try their luck on both lakes, with most bass anglers plying their skills at Grand Marais Lake. Bluegill and channel catfish are also taken from the lake. Shoreline anglers prefer live bait, while bass anglers may use gas motors with 10 or less horsepower to probe the structure with spinner baits, buzz baits and rubber worms.

Whispering Willow Lake at the north end of the park, has a small bait concession stand and is stocked twice annually with rainbow trout. Local anglers find corn the most successful bait during the spring and fall.

There is no camping or hunting at the urban unit.

24 Horseshoe Lake Rec. Area

Land: 2,850 acres   Water: 1,200 acres

Horseshoe Lake is a very old and shallow lake on a low flood plain which follows the Mississippi River to the Kentucky border. Before the present system of levies was constructed, heavy spring floods would often cause the muddy runoff to quickly overflow its banks. The power of moving water cut wide new channels through the wet bottomlands. During this process, Horseshoe Lake was formed.

The park could be a staging point for families who don't mind rustic camping to visit the many attractions in the St. Louis area. The park is only minutes way from the Missouri Botanical Gardens, the Arch, shopping, golf, museums and much more (see listing under nearby attractions).

There is evidence of human habitation as long ago as 8,000 B.C, during the Archaic Period. Perhaps, however, the most impressive Indian history, occurred during the period of 800-1600 A.D. when the "Mighty Metropolis," known as Cahokia Mounds, were built. Ask the park staff to direct you to a remaining mound located inside park boundaries.

Information and Activities

Horseshoe Lake Rec. Area
P.O. Box 1307
Granite City, IL 62706
(618) 931-0270

Directions: Take exit 6, Route 111 north 3.5 miles to the park entrance on the right. The tiny park office faces the lake and inside there are a mounted aerial photo of the area and informational brochure rack. The office is open by chance; when the staff is working in the park, you can register your boat at the office.

Campground: The 48-site rustic camping area, across the narrow causeway on Walker Island, is rarely filled, even on major summer holiday weekends. Campers must secure a permit from the park office, which is the first left once inside the main park entrance. Large RV rigs should use caution on the drive into the campground.

The oblong island is part agricultural and part wooded in the old and shallow lake that was formed when an old river channel was closed off to form an owbox-like lake.

The gravel causeway to the island that bisects the lake splits some large crop fields, and winds back to the camping area. The first sites (1-10, non-electric) are on the left, along the rather dusty road facing a farm field and have little shade or privacy.

Sites 11-15 are wide open with no shade, a few picnic tables and no grills. Site 18 begins a shady camping area, complete with vault toilets, gravel pads, a privy at site 20, and other usual amenities. Site 25 is situated under a canopy of maple trees, overlooking the other camping sites and a lightly

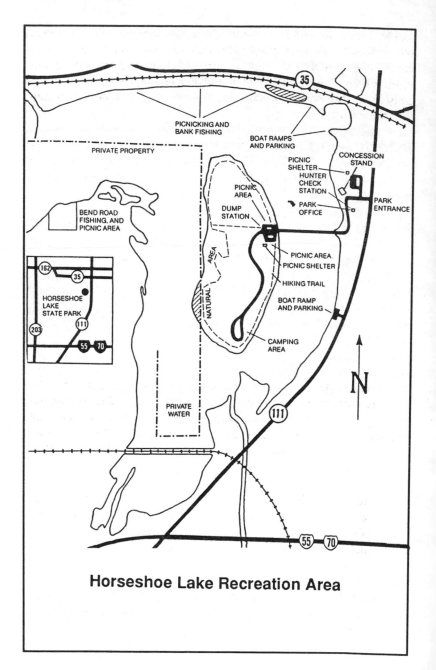

PICNICKING AND
BANK FISHING

BOAT RAMPS
AND PARKING

PRIVATE PROPERTY

CONCESSION
STAND

PICNIC
SHELTER

HUNTER
CHECK
STATION

PARK
ENTRANCE

PICNIC
AREA

DUMP
STATION

PARK
OFFICE

BEND ROAD
FISHING, AND
PICNIC AREA

PICNIC AREA

PICNIC SHELTER

HIKING TRAIL

NATURAL AREA

HORSESHOE
LAKE
STATE PARK

BOAT RAMP
AND PARKING

CAMPING
AREA

N

PRIVATE
WATER

Horseshoe Lake Recreation Area

wooded area. Some of the camping sites in this area are clearly numbered, others aren't—allowing campers to seek a smooth and dry spot for tent campers, or a particularly shady and cozy location for a small to medium-sized RV rig. Some of the unmarked tent camping spots are only steps away from the lake's edge. Because this area is a floodplain, make sure your area is dry.

Boating: There is a 25-horsepower limit on the lake. Three boat ramps are located around the lake and all have sufficient parking and staging areas. Boating activity is generally light. There is no boat rental, concession stand or bait sold at the park.

Fishing: Angling from a boat in the lake is fair when water conditions and depth cooperate. Shoreline fishing is popular along the causeway and in front of the park office where tables and parking pads are maintained, but the park's staff says the shoreline fishing action is slow most of the time. The 2,100-acre lake is shallow, sometimes averaging less than 4 feet deep, but the rough fish action can be good for carp, drum and bullheads, with some largemouth bass, crappie and bluegill taken during the spring and fall.

Hiking: The four-mile-long hiking and bird trail on Walkers Island is a loop that basically follows the shoreline through farm grounds, shoreline natural communities, near a pond, along marsh areas, and through mature wooded terrain. At the park office you can pick up a brochure that describes five sites where birds are often sited and why. The interpretive descriptions offers some natural history and a birding checklist. Bring your binoculars.

Day-use areas: In front of the office, before you make the turn onto the causeway, are several places to park your car and fish the shore, with picnic tables near. Adaquate playground equipment and picnic shelters arc on the north shore.

Hunting: Dove hunting is September 1- 30, with a limit of 15 birds; waterfowl blinds are drawn in June of every year; youth dove and quail seasons are offered; for the pheasant season, call the site superintendent. A waterfowl hunting map details site regulations, zones and blind locations.

25   Illinois Beach State Park

**Land: 4,160 acres   Water: 6.5 miles of
Lake Michigan frontage**

Illinois Beach State Park does not fit the traditional niche in the state park system. It's a different breed of cat. Though not devoid of scenic and natural qualities or typical services and amenities, those qualities are simply obscured by the overwhelming presence of the Lake Michigan beaches and dunes.

The park leisurely stretches for 6.5 miles along the sandy shores of Lake Michigan in northern Illinois and encompasses the only remaining beach ridge shoreline left in the state. It's also a stretch of beach that becomes wonderfully hectic as thousands of Chicagoans and other visitors cool off on summer weekends.

After you've spent some time sunbathing and walking along the lapping waters past sandy ridges and sprawling marshes, wooded areas of oak and by some of the nearly 650 plant species that populate the dunes, a visit to the park's nature center is a wonderful way to learn lots more about dune ecology, area animals and plant life.

Many sandy ridges are crowned by black oak with an open, savanna-like appearance and many kinds of fragrant pines, introduced here a century ago. The aquatic plants, fish and sedges are occasionally punctuated by large colonies of prickly pear cactus and other colorful wildflowers. This unit is well known for its birdwatching, too.

If you aren't stirred by the unique natural history, you can be overwhelmed with all of the other things to do at the park. Interested in jogging or bicycling? Tennis? Miles of trails? Miles of shoreline? Sailing? Boating? People watching? Jet Skiing? Beach stone collecting? You name it, this park, located in an urban area, has it.

Information and Activities

Illinois Beach State Park
Zion, IL 60099
(708) 662-4811
Fax: (708) 662-6433

Direction: Just south of the Illinois/Wisconsin border on the shores of Lake Michigan, the main entrance is at the east end of Wadsworth. The main entrance for the north unit and marina is at the east end of 7th Street.

Information: The campground office, nature center, marina and main park offices all have brochures and maps and are generally open 8 a.m. - 4 p.m. on weekdays. The camp office is open during most daylight hours during the summer.

Campground: You may make reservations for about 40 sites that are available from May 1 - Sept. 30, seven days in advance by mail. There is a $5 non-refundable fee. Reservations may be made after Jan. 1 by mail or in person. The reservable sites are close to the beach, but they are on

The northern marina is large and modern.

a slight incline; you will need rig levelers for these sandy sites with gravel pads. The campground is open year-round and is full on most summer weekends. There are 22 sites which have 50 amp service.

Camping sites 99-102 overlook a small pond that would make a good kids fishing area. All campsites have gravel pads, fire grills, picnic tables and generally are shady, protected from lake winds and blowing sand. Sites with odd 400 numbers are backed up against a wooded buffer. The best sites are 400-409 (by reservation) in the pine trees. Sites 163-219 have a long-distance view of the beach, but they are very open. For a small family, sites 140-149 would work well. Hard-surfaced (overflow) sites 500-521 are near the beach, good for large motor homes. They are handicapped accessible. All 244 Class A camping sites have electricity.

About 100 yards from the beach just west of the sandy ridgeline, sites 160-219, there are two shower houses in the campground. Some newer hard-surfaced trails connect camping loops to each other and to the beaches. Sites 229-237 are pleasant sites, shady, and at the end of a cul-de-sac.

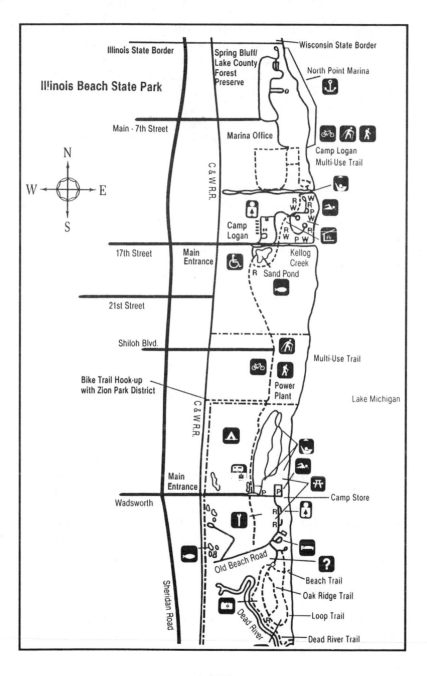

Illinois State Border

Spring Bluff/
Lake County
Forest
Preserve

Wisconsin State Border

North Point Marina

Illinois Beach State Park

Main · 7th Street

Marina Office

Camp Logan
Multi-Use Trail

N
W   E
S

C & W R.R.

Camp
Logan

R W
R
P
W
P
W
R
P

W
P

R
W
B

Kellog
Creek

17th Street

Main
Entrance

21st Street

Sand Pond
R

Shiloh Blvd.

Multi-Use Trail

Bike Trail Hook-up
with Zion Park District

Power
Plant

Lake Michigan

C & W R.R.

Main
Entrance

Camp Store

Wadsworth

P   P

R

R

Old Beach Road

Beach Trail

Oak Ridge Trail

Loop Trail

Sheridan Road

Dead River

Dead River Trail

Generally speaking, for an urban campground, it is nice. The park is close to amenities, enough shade, privacy and security. There is a small camp store that sells firewood, and has groceries and other items. This is the only campground on Lake Michigan between Milwaukee and Chicago.

Lodge/resort: The lodge has begun renovations to include nearly 100 rooms, conference space, indoor heated pool, restaurant and other amenities. The lodge is on the beach in the south unit. Call for additional information.

Boating: Most boating activity, except for Jet Ski rental/parasailing (call (708) 249-2334) at the beach house in the northeast corner of the main parking lot in the south unit, is located at the huge marina off 7th Street. This area is called the north unit and the marina is called North Point Marina, where there are 1,500 slips, a boat service center, food concession, slip rentals, 10-lane boat ramp, rentals and much more. There are also catamaran, sailboard and windsurfing lessons and rentals; call (414) 652-5334. The marina is a great place for campers to walk around too.

Fishing: In the north unit, Sand Pond is stocked with rainbow trout of catchable size. In the past the area has also been stocked with channel catfish and largemouth bass. A slip bobber and crawlers work well at Sand Pond. There is also a small fishing dock on Sand Pond that's great for youngsters.

You may also fish along the lake to the resort. Anglers with a boat should check with local bait and tackle shops for the latest information on Lake Michigan fishing conditions. Charter fishermen operate out of the marina offering half-day and full day outings for salmon and lake trout. There is also a fishing pier near the marina next to a pedestrian walkway that leads past the yacht club.

Hiking/biking: A newer 10-mile hard-surfaced biking trail system links amenities in the unit. Walking along the beach is popular, while users in the south unit can hike some of the five miles of trails that includes a 2.2-mile gravel-surfaced trail. In the north, Camp Logan is a 1.8-mile multi-use loop that cross-country skiers also use. There is no skiing allowed in the nature preserve.

Hiking in the nature center area is controlled, but interesting. Trails in the south unit in this area are Dead River Trail (1 mile) along the Dead River; Loop Trail (2.2 miles) through open oak forest and prairie; Black Oak Ridge Trail (.6 mile) along oak ridge and Beach Trail (.2 mile) through a forest, march and prairie ending at Lake Michigan.

Day-use areas: Interrupted by a nuclear power station, almost the entire length of the linear park has scattered day-use areas that include picnic tables, play equipment, beach and swimming areas and a concession stand. There is also a fishing pier, built jointly with Commonwealth Edison.

Nature: The unit's nature center is open year-round in the nature preserve. The interpretive center offers hands-on displays, multi-media and live programming and presentations, and is the gateway to the natural history of the park.

More than 260 species of birds have been recorded at the park since 1980. A bird list is available at the interpretive center. Hawk migration is one of the big birding events, where thousands of birds can be seen "kettling" and moving along their twice-annual migrations pathways.

Because the state park offers a full-time naturalist and considerable school programming, lots of educational brochures and posters are available for park users to learn more about dune ecology and the natural history of the area. The simple Duneland Plant & Animal Checklist brochure is a fun guide to help you identify plants and animals as you explore the park.

Nearby attractions: The entire metro Chicago area is only minutes away. Nature-related attractions in the area include the Chicago Botanical Gardens, Lincoln Park Zoo, swimming beach at Waukegan Harbor, Field Museum of Natural History, Adler Planetarium, Museum of Science and Industry, and Shedd Aquarium. There is a terrific Lake Michigan Corridor recreation map available from the Lake Michigan Corridor Council, 414 N. Sheridan Road, Waukegan, IL 60085-4096, or call (708) 662-2749.

26   *Illini State Park*

Land: 510 acres on the Illinois River

With the shady coolness and autumn colors of the dense stands of hickory, ash, walnut, oak and maple as your destination, Illini State Park lies along the banks of the gentle Illinois River. The trip is nearly half of the fun— especially crossing the erector set-like bridge that joins downtown Marseilles to the state park, spanning the 150-yard wide Illinois River. The narrow iron bridge offers a terrific view up and down the river, of the state park lands, a dam, Bells Island, and in the distance, the U.S. Army Corps of Engineer's locks.

By the way, there is a pedestrian walkway across the bridge which is a fun vertical trek if you aren't faint hearted. The bridge bounces and wooden deck boards clatter when medium-sized trucks driven by locals roar across on their daily rounds. After you've gotten the bridge crossing out of your system, you'll find the peaceful park a welcome stopping place to hold a family gathering, have a picnic, camp, walk along the river, or view the classic park buildings that were constructed by the Civilian Conservation Corps nearly a half-century ago. Some of the finest examples of their work in the state are here at Illini, complete with rock chimneys, plank floors and log construction. Many of these buildings are being restored and preserved for future park users to enjoy.

As at most units in this region, Native Americans were the original inhabitants. The rich forests and network of waterways offered them food, hunting, fishing and river-based transportation. They might have also been drawn to the area by the Great Falls on the Illinois River, at the north end of the park. In a mere two miles, the river drops three feet, creating a scenic set of rumbling rapids. Do you think the native people shot the rapids? I do.

Other bits of history that visitors can look for include reminders of America's Industrial Age such as the old Marseilles powerhouse, the historic Illinois-Michigan Canal that was completed in 1848 and transported goods until the railroad displayed them, CCC projects, and more. The park was dedicated in 1935.

Information and Activities

Illini State Park
2660 East 2350th Road
Marseilles, IL 61341
(815) 795-2448

Directions: One mile south of Marseilles on the south side of the Illinois River. Take the Townline Road exit south off I-80 five miles to park entrance.

Information: The park office, at the entrance of the Great Falls Campground is open 8 a.m. - 4 p.m. year-round. The park is closed 10 p.m. - 6 a.m.

Campground: The Whitetail Campground is one of two campgrounds

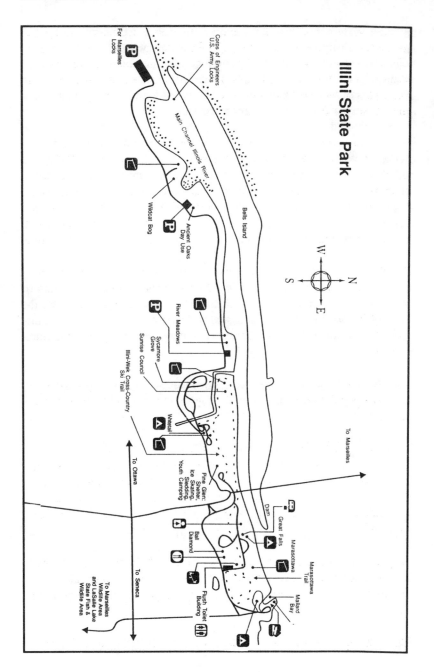

Illini State Park

and has 45 sites. Near the entrance to this campground, along an agricultural field, is the Pine Glen Youth Campground, which is open seasonally and reservable. The Whitetail Campground roadway is covered by a canopy of trees, almost tunnel-like, offering a shady retreat from the routine world. This is a privacy-type of campground with limited amenities.

Sites 22-25 are near vault toilets and an area where small trees are being planted in an effort to reforest and landscape the area. Sites 28-31 are near water; 32-34 are heavily shaded and private; at the end of this loop sites 35-37 are good for a large family that wants adjacent camping sites. Camp sites 38-40 are as private as possible. Sites 42-43 are also private and shady; each is separated by vegetation and has picnic tables, grills and nearby toilets and water sources.

The other loop in this section has sites that are well spaced and shady. Sites 11-17 are great for small RVs as they face a picnic and play area. Other small, intimate sites are 6 and 7, while site 9 can accommodate a large rig. A recycling station is located near site No. 1 where you can recycle paper, aluminum or glass products. A small creek meanders near camp areas and young tree plantings.

River Meadows picnic areas, complete with shelter and vault toilet, is situated along the Illinois River and is handy to campers in the Whitetail campground.

The Class A Great Falls Campground is near the park office along the river. All sites have electricity and nearby flush toilets and showers. The area has undergone recent improvements. Sites 1-15 are along the river offering an excellent view; there are 57 campsite in two loops. Most sites are shady and about half of the sites have a river view, but the sites are not as private as some locations in the Whitetail area.

The park does not take reservations and is full on holiday weekends, but there are often available sites on other summer weekends. Weekdays you can often have a good choice of campsites in either of the two camping areas.

Boating: A small one-land boat launch is at Mallard Bay at the east end of the state park. There are no motor restrictions on the Illinois River, but boaters should exercise caution around barge traffic and near the Marseilles Lock and Dam. At the launch are a vault toilet, picnic shelter, pop machine, 10 picnic tables and an enjoyable view.

Fishing: Fishing is only fair in the Illinois River that runs the length of the state park. Rough fish can be caught from shore and some anglers find spring fishing fair to good for crappies and bluegill. Most of the angling action is below the dam where some spring walleye, sauger and strippers are taken. You may shoreline fish along the river.

Anglers may want to try LaSalle Lake, 2,058 acres of water eight miles southeast of Marseilles managed by Illini State Park. The lake is open April 1 - Oct. 1, 6 a.m.-sunset. There are a concession stand, boat launch, bait, boat rental and good to very good fishing. Local anglers concentrate on the eight "holes," which can be up to 60 feet deep along rock rip-rap edge areas. Be warned: The lake was constructed to cool waters and circulate in 5-day patterns and has no boat or beaching areas. Windy days can cause warning system, and high voltage electrical wires that could damage your radios or depth finders if you get within 200 feet of them. Aside from all these warnings, anglers pack the lake on weekends and have reasonable fishing success.

Hiking: The Illini-Wek Ski Trail and the Marasottawa Trail near the Great Falls campground offer easy walks, as does a grassy shoreline along the river. There are no bridle or snowmobile trails.

Day-use areas: There are nine picnic shelters, two of which you can reserve for family outings, many picnic and open areas and play equipment along the main park road. In the youth campground there's ice skating, sledding and shelters for groups. There is a baseball diamond near the park office in the largest open space area.

Hunting: Only minutes from the state park is the 2,500-acre Marseilles Wildlife Area. Dove, squirrel and archery deer are the primary game species. A brochure is available at the park office regarding regulations.

Winter: An ice skating pond, sledding and cross-country skiing trail are available.

27 Johnson-Sauk Trail State Park

Land: 1,361 acres   Water: 58-acre lake

The biggest disappointment on my visits to the rolling hills of the Johnson-Sauk Trail State Park was that the grand round barn was closed. The magificant barn has been lovingly restored by an active group of volunteers and is open many weekends and holidays throughout the year.

Ryan's round barn, capped with cedar shingles, was built in 1910 near the entrance to the park. It towers skyward more than 80 feet and is nearly 85 feet diameter. Staff says there is a 15-foot ceiling-to-floor silo and some examples of old farm implements and educational materials inside the big barn.

The innovative structure once held a herd of 50 black angus show cattle and is on the National Registry of Historic Places. It won a Governor's award for volunteer accomplishments. The barn has a bunch of labor saving devices and is considered to be tornado proof, but I hope it is never put to that test.

The barn is open for tours on many weekends and if you know your schedule better than I do, you can call the Friends of the Johnson-Sauk Park Foundation about an appointment to make a tour at (309) 852-4262.

The reason religious groups built round barns at the end of the 1800s and into the 1900s was because they "left no corners in which the devil could hide." Maybe the devil will have better luck getting inside than I did.

Information and Activities

Johnson-Sauk Trail State Park
R.R. 3
Kewanee, IL 61443
(309) 853-5589

Directions: In Henry County, off Route 78, the park is five miles north of Kewanee and six miles south of Interstate 80. The park is about 20 miles from Ronald Reagan's birthplace.

Information: The park office, at the north end of the lake, is open weekdays, 8 a.m. - 4 p.m. The concession stand at the boat launch is open mid-May-October and staff there can answer many of your questions. The park closes at 10 p.m.

Campground: Campers should register with the campground host at site No. 1; registration hours are 8 a.m. - 10 p.m. Reservations are not taken at this small campground located on the west side of the 58-acre lake. All pets must be on a leash.

At the entrance of the campground, seen from the drive in, is a delightful grove of pencil-straight red pine. Under the looming pines is primitive tent camping—a cool, shady and very unique camping site that is rarely filled on non-holiday weekends. Beware that during certain times of the year, the pines can drip a little sap on camper's tents. Sites in this are 1-

31. Sites 8-10 have a good lake view, while sites 11-14 have a partial lake view. All sites have picnic tables. Self-contained campers could have great fun in this interesting grove.

Opposite the pine grove is a newer, less shady camping area beginning with site No. 34. Lot size is good, but shade trees are small in this area. Sites 51-56 have a view of a rolling valley and a reforestation area; site 58 also has a good vista. Sites 59-69 are backed up against the woodline and will offer shade or protection from the winds as needed. There is a small playground with eight swings and a slide nearby.

Emergency telephone numbers are: park rangers, (309) 853-5589; state police, 1-775-0428; sheriff, 1-937-3911; fire, 1-935-6222.

Boating: There is a well-maintained one-lane boat launch at the northwest end of the lake near the dam in front of the concession stand that rents 16-foot aluminum boats and sells bait and some grocery items. The small lake is an electric motor only fishing lake. The quiet waters of the lake makes it a good choice for lazy canoeing and family small boating.

Fishing: Near the round barn there's a small 3-acre stocked pond that can offer fast panfish and largemouth bass action during the early summer and fall. In the warmer summer days it's a good pond for kids to try quiet shoreline fishing with a bobber and redworms.

A lake map available at the concession stand offers information about lake depth and identifies underwater fish-holding structure that are scattered around the narrow dammed lake. Although the four-color parks brochure claims the lake is 21 feet deep, local anglers maintain that the average depth is actually about 14-16 feet. The southern third of the lake at 4-8 feet, and warms up quickly in early summer. The lake was built in 1956, and has about 1.5 miles of gentle shoreline and serves a 900-acre watershed area.

Fish species in the lake include largemouth bass, bluegill, redear sunfish, black crappie, white crappie, bullhead and catfish. Also, but less commonly caught, are northern pike, muskie, yellow perch, green sunfish and our friends, the "oooootrout," or carp.

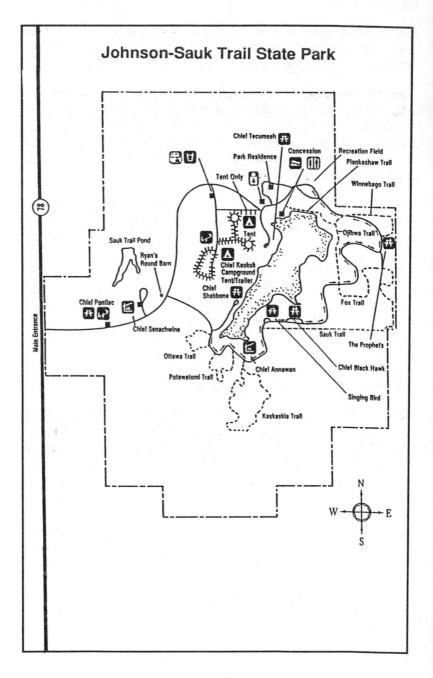

Johnson-Sauk Trail State Park

Bass must be 14-inches long and there is a limit of six per day; northern pike must be 24-inches with a limit of three daily; while you may take only one muskie daily and it must be at least 30 inches in length.

The little lake is a great kid's bluegill lake. Hang a gob of redworms with a bobber or a waxworm, and kids can catch 'gills all day long. It is a good largemouth bass lake; most locals use spinners and rubber worms in the shallows. You can try fishing for muskie near the surface when the water is warm trolling jerk baits or throwing Rattletraps. The lake is considered a very good ice fishing lake.

Hiking: The rolling prairie to pine plantations, bottomlands, lake shorelines and open spaces offers about 12 miles of hiking opportunity. The trails connect to each other and have great Indian names like Ottawa, Potawatomi, Kaskaskia and Winnebago. Cross-country skiing is encouraged on all parks trails.

Day-use areas: There are two picnic shelters (groups of 25 or more must obtain permission to use the shelters), 10 smaller picnic spots, two playgrounds (one at Chief Pontiac Picnic Area and the other at the campground), vault toilets, a recreation field and plenty of open spaces. Iceskating, tobogganing, snowmobiling on designated trails, and winter camping are also encouraged at the park.

Nature: The park is in a part of Illinois which was a huge shallow sea millions of years ago. Two glaciers covered this part of the state, with the last called the Wisconsin Glacier, carving and etching the land into the rolling and diverse form we know today. The park is near the edge of the Great Willow Swamp, an enormous wetland that covered the entire area between the Mississippi and Green rivers. The swamp, which is now virtually drained, was believed to have the most concentrated and varied wildlife populations in the central part of North America. This abundance of game and diversity attracted Indians, who quietly lived on the land. Later, market hunters and fur trappers blatantly harvested the region.

The area still has an excellent array of spring and summer wildflowers and birdwatching opportunities. The Kaskaskia Trail offers a terrific chance to see mammals and the woodlands.

Panfishing from small boats is popular at the park.

Hunting: Hunting is a popular activity at the park. Generally dove hunting is offered Sept. 1-15 with a daily drawing; archery deer from Oct. 1- Nov. 5 and later in the season until January on certain weekdays, by permit and registration only; and upland game season is typically Nov. 6-Dec. 31 with a daily drawing at 8:30 a.m. A pheasant put-and-take is also offered.

Many habitat improvement projects here and at other Illinois public lands were made possible by funds from the Pittman-Robertson Act of 1937, which earmarked funds for wildlife management with revenues diverted by taxes paid on guns, archery equipment and ammunition.

Special events: Annual Sauk Trail Heritage Days usually is held over the Independence Day weekend at Francis Park and in the state park.

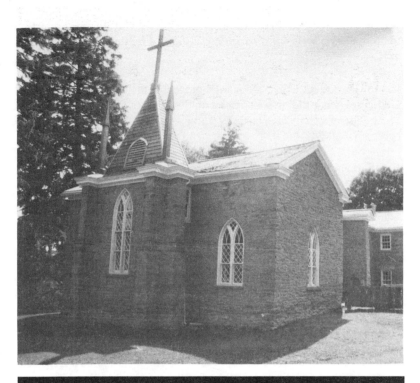

28 Jubilee College State Park

Land: 3,200 acres   Water: creek and ponds

The 93-acre Jubilee College State Historic Site is the hilltop centerpiece of the sprawling and rolling terrain of the state park. The entire park is situated in the Illinoisan drift-plain, which is deeply eroded into many complex valley systems, from near-level ridge tops and floodplains to steep sloping ravines.

The pleasing topography complete with bedrock exposures of sandstone and limestone, elevations of more than 600 feet, and a meandering creek make for a great park. It's easy to see why the founder of Jubilee College, Episcopal Bishop Philander Chase started the enterprise here in 1839. Away from temptation, Chase's rural college included a theological department, college for men, boys preparatory school and girls school. It was one of the first colleges established in Illinois, and also one of the first to close after a series of misfortunes climaxed by the bishop's death in 1862.

In 1933 the college and grounds were presented to the state; the two-story Gothic revival building was placed on the National Historic Register in 1872. Today the site is open daily 9 a.m. - 5 p.m. Tours are available by calling (309) 243-9489.

By 1850 Jubilee College covered nearly 4,000 acres and its buildings included several faculty homes, a two-story frame boarding house, a store, a print shop, and an L-shaped stone building that has been undergoing restoration efforts since the early 1970s. Bishop Chase developed a number of enterprises and was a successful fund-raiser, but after fires, lagging enrollment and business losses, the college faltered, then faltered again after some of his followers tried to breathe life back into it a few years after the bishop's death.

In 1986, after years of hard work by the Citizens Committee to Preserve Jubilee College and the state, the restored chapel, complete with pew boxes, walnut pulpit, an 1843 organ and recreated classrooms and dormitories, reopened and offers excellent living history and interpretive programming. This is one of the most interesting facilities in any of Illinois' state park.

Information and Activities

Jubilee College State Park
13921 W. Route 150, P. O. Box 72
Brimfield, IL 61517
(309) 446-3758

Directions: Located in Peoria County, between Kickapoo and Brimfield, just off U.S. Route 150, 15 miles northwest of Peoria.

Information: The park is open 8 a.m. - 9 p.m. The park office, in a ranch-style house, is open 9 a.m. - 1 p.m.

Classroom interior at old Jubilee College.

Campground: Jubilee's campground is open April 15-Nov. 15 and can accommodate any size recreational vehicle. Camping reservations are not accepted.

The campground has undergone considerable renovation in the past few years, improving important infrastructure, but leaving many of the sites shadeless. The younger trees are growing well, but it will be many years before they will cast long cooling shadows over most of the camping sites. Nevertheless, there are many fine camping sites in the scenic park and the park is rarely full. The showers are at the west end of the A and B loops.

Coyote Cove is a Class A camping area, and the best sites will be around the perimeter. The lanes or loops are designated alphabetically—A, B and C. Sites 7A, 34A and 35A are shady and private. In Possum Bend loop, which is called B-area, 7B is a good tent site, while 13B and 14B are lightly shaded. Most of the other sites are very open. In Woodchuck Ridge (C-area), sites 6C and 27C shady just inside the gate 11C, 12C and 13C are private, flat, and like many of the sites, offer a great view of the undulating terrain.

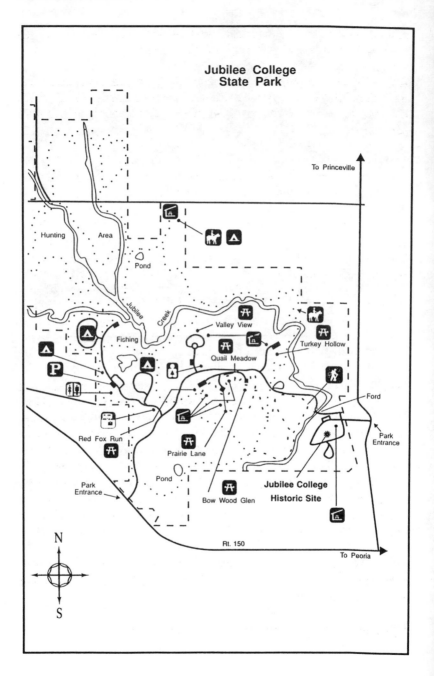

Jubilee College
State Park

To Princeville

Hunting   Area

Pond

Jubilee   Creek

Fishing

Valley View

Quail Meadow

Turkey Hollow

P

Ford

Park
Entrance

Red Fox Run

Prairie Lane

Jubilee College
Historic Site

Park
Entrance

Pond

Bow Wood Glen

N

S

Rt. 150

To Peoria

Although there are adequate vault toilets in the C area, it is about a half-mile walk to the shower house from this open area.

An equestrian camping area is located at the north end of the park, near more than 30 miles of trails that originate in the camping area. The area has a shelter house, plenty of water, toilet facilities, hitching posts and a pay phone.

Fishing: Very limited fishing is available in Jubilee Creek and in two small ponds. One of the ponds is stocked each season, and you must walk into them. The pond northeast of the park office offers some panfishing.

Hiking: There are about five miles of hiking trails at Jubilee State Park, plus another 30 hikable miles of equestrian trails which are well marked. Trails along the eastern side of the creek can be greasy, especially when it wanders along the sloping shoreline. Trails on the west side of the ford link with the often chewed-up horse trails that circle westward. Poor trailside directional signs make taking connector trails uncertain. Yet all trails arc concentric loops that take hikers back to main trails or where they started. The area is popular for cross-country skiing during the winter.

Day-use areas: The expanses of prairie lands welcome park users and waving grass and wildflowers are the perfect backdrop for picnicking, family gatherings or winter sports. There are a number of traditional day-use areas with picnic tables, timber structure playgrounds, charcoal grills, toilets and water that include the Foxwood Glen, Quail Meadow, Prairie Lane, Red Fox Run, tiny Turkey Hollow and others. There are huge mowed open areas along the main park road. Be prepared to drive up a 14 percent grade to the historic college across a small creek. This is a colorful park in the autumn as each ravine and valley is painted in crimson and yellow.

Hunting: About 450 acres at the park are managed for archery deer hunting and other small game. Call the site superintendent for hunting times, dates and species.

Special events: Olde English Festival and living history.

29 Kankakee State Park

Land: 4,000 acres   Water: 11 miles of Kankakee River

The ripples and topwaters of the Kankakee River attract fish and fishermen for derbys, recreational fishing on the weekend and, for many anglers, just sitting in the boat eating sandwiches and having the time of their life—catching fish or not. The tree-lined linear state park envelops both sides of the Kankakee River for 11 miles offering unspoiled settings, a wide channeled river that is rapidly cleansing itself, and many recreational opportunities for hikers, canoeists, hunters, fishermen and campers.

One of the most popular features of the park is canoeing the broad and gentle riverway. For youth groups, families and couples, slipping a paddle into the water is a magical experience and an ideal location for first-time canoeists to soak in the beauty and relaxing atmosphere. There are three lengths of trips you can take using rented canoes—a 2-3 hour tour, 3-5 hour outing, and a longer 20-mile, 7-10 hour trip that can be taken in one day or with an overnight stay at the Chippewa Campground.

The park has other interesting aspects for visitors. There are many prehistoric sites within the unit that were in a region of the state used by the Illini and Miami Indians at the time of the first European contact in the 1670s. By 1685 the Miami people were so numerous the Kankakee River was called the "River of Miami." Kickapoo, Mascouten and later the Potawatomi, Ottawa and Chippewa Indians later occupied the area, ultimately developing an extensive village known as "Rock Village" and "Little Rock Village."

Following the Black Hawk War in 1832, the Potawatomi ceded all of their land along the river to the United States. Most of the peaceful Potawatomi peoples left the area by the end of the decade, except for Chief Shaw-waw-nas-ee, whose grave is commemorated by a boulder along the nature trail at Rock Creek. Soon French Canadians and others came to the area. A railroad was almost built but the developers ran out of money, and the I & M Canal linked the area to the rest of the world. It wasn't until 1938 when Chicago resident Ethel Sturges Dummer donated the original 35 acres of land for a state park which now is a 4000-acre tract. The last major land acquisition was in 1989, and development continues.

Information and Activities

Kankakee State Park
P.O. Box 37
Bourbonnias, IL 60914
(815) 933-1383

Directions: Six miles northwest of Kankakee, along Routes 102 and 113. No swimming is allowed in the park.

Campground: The Potawatomi Campground is the Class A camping area comprised of four loops (Oak, Hawthorn, Osage and Hickory) along the north bank of the river. The area has showers between the Hawthorn and Osage entrances and a playground, dump station and limited river

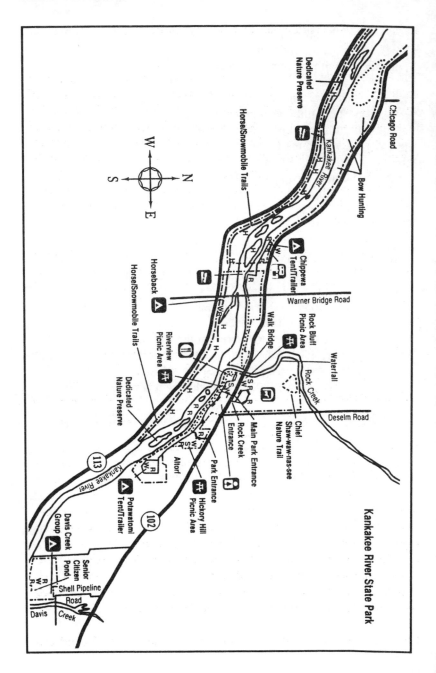

Kankakee River State Park

access. Alcohol is prohibited and quiet hours are 10 p.m. - 6 a.m. in the campgrounds.

The Hickory and Osage areas can be reserved in advance with a total of about 45 camping sites. All of the loops have excellent camping sites; all are private, notched out of the woods, flat and dry. Gravel pads, grills, tables and the visual barrier provided by thick vegetation, plus lots of shade, make this campground one of the most appealing in the state park system. Every site in these four loops is good, with the best sites at the end of the Hawthorn and Osage loops, near the Kankakee River. A path to the river is located between sites nine and ten in the Osage loop. Pedestrian pathways also connect each of the loops and the shower, which has a pop machine and extra parking.

The Chippewa Campground (Class B, C and E) is 2.5 miles from the main entrance and park office and offers a small boat launch, expansive open spaces and visitor parking. Camping sites 11-72 are medium shady with mature trees, while the 14 Class B/E area just east is very open and not private.

Camping sites 11-19 are shady with gravel pads, with all sites (11-35) in this loop getting heavy use. Site 10 is the best spot in the area as it's backed up against a natural area, near a small playground, and is somewhat private and shady. Sites 73, 74, 77 and 79 are shade covered and neighbor a thick wall of vegetation for privacy.

Boating: Unlimited boating is allowed in the river from the two launching ramps maintained by the park. Canoeists may rent 17-foot aluminum canoes outfitted with paddles and lifejackets. Trips typically start at the concession stand, where you will be bused to the "put-in" point on the river. At the end of the trip you will be returned. The Kankakee River is a Class 1 canoeing stream, which means that it provides an interesting variety of water conditions suitable for beginners or the occasional canoeist, without dangerous rapids or tricky currents. The canoe rental and concession stand is open Saturday and Sunday, 8 a.m. - 7 p.m. and Tuesday - Friday, 9 a.m. 7 p.m. Call (815) 932-6555 for canoe rental information. They have bait, tackle, firewood and a snack window.

Even on a short canoe trip, preparation is important. Wear light, loose fitting, comfortable clothing, and hats and long pants for sun protection. Rubber-soled canvas shoes, extra food and clothes, and your wallet should be in a waterproof bag that is tied or strapped to the canoe, just in case you soak your hat. Bring plenty of water, insect repellent and a smile.

Fishing: The size of the surface ripples on the Kankakee River will indicate the water depth, which helps in this particular river to locate the fish. Instead of random casting, look for weed beds and shoreline weed cover. Flat water typically indicates a shelf, and a dropoff is nearby. Work the rippling waters around shelves. Try casting topwater or semi-buzz baits, just inside the flats. Retrieving them over the break will produce smallmouths. Stick baits like floating Rapalas are great in these types of waters also. Try casting cross-current into the breaks and quartering downstream at various angles.

Weedless bass jigs also can be dropped directly behind the downstream flats, probing any underwater structure or dropoffs. Black or crawdad color jigs tipped with soft plastic or pork can be lightly jigged or crawled and rolled across the bottom for bass or walleye. Controlled live bait drifting is productive for bass and walleye, also. Drift the live bait as close to the breaks, ripples and edges as possible, trying to keep the bait moving at the same speed as the current. Think about drifting so that the live bait is presented as naturally as possible.

Many river anglers also start the day with shallow running lures, then progress to deeper running lures, and possibly switch to all live bait later in the day.

Hiking: Check with the staff regarding trail maps and about eight miles of trails on the north side of the river along Route 102 that aren't mentioned in the brochure.

The park's varied trails stretch for miles along both sides of the river for hiking, biking and cross-country skiing. The Area "A" hiking trails are five miles west of the park office on Route 102, with the parking area and trailhead south of Chicago Road and Route 102 junction. The slightly rolling trails follow a four-mile multiple loop system that travels through both timber and prairie. The loops are marked with ski trail signs and also have color coded emblems at the top of each sign identifying each loop.

There are 12 miles of bridle trails at Kankakee River State Park.

The far east loop is the archery range. When walking the archery trail, walk only counter-clockwise.

The Rock Creek hiking trails feature a self-guided nature trail, a 40-foot tall bluffline, waterfall, ponds, and creekside jaunt. The excursion also takes hikers by Chief Shaw-waw-naw-ee's grave and through a shady pine grove. The trailhead is at the Rock Creek Day-use Area off Route 102 or from the riding stable. Trails are marked by square construction fasteners painted orange and white.

A terrific biking trail starts at the Hickory Hill Picnic Area and travels 3.5 miles to the Chippewa Campground.

Stable: This is nestled in a wooded area on Deselm Road, three-quarter-mile north of Route 102, with a brown pole barn stable and paddocks that are occupied by gentle saddle horses swatting at flies and waiting for the next buckaroo to climb aboard. All rides are guided. You must have proper footwear. More than 12 miles of equestrian trails are in the area. Pony rides for the kiddies, cookouts, Polaroid photos and riding lessons are also offered by the stable. The small equine facility is open seven days, call (815) 939-0309.

Day-use areas: A daylong visit to the Kankakee park should start with a tour of the small nature center and talk with the full-time interpreter who prepares environmental education programming and offers classes, hikes and natural history information for all visitors. A tree guide, hiking trail maps, field guides and displays are located in the center.

Generally speaking, most of the day-use areas are on the north side of the river along Route 102 and include, a biking and hiking trail system, picnic tables and grills, river access points, a walk bridge, concession stand, camping and open spaces. One of the biggest day-use areas is near the park office. There are reservable picnicking shelters. Between the park office and campground there are extensive day-use areas with play apparatus, picnic tables, open spaces, trailway, shelters and toilets.

Hunting: Firearm hunting is permitted for duck, pheasant, quail, dove, rabbit, squirrel and raccoon.

30   *Kickapoo State Park*

Land: 2,842 acres   Water: 221 acres, 22 ponds

There are few Illinois state parks where you can go mountain biking, scuba diving, fishing in 22 ponds and lakes, camp, birdwatch or hunt all at the same unit. Kickapoo, once a wasteland ravaged by turn-of-the-century strip mine operations, is now nearly 3,000 acres that is healing and recovering from the damages.

During the past 50 years, trees and vegetation have gradually reclaimed the naked ridges of subsoil, and stagnate mine ponds have cleared. Kickapoo was the first park in the nation to be built on strip-mined land, and is therefore the first to be recovered and once again lush, active and heavily used by outdoor enthusiasts.

At first, the park, with its many ponds and winding roadways, is hard to navigate, but after a short stay visitors soon begin to discover many day-use areas, tiny fishing access points that are very private, almost hidden boat ramps and hiking trails. Just the web of roadways is a point of interest at the park.

The park also offers central Illinois residents and visitors a chance to fish for trout that are stocked in the ponds each year. Bring your panfish tackle, too. Bluegill, redear sunfish, crappies and bass also appear in the clear ponds, waiting for your wiggling bit of bait.

Information and Activities

Kickapoo State Park
R.R. 1, P.O. Box 374
Oakwood, IL 61858
(217) 442-4915

Directions: Six miles west of Danville, exit 206 or 210 off I-74 and go north. 25 miles east of Champaign in Vermilion County.

Campground: Alcohol is prohibited in all campgrounds and at each of the 217 camping sites. Reservations are accepted by mail or in person for a five dollar non-refundable fee for camping sites in the B (electric) and E (non-electric) areas. Quiet hours in the park are 7 p.m. to 9 a.m. There are Sunday worship services in the camp amphitheater at 8:30 a.m. No swimming is allowed at the park.

The campground is about 75 percent shady, generally level, and most of the sites are of equal size. In loop A, sites 3A and 4A are shady; 7A and 8A are backed up against wooded areas and near a horseshoe court and small playground area. Families would like 9A and 10A. The shower is handicapped accessible and is located at the entrance to the A loop.

The B loop is more shady, has gravel pads, and has sites near the showers, amphitheaters and restrooms.

In the C loop, camping sites 26 and 30 are large enough for big RV rigs, and there is lots of shade for campers in the sites marked in the 20s. Sites

21C-26C are backed up against a wooded area and lightly shaded. Sites 8C-12C are small and tightly packed.

In loop D (non-electric), sites 1D-8D are near the playground and tightly packed. Avoid sites 15D-18D and 24D-31D, which can be noisy due to their proximity to a sometimes busy access road.

The E loop, 1-34, a tent camping area, is down a small hill and offers average quality camping. The E loop sites are walk-in tent camping. Sites 1E-5E, 9E, 13E-17E and 34E and 35E are against a wooded area.

Sites in loop S, 1S-15S, have a good view of Long Pond. These are the most popular sites in the park, offering a good view, flat pads, a one-eighth-mile walk to the showers and plenty of shade to combat hot summer afternoons. The Red Ear camping area near Long Lake is very nice. Sites 1S-4S have water views and you can pull your boat right up to your camping site. Sites 7S and 8S are at the end of the loop, very private and shady. Sites 15S and 16S, 29S and 30S are also excellent camping areas in this light and airy part of the park. Check for camping sites that are level.

Firewood, bait and bike rentals are available at the concession stand. Emergency numbers: Illinois state police, (217) 867-2211; fire, sheriff and ambulance, call 911.

Boating: There are 12 boat access points on the small lakes: Emerald Pond, Long Lake, Middle Fork, Pond Six, Inland Seas, Sportsman's Lake, No Name Pond, Clear Pond, Deep Pond, Peelman Pond, High Pond, River Road and Possum Pond.

Canoe trips (with shuttle service) are available in and near the state park (Long Pond), with two-hour, one-day, and two-day trips. Call (217) 443-4939 or (217) 354-2060. Nearby Short Road Marina and Wynes Marina have complete boating and marina supplies.

Fishing: TJs Tackle and Bait, Davis Bait and Eastside Bait have bait and local knowledge of the ponds. Anglers will generally find small- and largemouth bass fishing good to very good, depending on the time of year.

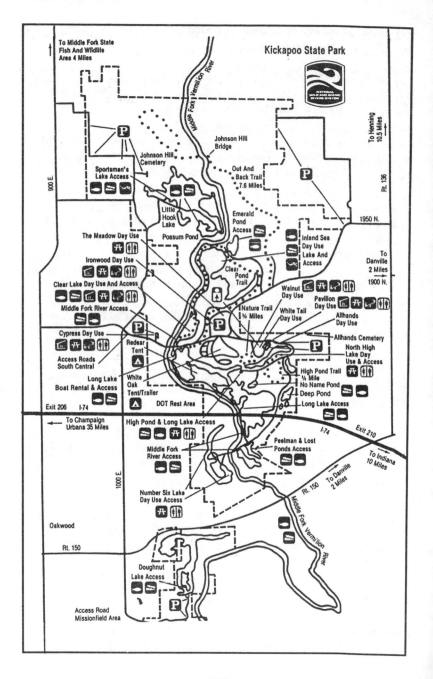

Kickapoo State Park

Hiking/biking: Mountain biking is encouraged on the five miles of designated trails at the unit. There is even a mountain biking club that organizes group outings, races and off-site trips. For more information, call (217) 548-2696. The special mountain biking trails and quiet hilly park roadways make this park an excellent destination for cyclists.

When the Middle Fork River was designated an Illinois and National Scenic River in 1986, it became protected by federal law and its historical and recreational importance was deeply seeded in the minds of staff and park users. Since this time, park trails have been improved and use is increasing. The primary walking trail is the Out and Back Trail, which is seven miles long and loops around a hill and retraces itself back to the trailhead. The trailhead is off the road that takes you to the Inland Sea and Emerald Pond, located just behind a small day-use area. The old iron Johnson Hill Bridge is of interest about half-way out on the trail where hikers can rest, fish or take in the views from the old span.

Also offered are one and two-hour horseback rides and hayrides.

Day-use areas: There are five main picnic areas with shelters around the scattered small bodies of waters. They all have water hydrants, picnic tables, toilets and grills. A variety of game court areas are maintained in the park, such as horseshoes, volleyball court, softball diamonds, Frisbee golf and scuba diving access.

The Eastside Pavilion is an area with the above amenities. Maple day-use area has trails, picnic tables and toilets and game areas. Cypress Area, Ironwood and High Pond (handicapped accessible) all have routine equipment like play structures, tables, toilets and water.

A cross-country course is an accurately measured one-mile loop that takes you by the shelter restroom, up and down a one-quarter-mile hill to the end of the course. There is a runners club at the park.

Scuba divers must obtain a permit from the park office and demonstrate proper certification before diving in the park.

Nature: Approximately 190 species of birds have been identified within or flying over Kickapoo and nearby Middlefork State Fish and Wildlife

Please don't feed the animals!

area during the past 20 years. A birding checklist is available and prepared by Steve Bailey (no relation to me) in cooperation with the Natural Heritage Department.

The handy list is easy to use and the legend indicates the relative abundance of each species during each season, and a key to general habitats the birds might be spotted in. The area has a good warbler migration. Osprey are occasionally seen, plus many other interesting species stop by the tiny lakes and ponds at the park.

Hunting: More than 1,000 acres including forests, grasslands, edge and croplands are available for hunters each fall. There are archery and firearm deer seasons, as well as seasons for squirrel, dove, woodcock, pheasant, rabbit, raccoon and opossum.

Nearby attractions: Hitching Post Stable (217-446-8575, open weekends), and Weldon Springs State Park. Middlefork State Fish and Wildlife Area only four miles away has hunting, fishing and 35 miles of horse and hiking trails.

31 Lake Murphysboro State Park

Land: 1,022 acres   Water: 145-acre lake

From the tiny downtown Liberty theater house to a small amusement park with go-carts and miniature golf, antique shops, apple festival, barbecue championship, home tours and fast food restaurants to the information-packed ranger station for the Shawnee National Forest, there are lots of things to do in this rolling and wooded part of southern Illinois.

The ranger station, on SR 149 just west of town, is open weekdays 8 a.m. - 4:30 p.m., and is the perfect place to learn about the wonderful amenities and places to visit in this portion of the sprawling national forest. While staying at the state park or one of the other forest campgrounds, consider day trips to any of the following areas: Pine Hills Recreation Area, Little Grand Canyon, Pomona Natural Bridge, Johnson Creek Recreation Area, Buttermilk Hill Beach, Oakwood Bottoms, Greentree Resort, Turkey

Bayou Campgrounds and many other natural area and trail systems.

Located in Jackson County, Lake Murphysboro State Park's beautiful rolling hills and woods surround a 145-acre star-shaped lake that is full of outdoor recreation opportunities.

Along the Big Muddy River, about one mile below the park, was located one of three saline lands given by the federal government to Illinois when it became a state. One of them was leased to Dr. Conrad Will, a prominent member of both the Illinois House and Senate in the early days of statehood, who operated the salt works until 1840 when the business was closed. Today, nothing remains of the town, Brownsville, except the village cemetery.

In 1950 the state built the lake, which has a maximum depth of 25 feet, and has 7.5 miles of shoreline made up of rolling hills with a wide variety of tree species. The lake has been stocked with fish over the years; underwater structures and other management techniques continue to keep the lake a good fishery.

Information and Activities

Lake Murphysboro State Park
R.R. 4, P.O. Box 144
Murphysboro, IL 62966
(618) 684-2867

Directions: Two miles west of Murphysboro off Illinois 149. Take exit 54A-B west onto Illinois 13 at Marion and go west through Carbondale to Murphysboro.

Campground: There are 54 camping sites in the Big Oak Campground and 15 tent sites as the north end. Showers are at the concession stand about a quarter-mile from the campground. There are three fishing docks in the campground, plenty of shade and the camping area is rarely filled on summer weekends. Staff says that sites 9-29 are the best, with sites 1-8 being small for pop-up campers or small trailers.

Sites 1-3 and 19-29 are surrounded by water on three sides. Sites 4-18 have a view of the tree-lined lake. Some of the sites in the 30s and 40s are pull-through sites. There's also children's play equipment in this part of the rolling campground.

Most of the sites have sparse gravel pads, picnic tables and fire pits. Youth camping is available at the park by reservation. Camping sites (and many other outdoor recreational opportunities) are also available in the Lake Kincaid recreation area that is only a couple of minutes from the state park.

Boating: Boat motors are restricted to 10 hp or less. Aluminum flat-bottom boats are rented at the small concession that also has bait, food and ice. The concession is open Friday-Sunday, 7 a.m. - 7 p.m. and Monday - Thursday, 8 a.m. - 6 p.m.

There's parking for about 20 cars/trailers at the ramp area and day-use amenities are near the parking lot. A small building with three showers is behind the concession stand at the boat ramp.

Fishing: A small fishing pier is only 50 yards from the concession stand and a great place for young anglers to try their luck in the panfish-filled quiet lake waters. You can use your small boat, or take advantage of the many man-made fishing docks and quiet shoreline fishing spots that are often productive places to catch panfish, catfish, carp and the occasional bass.

The concession operator monitors lake fishing and is the best source for up-to-date angling information, how-to tips and places to go. Learning where the underwater structures are is an important bit of knowledge to make your fishing day successful. The many shady coves of the lake offer plenty of places to explore for planted largemouth bass. A handicapped accessible pier is maintained by the park.

Many anglers fish near the dam using long pole, bobber and redworms. A gentle jigging action seems to produce well for the locals who regularly fish here.

Creel limits: redear and bluegill maximum of 25; largemouth bass must

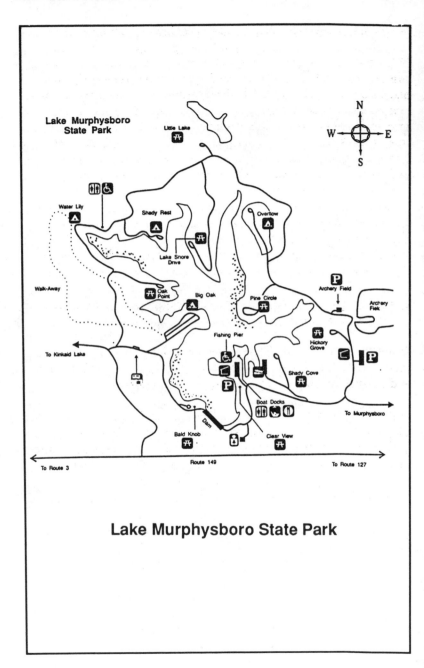

Lake Murphysboro State Park

be 15 inches in length; all other Illinois fishing regulations apply.

Hiking: The main trail is well-marked and ranges in difficulty from easy to moderately difficult. The 3-mile-long ravine and ridge loop is popular and follows a winding portion of the lake shore into the northwest wooded corner of the park. Access to this trail is from the Big Oak campground, at several pulloffs or the Oak Point picnic area. The trail is a complete loop and takes hikers through a cool and damp wooded area that is the home of nine orchid species, wetland communities, and a variety of song and some wading birds. There are also many small, unmarked trails through the wooded areas.

Large parts of the 7.5-mile lake shoreline are walkable along mowed day-use expanses with vault toilets and tables along part of the way. The main park road is also used by walkers for a shady, usually private stroll by the dam, boat docks and many picnicking areas.

Hikers can also walk the perimeter of the 15-acre Little Lake at the north end of the park. Bring your fishing rod and reel.

Day-use areas: Two reservable picnic shelters, two playgrounds and more than 150 picnic tables scattered along the lakes' edge offer campers and day-use visitors many private locations and vistas.

Nature: Wild orchids that include Showy Ladies Slipper, Yellow Ladies Slipper, Purple Fringeless, Twayblade, Puttywood, Coralroot and Ladies' Tresses are some of the varieties at the park. The oak/hickory offers many other flora and fauna communities for your examination.

Nearby attractions: Mississippi River and swimming at Lake Kincaid.

32 Le-Aqua-Na State Park
Land: 715 acres   Water: 40 acres

Don't get sidetracked by the cheese outlet stores, like Torkelson's, on your way to the state park with the cleverest name in the system—Le-Aqua-Na. Aqua means water. You knew that. Well, they took the name of the nearby town, Lena, Illinois, and, as man once made the lake at the park, some marketing guy held a "name the park contest" and the "winner" put the lake—or water—in the middle of the town's name.

Lena is a terrific little farming community of about 2,500 residents that comes compete with the Clover Patch Tea Room, grain elevators, milling, cheese outlets and a bustling downtown area. It's no wonder that most of the visitors to Le-Aqua-Na State Park come over from Chicago to immerse themselves in a rural farming town that remains much the way it did in the 1950s.

The park was developed as part of a statewide plan to provide Illinois citizens with close to home quality outdoor recreation. The park was started with a land acquisition program in 1948 and was dedicated as a 715-acre state park 10 years later.

The park is in Stephenson County, where three engagements of Black Hawk took place within a couple of miles of the quiet state operated park. Soon after the war ended settlers quickly populated the fertile area, with William Waddams building the first home in the county just west of the park site, along a trail that was to become the principal east-west route across northern Illinois for stagecoach and early automobile travelers. The historic highway can still be seen by area visitors.

Information and Activities

Le-Aqua-Na State Park
8542 North Lake Road
Lena, IL 61048
(815) 369-4282

Directions: In Stephenson County, west of Route 73 on Lake Road, the park is six miles south of the Illinois-Wisconsin state line and about 2.5 miles north of Lena.

Information: The park office is at the end of the first road to your right upon entering the park. The office is open 8 a.m. - 4 p.m. weekdays. Reservations and information about the campground are available here.

Campground: Reservations will be accepted by mail beginning January 2, and in person reservations will be accepted beginning February 1. Sites may be reserved from May 1 through October 31. There is a non-refundable $5 reservation fee. Mail-in reservations must be received seven days in advance. The seven-day time period does not apply to in-person reservations. Sites 1-43 can be reserved.

About 140 of the 178 camping sites have electricity and they are grouped in three designated areas. The Class A sites have gravel pads, and nearby shower buildings with flush toilets and water. Class B campers can use

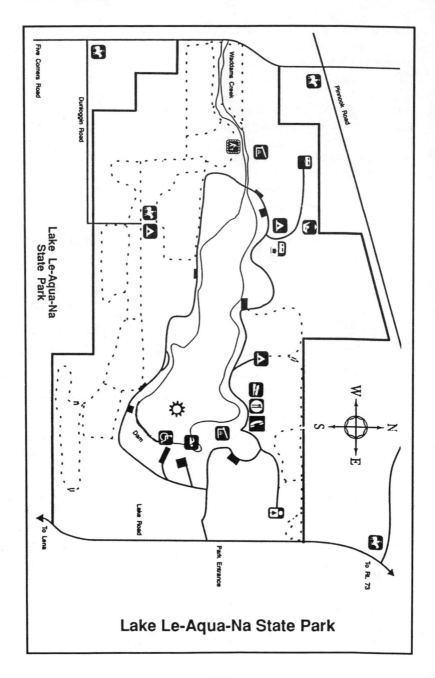

Lake Le-Aqua-Na State Park

the showers.

The small Pine Ridge camping area overlooks the narrow lake and has mostly Class B sites where many tent campers can enjoy the open area. Site number 4, 5, and 8 are popular sites.

There are 150 camping sites in the clean Hickory Hill area north of the Class B campground. This area is busy on the weekends and always full on holiday weekends. The area is fairly new, with light shading. Sites 27 and 28 are very nice locations, while 8-28 are open; 29-34 have some shade in back of them. Sites 35-41 are good sized and near the shower building. Light to medium shading marks the sections with sites in the 50s and 60s. Sites 83-86 are against agricultural fields, while very private locations are sites 87-89, with a small gully and wooded area nearby. High Point hiking trail begins in this area.

Site 91 is surrounded by a roadway, but actually is private and convenient. Those at the end of a lane like, 103 and 104, are secluded and wooded. Areas with the least shade are sites 112-118 and 124-135. Most sites can accommodate RVs. Generally speaking, the campground is open, lacking privacy. Nevertheless, if you take a drive through first, you can find some pleasant camping sites.

RV drivers should gear down on the sometimes steep and winding roadways.

Big Buck Campground is separate from the others and is maintained for equestrians. It is accessed from county roads bordering the park.

Boating: No gas-powered boat motors are allowed on the quiet little 39.5-acre lake that was built in the mid-1950s. Small boats can enjoy the waters and its 1.4 miles of wooded shoreline, nearby concession stand and many day-use areas along the shore. The small boat launching ramp is at the northeastern side of the lake, next to the restaurant. You can rent paddle boats, canoes, and rowboats at the concession.

Fishing: There is no fishing at the beach, but angling is considered good to very good on the rest of the lake that reaches a depth of 20 feet at the southeast end. The average depth of the lake is about 11 feet. Walleye, northern pike and channel catfish are periodically planted in the popular lake, and brush piles and fish cribs have been installed to encourage further natural reproduction and offer cover. The lake has a good population of largemouth bass, bluegill and crappie that can be taken from shoreline, at the handicapped fishing pier, which is a great place for small children to fish from, and from small boats that can find the underwater structures.

Strict fishing regulations help to ensure quality fishing. You may take one 14-inch or larger large- or smallmouth bass per day; six walleye per day; and three 24 inch or larger northern pike daily. There is no limit on the size of black crappie (limit 25 daily), catfish (limit six per day), or bluegill (10 per day). Occasionally rock bass and redear sunfish are also taken.

Local catfish anglers soak their bait with cooking oil—it's worth a try. Some big carp are also taken at the lake, usually by a little kid, according to the bait shop attendant.

Anglers also benefit from the good management of the lake and the use of an axial-destratifier, a device that mixes the lake water to keep oxygen levels high at all depths.

Many campers bring their flyrod along and cast small surface poppers that often attract the attention of bass and panfish. Try using your flyrod along the dam area in the evening. Locals say white and yellow poppers are good choices for this lake. Kids can have lots of action with red worm and a bobber.

Hiking: There are seven miles of trails, some of which pass along the shoreline. Most of the trails are on the south side of the lake, with trailheads located on the main park road. Hiking is generally easy.

The trail near Waddams Creek, at the west end of the park, is a pleasant walk. Horses, hikers and cross-country skiers share the trails.

The 13-mile Stephenson-Black Hawk Trail, which follows county and township roads, passes by the north side of the park and offers a loop that takes about 8 hours to walk, or 3-4 to cycle. The trail is roughly circular and can be traveled at any starting point. A self-guided brochure detailing points of interest along the way is available at the park office. Wild turkey can often be heard and seen by hikers.

Day-use areas: Beaches are rare in the state parks of Illinois, and when you do find them they are popular, just like the sandy, horseshoe shaped cove that was made into a beach in 1985. There is no lifeguard and the beach is open 8 a.m. - 8 p.m. from Memorial Day - Labor Day. There are many picnic tables near the beach.

Two picnic shelters can be reserved and have electricity. All other picnic sites have grills and trash barrel; many are near toilets. Virtually all of the picnic areas have a lake view and parking.

The day-use area is big enough to keep people spread out, but small and safe for family gatherings and camping.

The Lake View Restaurant, with seating that overlooks the lake, has great burgers, ice cold drinks and a super friendly staff. Piers and the boat ramp are nearby.

An outdoor church holds services periodically during the summer.

Nature: Towering hickory, oaks, walnut and other hardwoods are thick, along with large tracts of pine plantation. The area supports many wildflower species during the spring and fall, as well as most common wildlife. Of special interest is the chance to see badgers at the park.

The feisty diggers are secretive and underground a lot, so they are difficult to spot, unless you are patient and talk with the park rangers to find out where active dens are. It's said that an adult badger can out-dig a man with a shovel. If you have ever seen the front claws on this barrel-shaped critter, you'll see why they can dig like a steam shovel.

Hunting: Doves, in season. Call ahead for details.

33   *Lincoln Trail State Park*

Land: 1,022 acres   Water: 145-acre lake

Named after the trail Abraham Lincoln's family followed en route from Indiana to Illinois in 1831, the region was also used by three Native American groups, the Miami, Kickapoo and Mascouten before the lands was ceded to the United States in the early 19th century. In 1955 the state created the 145-acre, 41-feet-deep lake, which was the third man-made lake created in Illinois using federal funds from the Dingell-Johnson Act. The park was dedicated in 1958 and has been constantly upgraded since.

Today, visitors enjoy fishing, a waterfront cafe at the boat ramp, rental boats, raccoon hunting, tent or modern camping, a nature preserve, huge American beech trees, shady picnic areas and the jagged shorelines of the tree-lined lake. Old Abe would like the park.

The Lincoln Heritage Trail was authorized 50 years after Lincoln's death. The Illinois State Historical Library was charged with the responsibility to mark the exact route traveled by Abraham Lincoln from Kentucky through Indiana to Illinois. Another 50 years passed before the 1,000-mile long trail was opened in 1963. More than 3,000 markers direct travelers from around the world that come to use the scenic route, with some travelers stopping off at the state park. The park is west of the trail as it follows Route 1. A few miles north of the park, the trail branches onto a county road heading west toward Clarksville.

Fishing and camping are the two main attractions of the park, but visitors will soon be captivated by the deep ravines of the nature preserve that almost overflow with a lush beech-maple forest that has changed very little since Lincoln's time. The towering American beech trees, unusual ferns and abundant wildflowers, plus winter sports and clean day-use areas, make Lincoln Trail State Park a great stopover and gateway park to the wonderful southern portion of the state.

Information and Activities

Lincoln Trail State Park
R.R. 1, P. O. Box 117
Marshall, IL 62441
(217) 826-2222

Directions: West of Route 1, two miles south of Marshall in Clark County. Take Route 1 south off of I-70 for about three miles to the park entrance.

Information: The park office at the entrance of the park is open daily. It has lake maps, campground maps, birding lists, and other brochures and useful information about the park.

Campground: There are two pleasant Class A camping areas, Plainview and Lakeside, totaling 218 sites which are typically full on the weekends, and always full on summer holiday weekends. As usual in Illinois state parks, the Class A camping sites have electricity, nearby showers and toilets, tables, waters, fire blocks and a sanitary dump station. The

Lakeside campground also has a tent camping area.

In loop D, there are four tent sites at the end of the peninsula near a walkway to a small dock anchored at the shore in a tiny cove. Virtually any site in loop D is great. This is the park's most popular area. Loop E also has four tent sites with a water view; loops C and A have additional tent sites that are also quite adequate.

For campers with big RV rigs, a number of pull through sites are maintained in Loop G. Sites in loops F and H are generally shady, but more compact and farther from the water. A group camping area accommodating tents is available to organized adult or youth groups by reservation.

Firewood and limited camping supplies are on sale at the boat ramp concession which is open April - October.

Boating: You can bring small boats or rent a 14-foot johnboat at the launch, with parking for about 25 vehicles. The lake has a 10 hp limit. The many coves of the lake offer small boats plenty of chances to fish or merely enjoy a leisurely tour of the wooden shorelines and watery open areas. Rental docks are available and a newer concession stand offers food and supplies. The ramp area is a focal point for activity and a place to meet other park users, fishermen, campers and boaters.

Fishing: Fishing in the 145-acre lake that reaches a depth of about 35 feet is considered good. The lake has some underwater structures, some flooded timbers, many narrow covers and very good locations for spring angling in the shallows and around beds.

A good population of largemouth bass exists in the lake, but the average size has steadily decreased since 1986 due to overharvesting. A slot length limit is helping to restore the bass fishery. Fish 15 inches are protected. Locals find rubber worms with scent and buzzbaits good producers.

About 7500 channel catfish are stocked annually and anglers find cheese bait to be the best terminal tackle to use on the big cats. They are taken in all parts of the lake.

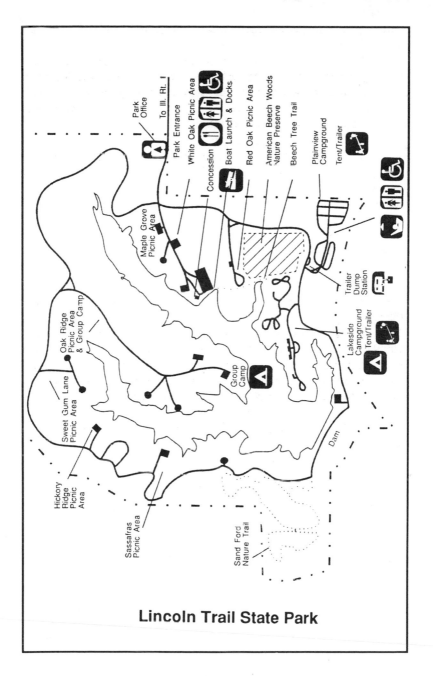

Lincoln Trail State Park

Park Office

To Ill. Rt.

Park Entrance

White Oak Picnic Area

Concession

Boat Launch & Docks

Red Oak Picnic Area

American Beech Woods Nature Preserve

Beech Tree Trail

Plainview Campground

Tent/Trailer

Maple Grove Picnic Area

Trailer Dump Station

Oak Ridge Picnic Area & Group Camp

Lakeside Campground Tent/Trailer

Sweet Gum Lane Picnic Area

Group Camp

Hickory Ridge Picnic Area

Dam

Sassafras Picnic Area

Sand Ford Nature Trail

Lincoln Trail Lake is a good to very good crappie and bluegill lake, especially in the upper reaches where local anglers use small worm rigs and crickets. Fly rods and crickets in the spring are great fun. I caught several hand-sized bluegill one morning in early May one year. Also, lots of three-quarter-pound crappies are taken, many from the shoreline.

Redear sunfish are also found in the lake up to one pound, with most eatable fish sized at one-half pound.

Hiking: There are no bridle trails and the hiking trail system is not greatly developed. The Beech Tree Trail has lots of stairs, but is wooded and moderately difficult in all other regards. It is located near the nature preserve on the east side of the park, near the campground entrance.

The two-mile-long trail near the dam is pleasant and also connects to the two-mile Sand Ford Trail south of the Sassafras Picnic area on the west side of the lake. Both of these trail are fairly easy.

Day-use areas: Swimming is not allowed at the lake, but there are plenty of lakeside places to rest under a shady tree and cool off in the summer, or strike out for an ice fishing effort in the winter. There are two main picnicking areas with shelters, but there are many picnic tables with grills spaced about the park, most with a lake view and a cool breeze. Kids will enjoy the play equipment, open spaces and chance to romp about the mowed day-use areas.

Nature: The American Beech Woods, an Illinois nature preserve, is a wonderful area to explore and features dozens of herbaceous plants, seven species of ferns, three species of orchids, four species of grasses, 10 species of shrubs, lots of vines, significant wildflower populations, about 150 species of birds and many common mammals.

The short, one-half-mile Beech Tree Trail will take you from the boat dock and concession stand near the preserve.

Hunting: Raccoon hunting, by a draw system, is offered during the fall season. There is no deer hunting at the unit.

34　Lincoln Trail Homestead

State Memorial Park
P.O. Box 705
Mt Zion, IL　62549
(217) 963-2729

The underdeveloped (no park office) and backroads park is a small day-use unit with the feature attraction a plaque and memorial commemorating Abraham Lincoln's first Illinois homestead.

A red granite boulder with green-colored bronze plaque marks the spot only a few steps from the Sagamon River where the old Whitney Dam and Mill stood and the Lincoln cabin was originally constructed.

The Lincoln family, in March 1830, came to this area and lived here for a relatively short time, where the parents returned to Cole County and Abe set out on his own career.

An American flag flaps in the breeze above the small monument that rests in the middle of a 30-foot square flag stone area, and a walkway down to the river is one way to retrace Abe's steps that he probably made hundreds of times on his way to the river as young man.

There is a small picnic shelter, about a dozen picnic tables and some children's play equipment in the day-use area.

Bring a picnic lunch and your fishing pole; there are a few sites along the swift little river that bank fishermen can use.

Directions: The park is open 8 a.m. - 10 p.m. The park is on 600E (C.R. 27), south of Route 51, about three miles from Harristown. The Lincoln Memorial Highway ends at the park. The highway route follows the Lincoln family and their migration from Indiana to Illinois in the spring of 1830.

35 Lowden State Park

Land: 273 acres   Water: Rock River

Half of Lowden State Park, which is named for Gov. Frank O. Lowden who served the state during World War I, is an open, day-use area. The other half of the small unit consists of camp sites and an overlook where a nearly 50-foot-tall concrete-reinforced statute casts a shadow onto the Rock River and stands as a tribute to Native Americans.

Art Lorado Taft was the creator and John Prasuhn was the builder of the statue on the west end of the park looking down on the river from a bluff top. The statue is 60 feet high; the body alone is 44 feet tall. It weighs 270 tons of steel and concrete. Inside there is a seven-foot-wide chamber and the concrete was actually poured from the inside out using the chamber as an access point. The jumbo work was completed in Dec. 30, 1910.

At the base of the statue there is an information board that talks about the freezing weather and efforts to pump water up from the river below during the early part of the century. In many ways the statute is a tribute to working in difficult conditions and the blend of engineering knowhow in the creation of an art form. The figure is the second largest monolithic statue in the world, even after lightning hit it and it was repaired during the mid-1940s.

Legend says that Chief Black Hawk, after the Black Hawk war, reflected on the beauty of the area and admonished his captors to care for the land as he and his people had. The state has done a good job, and in most ways, I think the Chief would be proud that the park is preserved and open to the public so that all creeds, races, young and old can continue to enjoy the beautiful views of the Rock River and that the bluffs grace the shorelines and offer a majestic reminder of how our Native Americans once saw them.

Information and Activities

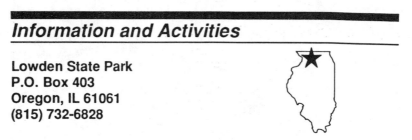

Lowden State Park
P.O. Box 403
Oregon, IL 61061
(815) 732-6828

Directions: Located about 2.5 hours west of Chicago, just east of Oregon on Route 64.

Campground: The campground is south of the park office near a dump station. There are 89 electrical sites and 44 non-electric sites. A shower building near the main campground called the Shady Rest Camping area also near the office, while additional primitive camping is available across the road (east side) at the White Oaks (41 non-electric) camping area, or the Sun Valley sites southeast of the statue. There is also a group of private walk-in camping sites at the White Oaks area. If you don't need electricity, use White Oaks for a more private outdoor experience.

In Shady Rest, all sites have gravel pads, picnic tables, a fire ring and electricity. There are flush toilets and showers. Virtually all of the sites

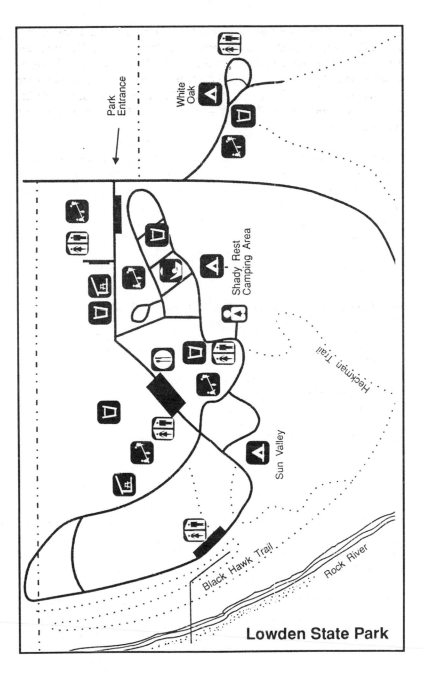

Park Entrance

White Oak

Shady Rest Camping Area

Heckman Trail

Sun Valley

Black Hawk Trail

Rock River

Lowden State Park

189

in this area are large enough for motor homes and large camping trailers. Sites have little privacy. Sites 92-100 back up against the woods, while most other sites have shade from large mixed-deciduous trees, but little side-to side privacy.

This is not one of the better campgrounds in the system, and staff indicated that improvements are planned in the next couple of years. Road work and other infrastructure improvements will help attract more campers to this small unit.

Boating: A ramp is south of the park accesses to the Rock River. There is no horsepower restriction on the river.

Fishing: Anglers congregate below the dam on Washington Street near the bridge. Smallmouth bass must be released, while anglers have good luck on rough fish. Many locals use chicken livers for channel cats, and the occasional walleye is taken from the relatively shallow waters along this part of the river. Small boats do use the area and can do well on sportfish during the spring.

Hiking: There are about 3.5 miles of trails at the park with nearly a half-mile of foot trails that wander north and south along the bluff near the statue. Other trails are fairly flat loops. The Pines Trail, on the east side of the park near the White Oaks camping area, is the most interesting trail as it leads visitors through some natural areas and along the park boundary. The hiking paths, due in part to the high college student population in neighboring Oregon, make them well used. The 101 steps will take you down to the river from the Black Hawk Trail, near the towering statue.

Day-use areas: About half of the main park area is comprised of adequate picnicking areas, play equipment and a dirt-surfaced basketball court nestled under large trees and serviced by vault toilets, lots of trash barrels, grills and drinking water. A small set of play equipment with 10 swings and a slide is near the park office.

The Larado Taft Campus outdoor education center offers residential environmental education programming for area schools and other groups.

36   Matthiessen State Park

Land: 1,938 acres

Matthiessen State Park is managed by Starved Rock State Park and is an impressive link in the 30 miles of outcrop shoreline, dells and riverways that lies between La Salle and Ottawa. The park is not nearly as developed as its big brother, Starved Rock, but is every bit as charming and far more intimate. In fact, the park is a great natural area that includes "the Dells," a large day-use area, and trails.

The park has two areas, Vermillion River, a day-use areas and the Dells. Vermillion includes a model airplane field, four picnic shelters with dozens of picnic tables, a baseball field, play areas, vault toilets, plenty of open spaces, and about one mile of sparse shade and open spaces. Parking is allowed on the road shoulders and the area can accommodate large family gatherings or group picnics.

North of this area is the Dells Area, which is lushly wooded and abundant with flora and fauna. There is no camping at this state park, but the trails, waterfalls, canyons, streams and low use combine to delight visitors. It also is a paradise for geology buffs, birders, nature photographers and day users.

The park was named for William Matthiessen, a businessman from La Salle who originally developed about 176 acres, employed 50 people and operated the park under the name of "Deer Park." The old park housed penned-up deer, a long narrow canyon and a stockade, which has been renovated. After Matthiessen's death the park was donated to the state and opened to the public in 1943. Matthiessen State Park is an excellent day-trip destination for campers staying at Starved Rock or visiting the canal corridor area.

Information and Activities

Matthiessen State Park
P. O. Box 381
Utica, IL 61373
(815) 667-4868

Directions: South of Starved Rock State Park, take Route 178 south off from I-80 about five miles to the entrance. The park is about four miles southeast of La Salle.

Information: The park office is open weekdays from 8 a.m. - 4 p.m.

The Dells Area: There are many unusual and beautiful rock formations that feature exposed sandstone. The main canyon, consisting of the Upper and Lower Dells, and offers a great walking tour of moderate difficulty that takes you by a canyon with a 60-foot waterfall, across a pedestrian bridge, flowing springs and tree-canopied areas.

Boating: The Vermillion River, after a hard rainfall, quickly becomes a roaring whitewater river and kayakers love it. They put in at a low bridge

Footbridge near the falls.

off Route 178 and can work about 14 miles of the river that wipes up into some fast and powerful water. No boat rentals or launches at the park.

Fishing: The Vermillion River has fair fishing for large and smallmouth bass and crappies. You can hike back to the Lower Dells where waters are about four feet deep and fishing is considered fair to good. Bait is available in Utica on Route 178.

Hiking: The trail to the waterfalls is behind the stockade. There are eight miles of trails that are well-marked, mostly wooded, chipped and relaxing or vigorous depending on the loop. Large trail maps placed along the trails and easy to follow. Trails along the upper bluff tops are easy hiking, but the trails into the interior of the Dells may be difficult, particularly during the spring. There is one double canyon at the park.

Bridle trails: There is a horse rental on Route 71 and on the north side of the Dells Area is a parking lot with hitching post and staging area with access to about nine miles of bridle trails. These trails may also be hiked.

Day-use areas: Both portions of the park have picnicking areas, water fountains, field archery range, radio-controlled model aircraft fields, and open spaces. A restored fort and stockade, which represents the type of

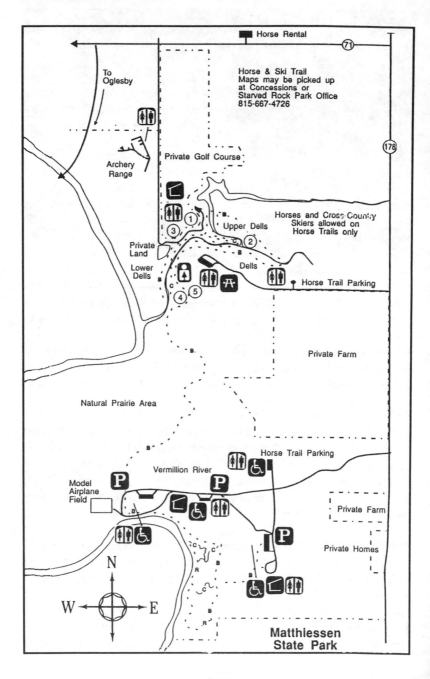

Horse Rental

71

178

To Oglesby

Horse & Ski Trail
Maps may be picked up
at Concessions or
Starved Rock Park Office
815-667-4726

Private Golf Course

Archery Range

Upper Dells

Horses and Cross Country
Skiers allowed on
Horse Trails only

Private Land

Lower Dells

Dells

Horse Trail Parking

Private Farm

Natural Prairie Area

Horse Trail Parking

Vermillion River

Model Airplane Field

Private Farm

Private Homes

N

W E

Matthiessen
State Park

forts built by the French in the Midwest during the 1600s and early 1700s, are near the newer restrooms at the end of the drive at the Dells area.

Nature notes: Morel mushroom collecting is almost as much fun in the spring as watching the cliff swallows darting for insects along the canyon walls and over tiny streams that produce insects and nourishment for flora.

This is one of the finest, least used natural areas in the park system. Frankly, I almost hate to oversell or overpromote the area. I'm a bit selfish about this little park. Nevertheless, visitors should look for the many interesting types of mosses and liverworts which cling to the damp and shady vertical walls. Also note the array of fern species that enjoy the rich soil and moist, cool ground.

On top of the dry shady bluff tops near the canyon edge, black oak, cedar and white oak provide a shady canopy. Towering wispy white pine and white cedar were carried this far south by glacial activity thousands of years ago. Closer to ground level you'll discover serviceberry, northern honeysuckle, tanagers and waxwings that often feed on the berries these shrubs produce. Birding is considered excellent, especially during the spring warbler migration as the birds follow the river corridors northward to summer nesting areas.

As you move farther from the bluffs, burr oak and hickory grow densely along various edges, producing yet another unique area to explore featuring witch hazel, black huckleberry and bracken fern. Wildflower lovers will enjoy both spring and summer seasons. In the spring jack-in-the-pulpits, pastel-colored hepatica, wild geranium and other wildflowers cover the forest floor. In open areas black-eyed susans and spiked trefoils will bloom throughout the summer.

Animals watchers will be amused if they spot a flying squirrel during the twilight hours, whitetail deer along the edge areas, or raccoons spending most of their time in trees plucking berries from thin branches. Bring your binoculars and field guides.

Nearby attractions: Golf course, three other state parks in La Salle County.

37 *Mississippi Palisades*

Land: 2,500 acres

The word palisades is used to describe a line of tall, steep cliffs usually seen along a river, and the Mississippi Palisades, two miles north of Savanna (motto: "A Sportsmen's Paradise") in Carroll County tower above the famous riverway, offering visitors sweeping vistas found in no other Illinois state park.

The natural features of the park, which include sink holes, limestone caves, bluffs and wooded ravines that dissect the unglaciated terrain are just some of the reasons this park, and the entire northwestern corner of Illinois, are the most scenic places in the Midwest. Located on the southernmost limit of the paper birch tree's range, the park is a showcase for spring wildflowers that dapple the slopes with blooms of trillium, bluebell, lobelia, shooting star and yellow ladies slipper. Animal watchers and other park users may also see flocks of wild turkey gobbling about or the crow-sized pileated woodpecker drilling huge holes the size of coffee cans in trailside trees.

The north section of the park represents one of the largest forested expanses in the state. Located near the confluence of the Mississippi and Apple rivers, the U.S. Department of Interior designated acreage here in 1973 as a national landmark.

Route 52/84, which travels north through Savanna, passes the old train car that serves as a visitor information center; the route is part of the Great River Road program that features routes near historic rivers and the communities that have sprung up along them.

Whether you take the auto tour (information is at the south entrance, in front of the large picnic shelter), or do some vertical hiking, wildflower walking, or climbing the cliff faces, Mississippi Palisades has many attractions and features that will engage you, move you and keep you on your feet. This is a busy park with a clean, very nice campground.

Information and Activities

Mississippi Palisades State Park
4577 Route 84 North
Savanna, IL 61074
(815) 273-2731

Directions: North of Savanna, on Route 52/84, about three hours directly west of Chicago.

Information: The park office, at the north entrance of the park across the street from the mini-mart park store, is open 8:30 a.m. - noon and 12:30 p.m. - 4:30 p.m. weekdays.

Campground: Campers pulling large trailers or those with under-powered rigs should watch warning signs carefully; the many steep and tight-cornered turns might be impossible for you to navigate. Drivers should also look out for hiking and horse crossings along park roads.

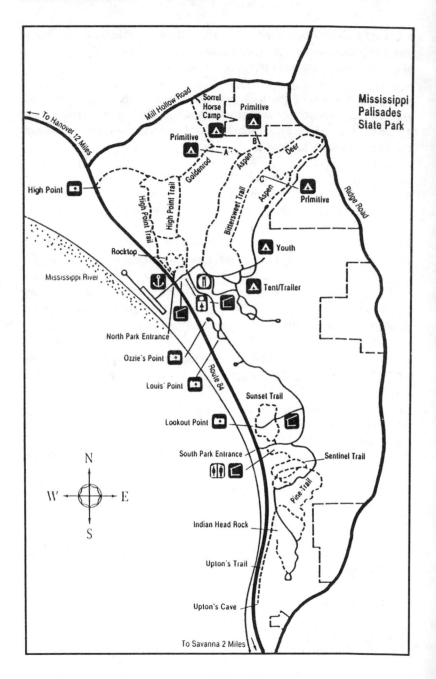

Mississippi Palisades State Park

The 240-site campground does not take reservations and is typically filled on holidays and many other summer weekends. 106 sites have electricity and there are three shower buildings, three primitive walk-in sites and an equestrian camping area. Entry to the campgrounds is restricted to registered campers; quiet hours are from 10 p.m. to 7 a.m. Fires are allowed only in the campfire grills provided at each site. You may gather dead and downed firewood only. Shower buildings are open from May 1 to October 31. There are two sanitary dump stations and flush toilets at the shower buildings. A youth camping area is available by reservation only.

The hunter check-in station is at the entrance of the campground.

The campground is situated along narrow valley corridors, offering both shady and open camping sites. The loops are organized as concentric circles.

Camping site 17, which is actually the first site you will see upon entering the park, is convenient to the restrooms and can accommodate a very large rig. Sites 32-41 and 44-46 are also large with gravel pads, while sites 30-35 are smaller grassy locations suitable for pop-up campers. Sites 48-59 are tent sites, while sites 60-63 are medium sized with gravel pads. All sites have picnic tables and campfire grills.

Sites in the 60s are good for trailers, 79-81 are excellent for trailers with site 83 an excellent camping site with shade and privacy. Near site 121 is a shower building with parking and a recycling station. 112-118 are small grassy sites, ard sites 110-111 are very private at the end of a loop.

Sites 175-176 are adjacent to a small creek and are shady. At 184 is a shower building. Sites 183-193 are not very shady.

Sites 187-215 are nice for small RVs, nestled under a canopy of trees. Tent campers will like sites 222, 224, 225, 227 and 230.

Pull-through sites are 64, 82, 88, 130, 139, 173, 174, 197, 204 and 206.

Boating: The three-lane Miller's Hollow Boat Access is across the street from the north park entrance and a boat repair, rental and marine supply vendor operates near the wonderful little restaurant at the ramp area. There are two booths at the little restaurant that have a sprawling view of the Mississippi River that is just steps away. There is no horsepower limit in Pool 13, a long section of the Mississippi River. There are picnic tables at the launch, great for watching novice boaters trying to launch their craft, back up the trailer, panic and much more.

Fishing: Tournament bass anglers flock to Pool 13 and often launch from the Miller's Hollow ramp. Fishing in this pool of the Mississippi River is considered good to very good, except during high water. Catfish and carp are the most commonly caught fish, but anglers can refine their techniques to lure bluegill, carppies and bass to the surface. Some walleye and northern pike can be taken during the spring and fall. Fish walleye with an 1/8-ounce jig head tipped with a minnow, slipping against the stream on the bottom.

Hiking: You'll find about 15 miles of backcountry hiking trails that traverse the high park, cresting the palisades and wandering along a forest and through bottomlands. Flat landers need to get in shape for some of the trails; the local hikers call some sections of the South Trail System, "vertical hiking" and your burning lungs and pounding thighs will attest to the challenge.

The 9.2-mile North Trail System is generally easier to walk than the severe trails in the south portion of the lofty state park. Access points are found near the campground and at three other places in the campground. All of these trails are signed and loop back to the campground. As you begin your ascent to the upland wood, notice the gradual changing sequence of plants and animals occupying different zones or habitats. The observant hiker will notice tall grass, prairies, stands of paper birch trees or maybe catch a glimpse of the illusive pileated woodpecker, deer or migrating warblers during the spring and fall seasons.

The 4.6-mile South Trail System is rated moderate to extremely difficult. These trails traverse the bluff edges at various locations, so extreme caution should be exercised. Like all outdoor sports, get training, know your limitations, use good equipment, wear proper clothing and don't take chances. The primary access points are reached by trail head signs off of major park roads. Spur trails are numerous and unmarked. From the abundance of spring and woodland flowers on Sentinel trail to the sweeping vistas offered by Sunset trail, the south system is as challenging and diverse as the Mississippi itself.

Day-use areas: From the auto tour that takes you to overlooks like Ozzies Point, Louis' Point, Lookout Point and many others to vertical hiking trails, the park has extremes, and that's great. You can find dozens of shady picnicking sites along main roads, a mini-market store, drinking fountains, and the 1930s craftsmanship of the Civilian Conservation Corps Two large picnic shelters are available for groups, and wildflower lovers will be in heaven.

Rock climbing, one of the fastest growing sports anywhere, is popular at the park. Climbers can leave pieces of their knee skin on many climbing areas, but the 52-acre nature preserve is delicate and you should talk with the site superintendent before climbing there. Please climb gently.

For more information contact the Mississippi Palisades Climbing Coalition, 103 Evergreen Lane, Oswego, IL 60543, (708) 554-8423.

Nature: The wooded ravines, whose brilliant hues splash the cliffs with color each autumn, and delicate ferns and tiny wildflower blooms dot the deep ravines as paper birch leaves ripple atop the white trunks and the birds sign. Because the park escaped glacial sculpting of the land in all other directions, the topography and habitats are delicate, diverse and unlike any other region in the state.

Sentinel Nature Preserve, in the park is the 200th nature preserve dedicated by the state of Illinois and contains some wonderful natural communities that include mesic and dry-mesic upland forests, a loess hill prairie, a cave and small sinkhole, and outcrops and dolomite cliffs.

The original Palisades Park acquisition was made in 1929 with the purchase of 420 acres. Subsequent purchases through the 1970s have increased the park's acreage to about 2,500, which includes one of the largest forests in the state, a protected nature preserve and other fragile tracts.

There is interesting geology across the entire park, but especially in the nature preserve including bluff-face palisades, a free-standing dolomite column known as the Sentinel, and a sink hole/cave structure. Small limestone outcrops also occur scattered above the side slopes and provide important cliff habitat for many plant species.

Another natural community in the Sentinel Preserve of special interest to naturalists is the Mesic Upland Forest on the north facing slopes and ravines of the preserve. Red oak, basswood and sugar maple dominate the forest in this area. Thick and diverse wildflowers grow here, including Virginia bluebells mixed with Dutchman's breeches, wild ginger, bloodroot, large white trilliums, miterwort and bellwort. Airy ferns include maidenhair, lady, bladder and interrupted ferns. Three endangered species here include American bugbane, ill-scented trillium and Canada violet.

The Dry-mesic Upland Forest predominates on the ridge, blufftops and southern exposures of the preserves slopes and features mature second growth white oaks and sometimes bare rocky soil that supports red trilliums, spring beauties, columbine and mayapple. The rare jeweled shooting star wildflower can also be seen in this area.

The Loess Hill Prairie occurs as only a remnant on a south facing slope just off the bluff line. The prairie is dominated by little bluestem and side oats gama. Common flora found here include Ohio spiderwort, purple prairie clover, rough blazing star, field goldenrod and silky aster. Some prescribed burning is conducted in this area in an effort to maintain the communities and keep out invasive plants.

The Upper Mississippi River National Wildlife and Fish Refuge extends for more than 260 miles and consists of about 200,000 acres of wooded islands, waters, marshes and bottomlands from Wabasha, Minn., to Rock Island, Ill. The 90-mile section that includes Pools 12-14 in the northwestern corner of Illinois is some of the finest habitats for flora and fauna, and some of the best facilities anywhere for the estimated 3 million annual visitors to the linear refuge.

Information about the local section of the huge refuge is available in the basement of the post office in downtown Savanna, Upper Mississippi

Refuge, P.O. Box 250, Savanna, IL 61074 or call (815) 273-2732. In Pool 13, which extends northward from near the Mississippi Palisades State Park, there are hundreds of miles of boating and canoeing accessible from many ramps. Hunting of ducks and geese is considered some of the finest in the world, while half of the three million visitors to the refuge go fishing. You can even obtain a trapping permit. Take a scenic drive. There are many campgrounds and lots of spots to go picnicking.

Wildlife observers will find no better area to look for some of the 292 bird species, 57 species of mammals, 45 species of amphibians and reptiles, and 118 species of fish . Whenever you are visiting a state park on the western side of the state along the Mississippi River, you are usually just minutes from huge expanses of federal refuge that offer all kinds of outdoor recreation opportunities. Be sure to request maps, bird lists, fish brochures, and a handy brochures on reptiles and amphibians in the area.

Hunting: Hiking trails are closed for a special three-day hunt annually. Turkey hunting is considered very good in the 1,500 acres that are hunted. Call for more details.

Nearby attractions: Ridge Road to Elizabeth is a scenic drive, Mt. Carroll Historic District, lock and dam No. 13; and Old Mill Park. There are six boat launching ramps in Carroll County along the Mississippi River, and the Thomson Causeway and Blanding's Landing both have excellent camping facilities.

38   Moraine Hills State Park

Land: 1,690 acres Water: Fox River, Lake Defiance

Lake Defiance, a 48-acre lake near the center of the park, was formed when a large section of ice broke free from the main glacier and slowly melted, leaving behind deposits of sand, gravel, rock and clay, a mixture known as glacial till. The rolling hills, known as moraines, throughout the park are composed of this material and are now covered with thick vegetation and lush oak and hickory forests.

Scattered within the glacial till were many huge blocks of ice which melted as the climate continued to warm about 15,000 years ago. These depressions left by blocks of ice quickly collected and stored the meltwater from the glacier.

Marshes and bogs formed in the poorly drained shallow depressions, and lakes formed in the deeper basins which had good drainage and a sustaining water supply like springs, streams or rivers. Lake Defiance is a fairly deep lake created by the glacial action and is called a "kettle hole" lake. It is about 15 feet deep. The pristine lake is fed from the north by Pike Marsh, and from the east by a network of sprawling wetlands.

Complete with great bike trails, boating and fishing, bird watching and opportunities for nature study and wildlife photography, Moraine Hill is within the largest moraninic system in northeastern Illinois, the Valporasio Moraine. This huge geologic feature, with its characteristic rolling hills, lakes and wetland area covers a 10-mile wide expanse which extends to the southwestern edge of Lake Michigan.

Because of the diverse geological features that characterize the land, flora and fauna are rich in variety and abundance. From the Leatherleaf Bog, which is a floating mat of sphagnum, to Pike Marsh, a peat-filled 115-acre area comprised of sharply contrasting plant communities and fen, Moraine Hills State Park is truly one of the most interesting units in the system.

Roughly half of the park is composed of wetlands, lakes and rolling moraines, and much of the other half of the park has excellent trails, a nature center, fields and fine day-use areas. Major land acquisitions began in the early 1970s and by late 1975, the park facilities were opened.

Information and Activities

Moraine Hills State Park
914 S. River Road
McHenry, IL 60050
(815) 385-1624

Directions: In the northeast corner of Illinois, in McHenry County, three miles south of McHenry, the park entrance is off River Road. The park is centered between Routes 31 and 12.

Information: Office hours are 9 a.m. - 4 p.m. daily, and park hours vary by season. The park office, in a stately old house with white columns, has an interpretive center and concession stand. Volunteers are always needed at the state park; if you are interested in helping call (815) 385-5428. Cross-country skies are rented at the lower level of the park office, and the concession is open only on weekends. There is also a concession stand at the McHenry Dam area.

Campground: none.

Boating: Cartop boats are permitted on Wilderness and Tomahawk lakes and the Fox River using electric trolling motors only. Boat trailers are prohibited in the park. You may rent a boat at the McHenry Dam and Lake Defiance concession (there are about 15 boats available). Private watercraft are not allowed on Lake Defiance.

The rules are strict about boats, and there are no boat ramps on any of the lakes at the state park.

Fishing: Lake Defiance is surrounded by fragile peat soils. To protect you and this delicate natural resource, bank fishing is not allowed. So do not walk or wade around the lake, or release minnows into the lake. Lake Defiance has three fishing piers, 1.2 miles of shoreline, and five areas where underwater fish attractors (brush, etc.) have been created to enhance angling. Locals often gravitate to the east side of the lake for the best action. Fishing is considered fair in the small and delicate glacial lake and there is a simple map of the lake and its structure and depths available at the office (maps of Tomohawk and Wilderness lakes are also available).

Creel limits at Lake Defiance: largemouth bass, 14-inch minimum, three daily; panfish, no limits; northern pike, 24-inch minimum, three daily limit; channel catfish, six daily.

For better fishing opportunities, try the McHenry Dam area, two miles from the park office and open 6 a.m. - 9 p.m. daily. Complete with a concession/bait stand, rental john boats and improved shoreline, many anglers fish from shady benches along the Fox River. Check creel limit regulations at the dam.

Many species can be taken at the dam, including catfish on minnows.

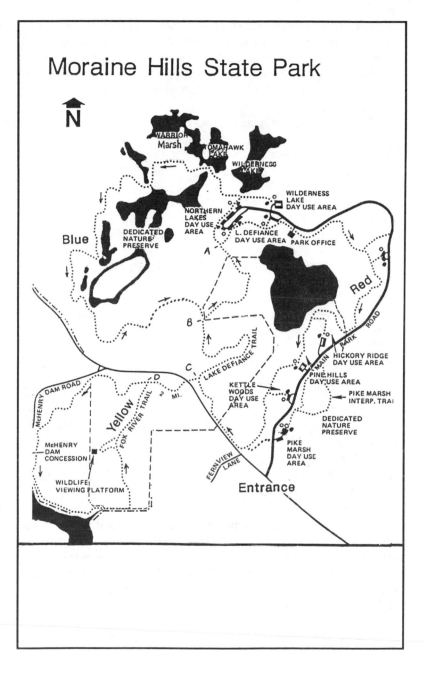

Moraine Hills State Park

Local anglers recommend live bait from shore that include wax worms, crickets, leeches, crawlers and red worms. The bait shop attendant says you can catch plenty of fish right from shore, when the fish are on the bit. If they aren't on the bit, take a nap instead. Directly across the river from the bait stand can be very good panfishing among the large boulders scattered along the shore. Walleye stack up in front of the dam during the early spring, and jig and minnows work well.

Food, restrooms and picnic areas are along this day-use area at McHenry Dam.

Hiking/biking: Stone chipped hiking and biking trails are color-coded and one way. Dogs must be leashed and have a proof of rabies certificate. Roller blades are not allowed on the trails at Moraine Hills.

The excellent prepared trails are a welcome change for mountain bikers, who are often not allowed on interesting state-owned lands. The hilly and gently rolling terrain, combined with good wildlife management, offer cyclists wonderful rides along smooth trails and a unique glacially formed terrain.

The unit has about 11 miles of trails consisting of three main loops and include the interpretive trails. Trailheads are at all day-use areas.

The Leatherleaf Bog Trail is nearly 3.5 miles long and offers hikers a wonderful example of kettle moraine topography and has a diverse plat of plant specimens. Circling Lake Defiance is a four-mile trail that connects the Northern Day-use Area with the Lake Defiance Day-use Area. The 2.5-mile Fox River Trail travels across a prairie area and along a wetland to the Fox River.

Pick up a copy of the Lake Defiance Self-Guided Interpretive Trail guide, a three-panel brochure that is richly detailed and features seven learning stations. You will learn about plant succession and the ever changing plant communities, aquatic plant life, an observation blind that is great (depending on the season) for spotting waterfowl, wetland information, and the story of trembling trees.

Day-use areas: Unlike many state parks, there are no reservable picnic

Elevated boardwalks cross diverse wetland areas.

shelters at Moraine Hills, but because there are so many fine day-use areas, it rarely is a problem to find an adequate area. Picnic shelters are at the Pine Hills and Pike Marsh day-use areas, while playground equipment is at McHenry Dam, Whitetail Prairie and Pike Marsh Day-use Area.

Nature: Inside the huge brown converted house with flagstone trim is an interpretive center with displays. A small observation room has an active beehive and overlooks Lake Defiance. Other displays and educational features of the pine-paneled facility include a video presentation, mammal mounts, projectile points and archeology information, hands-on nature trivia touchboard, rock and mineral display, ice age fossils, raptor mounts, wood duck nesting box, colorful interpretive posters, brochure rack, bluebird nesting box exhibit, and a number of other educational static displays. Some educational programming is offered by the staff.

The low-lying bogs and deciduous forests (oak, hickory, ash, cherry, dogwood and hawthorn) offer a diversity of habitats that is reflected by the number of different bird species throughout the park. Birding is best in the morning, bring your binoculars and carry the handy bird checklist compiled by the parks staff.

The Moraine Hills Wetland Enhancement Project, which can be seen from the park office, is a conservation project undertaken for the perpetuation of American waterfowl resources it was initiated in the early 1990s by Duck Unlimited in cooperation with the Illinois Department of Conservation. Funds for this project were generously donated by Ducks Unlimited. The project provides habitat vital for the survival of waterfowl and endangered and threatened birds. Nesting habitat is provided for wood ducks, Canada goose, blue-winged teal, common moorhen, black tern and yellow-headed blackbird. Food and rest areas are furnished for waterfowl and wading birds during the fall and spring migrations.

Habitat at the park, is enhanced by controlling water levels and plant growth in five marshes. These 220 acres of wetlands are part of the park's 800 acres of wetland complex. The five marshes are Opossum Run, Goose Island, Raccoon Island, Yellowhead and Black Tern.

Winter: Ice fishing, 10.2 miles of cross-county skiing trails.

Fishing at McHenry Dam, two miles from the park office.

39 Moraine View State Park

Land: 1,687 acres   Water: 158-acre lake

When the glaciers of the last Ice Age swept though central Illinois nearly 14,000 years ago, they shoved massive amounts of rock and earth debris in front of them like a giant snow plow, leaving in their mighty path long and expansive ridgelines that ripple across the landscape. These irregular crests are called moraines, and on their gentle swells and in their broad valleys they are now dotted by scattered groves of hardwoods, town and cities, and at least one very nice state park.

The local moraine, called the Bloomington Moraine, one of the four largest in the state, reaches across Illinois from the Illinois River at Peoria east to the Wabash River in neighboring Indiana. In the middle of the sprawling terrain and natural feature is the fully developed state park, east of Bloomington off I-74.

As the early Europeans filtered in to the area, they found peaceful Kickapoo and Potawatomi tribes sharing the countryside. But following the War of 1812, the tribes signed a treaty with the settlers allowing them to continue to live on the lands. But, sadly, as the settlers poured in, the remaining 630 Kickapoo living here were moved to a reservation in Kansas.

After what amounted to kicking out the Indians, the white settlers quickly set about draining the lands, clearing the scattering of woodlands, and farming the rich soils left by the glacial retreat.

By the middle part of the 20th century, it became apparent that the heavily altered agricultural lands needed further manipulation to maintain an adequate supply of water for its continued well being and growth. By 1962, construction began on Dawson Lake, named after the families of early settlers, and it was opened in 1963.

Information and Activities

Moraine View State Park
R.R. 2
LeRoy, IL 61752
(309) 724-8032

Directions: Five miles northeast of LeRoy in southeastern McLean County, minutes east of Bloomington.

Information: The park is open 7 a.m. - 10 p.m. daily. The park office is open weekdays.

Campground: The Gander Bay Campground on rolling terrain is a favorite for large RV rigs. About 75 percent of the sites are well-shaded and all have picnic tables, fire grills, gravel pads and nearby amenities. The campground is one big loop, with sites on the perimeter designated as "P" sites, and six lanes (A-F) that are listed alphabetically. This is a very nice campground. Virtually every site is good, high, dry and near

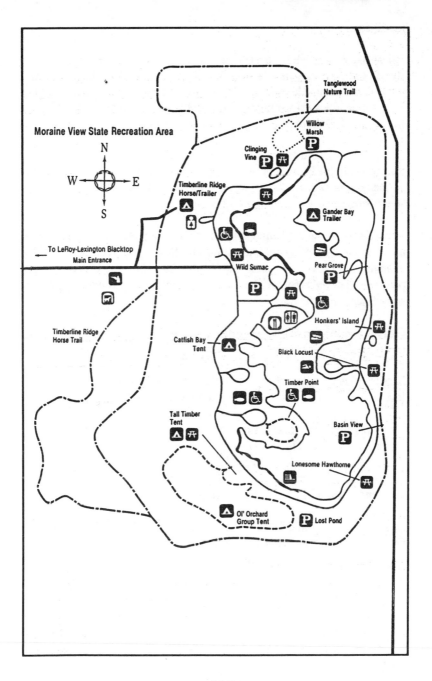

Moraine View State Recreation Area

N
W · E
S

Tanglewood
Nature Trail

Willow
Marsh
P

Clinging
Vine
P 🏕

Timberline Ridge
Horse/Trailer
△
🚻

Gander Bay
Trailer
△

To LeRoy-Lexington Blacktop
Main Entrance

Wild Sumac
P
🏕

Pear Grove
P

♿

Honkers' Island
🏕

Timberline Ridge
Horse Trail

Catfish Bay
Tent
△

Black Locust
🏕

Timber Point
♿

Tall Timber
Tent
△ 🏕

Basin View
P

Lonesome Hawthorne
🏕

Ol' Orchard
Group Tent
△

Lost Pond
P

facilities.

All of the P sites back up against wooded areas and offer pretty good shade, some privacy, and typically dry sites. Sites 15-20P have a nice view of the lake and lake access. The campground creel clerk often camps in this area. There is a small one-lane boat ramp for campers in this area, complete with about 40 feet of floating mooring dock.

Site 10P is adjacent to the boat launch and there is a small parking area for boat trailers. From this camping site you would have a great view of all the fishing and small boating action. Sites 24P and 25P are excellent shady sites, near the water, and private.

Site 7C is on a peninsula and particularly private, large enough for most any size RV unit. Play equipment for children between lanes C and D is available for campers at each loop. Sites 1A, 10A and 16A are shady, private and popular for tent or small RV campers; 5B is a similar site on a knoll and very private.

Catfish Bay is always a popular place for those who love primitive-style camping. There is parking for 18 cars, and there are 22 walk-in camping sites. The vault toilet in this primitive camping area has handicapped handles inside. Swimming is allowed only at the beach. The sites are level and dry; you must camp in designated tent sites.

The Timber Ridge Horse Camp is the first road to the left upon entering the park. Most sites have electricity and hitching posts; favorites are 21 and 24-26. The area has additional lighting, vault toilets, picnic tables and plenty of water hydrants. Sept. 1- Jan. 16, all riders must wear an upper garment of solid orange and an orange or red cap.

The concession stand is open weekends, 6:30 a.m. - 7 p.m. and sells firewood and snacks. There are a number of campground visitor parking lots, which is very convenient.

Emergency numbers: state police (815) 844-3131; county police, 888-5000; ambulance, 962-2341; fire, 724-8341.

Boating: The busy two-lane launching ramp on the east side of the lake allows small boaters to probe the lake for sport fish. A 10 hp or less motorcraft limit is in effect on the lake. Sailboats and windsurfers are becoming increasingly evident on the windy little lake and also share the small ramp area that has a concession stand that rents small craft. Campers are encouraged to bring their small boat and leave it parked at the mooring docks in the campground.

The primary boat ramp is a two-lane launch with plenty of parking, and it's rarely crowded. Paddle boats, john boats and canoe rentals are offered as is seasonal docking, which is mostly occupied by pontoon boats. There are eight picnic tables at the launch.

Fishing: There's considerable vegetation in the lake, including lots of surface plant material. Local anglers fish the dam area year-round, and work some of the five miles of shoreline in the spring casting for largemouth's. There also are some northerns in the lake. Local bait dealers offered no special tips or techniques for attacking the lake.

Creel limits: largemouth bass, 15-inch minimum, six per day; walleye, 14-inch minimum, six per day; northern pike, 24-inch minimum, three per day; channel catfish, six per day; crappies, 9-inch minimum, 15 per day; bluegill and redear sunfish, total of 25 per day.

Hiking/bridle trails: Outlaw Outfitters Riding Stable (P.O. Box 130, LeRoy, IL 61752, call 303-724-8043) offers horseback rides for ages eight years and up. The small stable is open seven days, mid-mornings to 6 p.m. They also offer a special Friday evening adult ride. In addition to trail rides, the stable offers horse drawn hay rides, private rentals, buggy rides, corporate outings and sleigh rides in the winter. There are 10 miles of bridle trails at Moraine View.

The half-mile, easy and flat Timber Point Trail and a shorter one-quarter mile loop offer physically challenged park visitors a chance to enjoy a wooded trail and seasonal wildflowers. Tall Timber Trail is a 1.5-mile trail for backpackers or other hikers; it also provides a small primitive camping area.

Moraine View's best trail is the half-mile Tanglewood Nature Trail. A brochure available at the park office details 13 interpretive spots along the walkway that passes a beaver pond, three streams, a recessional moraine, along a floodplain, through a prairie much like the one that once covered two-thirds of the state, and past a number of other interesting natural communities.

Day-use areas: Small wetland areas along the main park drive dot the rolling area, offering wildlife viewers a wonderful opportunity to see songbirds and other native mammals or reptiles and amphibians of the area. Shore and wading birds are often seen patrolling the shallows of these moist rich areas. The Hawthorn Day-use Area has the best lake view and is a popular place for group and family picnics.

The white clapboard restaurant overlooks the lake, seats 50-60 people and sells a few fishing supplies. They rent small craft and there are three small wooden floating docks in front of the restaurant where boaters can moor their boat for breakfast, lunch or dinner.

The Sumac Day-use Area is handicapped accessible and has a kiddy playground and shoreline access for fishermen. The asphalt main park roadway is often a tunnel of trees that is used by cyclists and walkers.

A 100-yard-wide swimming beach is open Memorial Day-Labor Day and has a small admission fee, shady parking and coarse sand, but no lifeguard. Pets are not allowed on the beach.

Hunting: Pheasant (released), dove, squirrel, rabbit, rail, woodcock, turkey, snipe and archery deer are hunted. About 1,200 acres are open to hunting with major habitats including forest, shrubs, grasslands and croplands. Call the site manager for additional information.

Nearby attractions: Wildwood Campground, south of the state park.

40 Morrison-Rockwood State Park

Land: 1,152 acres   Water: Carlton Lake, 77-acres

The little 77-acre watershed impoundment, known as Carlton Lake, is stream fed, an average of 12 feet deep, tree-lined with a rolling shoreline and an 1800-foot dam, and, maybe most importantly, home for big muskie.

We'll talk more about fishing when we get to that section, but knowledgeable anglers, many from the Chicago area, are attracted to the lake by other amenities, too, like a terrific, clean campground, an expert concessionaire that always has the latest fish story and a "hot" tip, a downright pretty landscape, and the little town of Morrison, with its stately homes and four-block-long freshly painted downtown. Homes along Lincolnway are worth a slow walk by on a warm summer evening. There are couple of ice cream shops in the downtown area that make the walking tour even more fun. One of the finest homes is at Grape Street and Lincolnway.

Morrison-Rockwood State Park, located in Whiteside County, was dedicated in 1971. The name of the park is a combination of the nearby town and the nearby wooded portion of Rock Creek. The lake was named for L. Carlton Andersen, who promoted the area before the state took over the former conservation area in 1971. This is the first time I can think of that a lake was named after someone's first name. I think Bill's Lake would be a nice name for a lake someday.

Actually, the lake is marvelous, and the park shows the caring of staff and people of the surrounding communities. In fact, the iron entrance sign was hand-crafted by a Morrison blacksmith in the shape of the state, and mounted on a stone. The sign is an attractive and welcome change from standard signage. Just another personal touch that makes this a very nice park to visit, fish, camp or lazy-away a long weekend.

Information and Activities

Morrison-Rockwood State Park
R.R. 4
Morrison, IL 61270
(815) 772-4708

Directions: Take Route 78 from I-30 at Unionville to the entrance. The park is about 2.5 hours west of Chicago.

Information: The park office is on the south end of the lake, just inside the entrance gate on the right. The park is open 8 a.m. - 4 p.m. or by chance if the staff is working in the park. The concession at the northeast side of the lake is excellent and has considerable information about fishing and the surrounding park.

Campground: Often filled on holiday weekends, the shady and mature campground typically has available sites on weekdays and other weekends. The campground is on the north end of the lake and is accessed by the tree-lined main park road, just past the remote control airstrip that has a windsock, runway and everything. There are 95 camping sites.

Camping sites 1-25 are shady, good sized, and fairly private complete with picnic tables. There are many newer improvements in the campground.

The loop with sites 26-95 has gravel pads, good separation between campsites, fire pits, showers, mature trees, and a few pull-through sites. Sites in the 40s have grass pads. Lots 68 and 69 are large campsites suitable for large rigs and are near vault toilets. Sites in the 70s are shady and large enough for big rigs. More than half of the sites have grass pads. If you are checking in after a big rain, you may want to inspect the sites for softness.

Sites 82-87 are my favorite sites, near toilets, very private on a small intimate loop.

There are also overnight camping sites with a shelter for horse owners at the southwest corner of the park.

Boating: Canoes are rented at the concession stand and there is a 10 hp limit. A tow-lane concrete ramp offers access to the no-wake lake near five picnic shelters and a quality concession that sells food, bait and other supplies. There's plenty of parking and maneuvering room at the ramp area. Fishing is prohibited on the three floating boat ramps.

Fishing: The lake is maybe the finest small fishing lake in the state park system, especially for families with small children or disabled members who can use the fishing pier donated by the local Lions Club.

Fishery biologists have long taken an interest in Lake Carlton and one recent study showed why. Lake Carlton has 254 pounds of fish per acre, while the average Illinois lake has only about 120 pounds of fish per acre. Regular anglers says it's because of the jumbo muskie that hunt the underwater terrain like the submarines from Red October. Locals claim more 40-inch muskie are taken from this lake than any other in the entire region. By the way, these big fish, seem to be evenly distributed around the entire lake, but the most scenic as well as excellent fishing area is the south side.

Try trolling a crankbait at 12 feet deep, toss bucktails and jerkbaits, or try

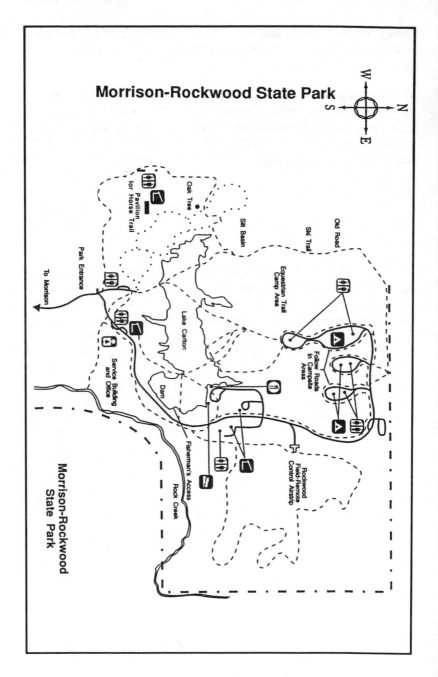

Morrison-Rockwood State Park

lively pike minnows for muskie. Bass will take rubber worms, while bluegills go nuts over redworms. Kids can have fun trying for catfish using doughballs on treble hooks.

Hiking: There is a 3.5-mile nature trail that offers an excellent view of the lake and wanders near an old quarry. The hike is easy to moderate in difficulty. The bridle trail is 14 miles long; hikers and cross-country skiers can share the trail that meanders around the thousand-acre state park. There are about 12 miles of cross-country skiing trails.

Day-use areas: There are many lakeview picnic areas and two reservable shelters for groups of 25 or more. One of the pavilions has a fireplace and electricity. Kids are welcome to sled on the hilly trails or ice skate during the winter season.

Nature: More than 160 species of songbirds, plentiful stands of hardwoods, and vigorous blooms of spring wildflowers are on display under a canopy of hickory, ash, oak and walnuts. Waterfowl are often seen, especially during the spring and early summer nesting season along the shallow and other parts of the lake.

Hunting: Very limited shotgun deer hunting is available.

Nearby attractions: Casino riverboat in Clinton; AA baseball team in Clinton, a farm team of the San Francisco Giants.

41 *Nauvoo State Park*

Land: 148 acres   Water: 12-acre lake

Nauvoo, which means a "beautiful place" in Hebrew, used to be the largest city in Illinois.   Today it is one of the finest community preservation sites in mid-America, complete with wonderfully restored specialty shops, homes, stores, churches and cultural centers.

The small Nauvoo State Park is virtually across the street from the large preservation and visitor district and is often used by visitors for overnight camping and day-use while they visit the historic town.

Years ago the Sac and Fox Indians called the place Quashquema, after their chief. When the prophet Joseph Smith led his Mormon followers here in 1839, he renamed it Nauvoo. During the 1840s the community flourished to become the 10th largest city in the nation. After the Mormon exodus, the French Icarians tried a short-lived experiment in communal living. Soon French, German and Swiss settlers recognized the fertile area and started the vineyards and the wine industry that grew until the dry days of the 1920s.

The Benedictine Sisters also started a school for young ladies in Nauvoo. Today St. Mary's Academy is a residential school for teenage girls. After repeal of Prohibition, the wine industry was reestablished, about the same time old wine cellars were concerted into caves for aging Nauvoo blue cheese.

In the mid-1900s, the descendants of those early settlers returned with pride and determination to restore the homes and shops of their forefathers to their former glory.

Today visitors to the area will find more than two dozen restored homes and shops open to tourist, old time crafts have been revitalized and demonstrations are given daily, and living history programs are conducted for a variety of special events in the beautiful area.

Information and Activities

Nauvoo State Park
P.O. Box 337
Nauvoo, IL 62354
(217) 453-2512

Directions: Near the banks of the Mississippi River along Route 96 on the south edge of Nauvoo.

Information: Park office hours are weekdays, 7:30 a.m. - 3:30 p.m.; weekends have flexible hours. The longtime staff know the park and community well and are very helpful. The museum at the park is open May - October.

Camping: There are no showers at the park and sites are not marked. The Class C camping area is located just before reaching the little brown building that served as the park office for many years. There are 75 sites

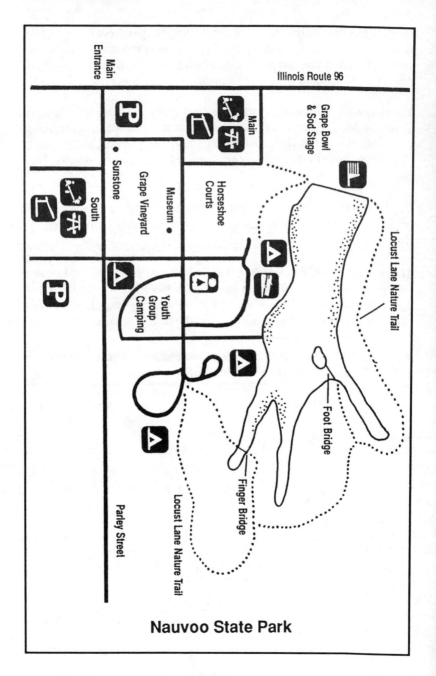

Nauvoo State Park

in this area and no reservations are taken at the park. Holiday weekends the camping areas are usually full; during the remainder of the summer you can usually find a quality site.

The White Pine area, which can accommodate about 75 campers is well shaded, rolling, and a quiet area that is excellent for family weekend adventures in this culturally rich area. At the north end of the camping area is limited shoreline access for bank fishing. Camping under the white pines is a great experience. Gentle breezes can make their way under the canopy of needles and limbs, while the shade is abundant and welcome during the mid-summer months in this part of the state.

Every site is nice and has fire grills, picnic tables and gravel pads The pit toilet even has linoleum on the floor. This is a good area for RV rigs, with nice views of the rolling terrain. Children's play equipment and winding roadways are also great for family play and activities.

The abundant red-headed woodpeckers that comb the pine and other trees in this camping area make this small campground one of the nicest in this part of the state. Firewood is not available in the park.

Emergency numbers: state police, (309) 833-2141; sheriff, 357-2115; conservation office, 357-2047; ambulance, 847-3347.

Fishing: The tiny lake is a fair early morning fishery for bluegill, crappie, bass and channel catfish. The entire perimeter can be used for shoreline angling. Some local anglers fish from the dam and into the finger-like areas with small boats. The nearest live bait is in Nauvoo or Hamilton.

Channel cats are stocked annually and typical stink-type baits are the most effective.

Boating: Electric motors only can be used on the small lake, and the one-lane boat launch is rarely busy. There are no boat rentals, bait sales or concession stand at the park.

Hiking: The 2.5 miles of foot trails are east of the lake. One trail circumnavigates the lake, called the Locust Lane trail. It also crosses the dam and wanders behind the campground. The hiking is easy and shady.

Day-use areas: Much of the park is recovered from a 1990 tornado that ripped across the 20-acre day-use area, tearing up buildings and the grounds. The old Ritter Press Room and Wine Cellar, a newer ball field south of the main park, and plenty of picnic tables are scattered in the 148-acre park in the two main picnicking areas.

The lovely brick, vineyard-sided museum is open daily 1-5 p.m. and houses a variety of period rooms, toy displays and information about the neighboring vineyard, the wine-making process and a wine cellar. The house that the museum occupies was built in the 1840s by Mormons and remodeled by the Icarians, and later owned by the Rheinberger family. There aren't many museums located in a more scenic site in the state. The vineyard is managed for public sampling and many wine-related programs are offered throughout the year.

Ice skating is allowed on man-made Lake Horton during the winter.

Nature: A small four-acre prairie around the superintendent's residence has four species of prairie grass, eight prairie wildflowers and is burned every few years to maintain a quality demonstration prairie plot. Birding is also good in the area. Spring and fall migrations along the Mississippi River corridor are big events for serious birdwatchers.

Hunting: none.

Nearby attractions: Cartage Jail, Great River Road Golf Course, camping in Hamilton along Scenic River Road, outlooks along Route 96, Breezewood Campground, B & Bs, bike touring on the Scenic River Road, Joseph Smith Visitor Center, Grape Festival over Labor Day weekend, many antique shops and Nauvoo.

42 Pere Marquette State Park

Land: 7,895 acres   River: Mississippi River

From the Lover's Leap lookout point you can see the famous St. Louis arch, unless, of course you are in love. You might also see bald eagles in the wintertime or crimson-colored bluffs in the fall. Spring and summers bring spectacular views of the Illinois and Mississippi rivers, fragrant wildflowers and agile rock climbers. Pere Marquette State Park has it all, a wonderful lodge, deluxe cabins, fine dining, horseback riding, hiking trails and more hiking trails, a nature center, camping, boating and fishing. And don't forget the fully stocked concession stand, history, nearby attractions, driving tour, McAdam's Peak, swimming pools and just lazy days under shady trees.

Pere Marquette was named Piasa Bluff State Park in 1932 when the state purchased the original 1,511 acres and began developing the park lands.

The name was changed after complaints from area interest groups and Father Jacques Marquette, a French Jesuit missionary priest was duly honored. He and Louis Joillet made the first recorded entrance by white men into the territory now known as Illinois in 1673. The intrepid explorers were traveling the Mississippi River in hopes that it would empty into the California Sea, which would open a new route to the Orient. Nice try guys.

After many mosquito bites and hundreds of miles of travel, they learned from the Indians the "Great River" flowed instead into the Gulf of Mexico. So they returned north and explored great rivers and the Great Lakes region. Their entry into Illinois is memorialized with a large stone cross and marker a few miles east of the park's entrance along Route 100.

Pere Marquette State Park is in the heart of wonderful country, surrounded by natural splendor and a rich history of animal and human habitation that goes back eons. Fossils found in the strata stripped bare by thousands of years of river currents reveals its history, while McAdam's Peak reveals its soul as twin springs flow from Ordovician-Silurian rocks deposited 350 million years ago.

Prehistoric use of the park dates back at least 11,000 years ago when Native Indians changed from nomadic hunters and gathers to agriculturists. The park has been surveyed by many archaeologists and a variety of interesting history has been found. The interpretive staff at the nature center can do a great job explaining the natural and cultural history of the area. The nature center also has a variety of displays, animal mounts and interpretive exhibits.

Information and Activities

Pere Marquette State Park
Route 100, P.O. Box 158
Grafton, IL 62037
(618) 786-3323

Directions: North of Grafton on Route 100. From Springfield, Route I-55 south to Route 16, west on 16 through Jerseyville to Route 100. South on Route 100 for 10 miles.

Information: Off Route 100, the park office is open daily, 8 a.m. - 4 p.m. The nature center is also an excellent place for general park information.

Campground: About one-third of the camping sites are shady Some sites along Route 100 might be a little noisy; otherwise the 80 Class A sites, of which about 70 can be reserved, have gravel pads, and are near the showers (open April 1-Dec. 15) and pay phone at the east end of the area. The Class A area is made up of three sections and all sites are about the same size, large enough for big RV rigs. The park offers two rent-a-camps and Class B camping in a separate area.

Group camping is offered at Camp Piasa, Camp Ouatoga and Camp Potawatomi from April - October by advance registration. Two of the group camping areas have pools, beds, dining halls, pots and pans.

Lodge/cabins: The Pere Marquette Lodge and Conference Center (618-786-2331), with handsome leather-backed chairs and a rich, rustic feel has wonderful sounds of giant flagstone clicking under your heels. It opened in September 1988 after major renovations totaling more than $11 million. Aside from 50 lodge rooms that are available to the public, there are also 22 guest rooms (seven lovely cottages). The restaurant, gift shop and lounge within the timber-structure lodge are open to the public and lodge or cottage guests may enjoy inside handicapped accessible swimming pools, whirlpool, saunas, exercise rooms and outdoor tennis courts. Other amenities include a nearby stable, playground, video game rooms, marina, retreat facilities, scenic overlooks, and more.

Features include the 700-ton fireplace in the Great Room Lobby, a 30-foot chess board, and the elegance of the structure that was originally constructed by veterans of the World War I under the supervision of the federal government. The site was acquired in 1932, and the structure was dedicated in 1941. Built of Nigaran dolomite, with Western red cedar pillars and bald cypress and "pecky" cypress finish, the roof of oak shakes is rived for form, that gives an impression of serene power.

Robert Kingery of the Chicago Planning Council saw to it that it was snugly set against a backdrop of 350-foot bluffs on the remnant of an

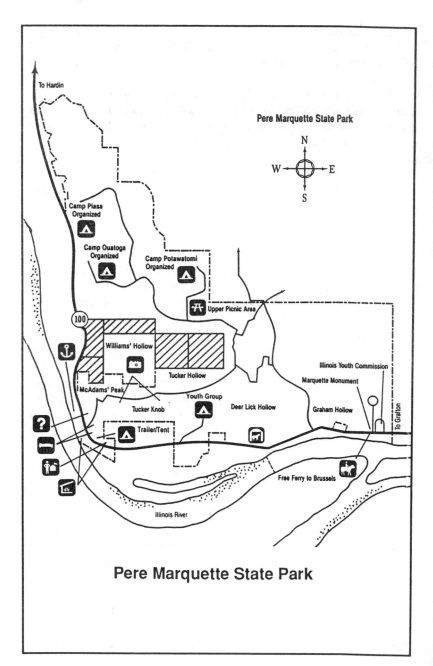

Pere Marquette State Park

To Hardin

Camp Piasa Organized

Camp Ouatoga Organized

Camp Potawatomi Organized

Upper Picnic Area

100

Williams' Hollow

Tucker Hollow

McAdams' Peak

Tucker Knob

Youth Group

Trailer/Tent

Deer Lick Hollow

Illinois Youth Commission

Marquette Monument

Graham Hollow

To Grafton

Free Ferry to Brussels

Illinois River

Pere Marquette State Park

ancient glacial lake terrace. Its site is also that of an old Indian village. A gigantic landscaping project planted 280,000 trees and shrubs around the lodge and ajoining terrain.

All of the furnishings in the lodge are of giant proportion, from the huge fireplace that soars 50 feet above its base to the bronze fixtures that were made by a former employee of the Czar of Russia. The impressive chandeliers weigh a ton each, and the furniture was custom made to fit into these enormous surroundings.

The lodge restaurant is open Sunday - Thursday 6:30 a.m. - 9 p.m. and Friday and Saturday, 6:30 a.m. - 10 p.m. The popular Sunday buffet is served from 10:30 a.m. - 8 p.m. Reservations are encouraged at the restaurant (and the lodge).

The 3000-square-foot banquet space can be divided into four rooms and allows the lodge to engage in considerable meeting and conference business. In fact, about 50 percent of the business at the lodge is business or meeting related. Plan ahead, make your reservations today!

Boating: A three-lane launch at the Pere Marquette Marina, (618) 786-3546) is maintained, and overnight docking is available. The marina also has an outdoor cafe which serves sandwiches, cold drinks and ice cream. The marina also has gasoline and boating supplies. There are more than a dozen launching ramps along the Illinois River corridor, mostly north of the state park. Call (618) 376-3303 for details about area public boating facilities.

Fishing: Stump Lake is mostly a bluegill and largemouth body of water, while nearby Fowler Lake has more rough fish.

Sport fishing is improving along the entire 273 miles of its length of the Illinois River from Kankakee to the Mississippi near the state park. The aquatic habitats are the basis for the diversity of sport fishing in this section of the river and along its length.

Tailwaters, found below each navigation dam, are fast and turbulent, caused by the passage of water though the dam. The tailwaters receive heavy fishing pressure because fish congregate in these rough waters.

White bass are particularly fond of tailwaters, and channel catfish and drum are often caught there.

Lake and slough habitats have little or no current and may have aquatic vegetation. Lakes have greater average depths than sloughs. These areas are good for bullheads and sunfish.

Side channels are departures from the main channel and may be as wide and deep as the main channel or so shallow they resemble sloughs. All side channels have current in them during normal water stages. Channel catfish like side channels.

Main channel habitat is the area between the edge of the navigation channel and the closest land or shallow water over submerged land. This is the most predominant habitat along the Illinois, and is so varied that most sport species can be found.

Largemouth bass, crappie, bluefill and green sunfish are common in the Illinois River. They are taken in all habitats.

Here are some local tips and techniques for fishing the area rivers: For crappies, use small minnows hooked high in the back on a small hook with bobber 2-3 feet above and fish near any structure. Use nightcrawlers in the early spring, later in the season (April - May) use leadhead jigs and spinners in combination with lip-hooked minnows. Early spring is the best time for crappies.

Bluegill are found in weed beds and other cover. Use a small bobber to keep the bait off the bottom. Worms, crickets and grasshoppers work well in the warmer months.

Stripers (white or yellow bass) are taken on jigs tossed into moving or rough water and along objects in the main channel. When the fish are schooling, use spinners with minnows or small artificial lures resembling minnows. Mornings and evenings are the best times before the fish head for deeper waters. May and August are the best months for the delicate stripers.

Largemouth are most frequently taken in the main channel border or lake

The lodge has 50 modern rooms and seven lovely guest cottages are nearby.

habitats. They like cover which might include weed beds, brush, fallen trees or willows. The best fishing in the Illinois in this part of the state occurs in May, early June and mid-September. Try white spinners with minnows.

Walleye and sauger are increasing in this part of the state. Small jigs tipped with a minnow and boat control are keys to success.

Catfish like to hold under old stumps or fallen trees, downstream around logs jam-ups, and in washout holes along the banks. Because cats have a great sense of smell, old stink baits, bloods baits, cheese and any other type of rank bait will gain their attention. Fishing for catfish picks up when other species slack off during the heat of summer.

Hiking: Overlooks from the blufftops facing the Illinois River offer hikers some spectacular views and both easy and quite rugged hiking trails. The state park's system of trails comprises more than 14 miles of interconnecting pathways that vary in length from one-half mile to two miles in length. Most of the trails can be accessed from the visitor's center and some of the trails can be slippery after a rain shower.

Fit hikers can try the half-mile Ridge Trail or the 15-station exercise trail. Other hikers can test their skills on many ridgelines and up and down slopes that expose fault lines, lush flora and many interesting wildlife communities. Hikers who want to get away from the crowds should use the Fern Hollow, Rattlesnake or Hickory North trails.

Bridle trails: The Pere Marquette Riding Stables, two miles south of the park lodge on Illinois Route 100, features "gentle" horses and group rates. Rides are about one hour long and they allow only walking and trotting the horses. The stable is open 9 a.m. - 5 p.m., call (618) 786-2156 for information or reservations. There are 27 miles of bridle trails in two areas.

Day-use areas: Serious cyclists routinely peddle the hilly park roads. Hikers and day-use visitors share the main roadway that winds through, up and down the park terrain. The asphalt surfaced biking trail system that parallels Route 100 is popular with all levels of cyclists as they tour the Mississippi River corridor. Rock climbers need permission to use the cliffs near the stables.

Nature: The scenic value of Pere Marquette is impressive. Many pull-offs and a driving tour offer visitors plenty of chances to see wildlife and gain an overview of the natural history.

The 54-acre McAdam's Peak Hill Prairie Natural Area is a rugged prairie, forest and limestone cliff community that contains Indian burial mounds and a wooded hollow that is a major roosting site for wintering bald eagles.

McAdam's Peak lies within the Middle Mississippi Border Natural Division, an area which apparently escaped Pleistocene glaciation. The interesting area is characterized by steep topography and many impressive outcroppings of dolomite, limestone and shale. The hills of the area are covered with a thick mantle of loess (wind-blown soils originating on the river floodplain) and varies in thickness from inches to 100 feet in depth. The yellow clay seen along the road to McAdam's Peak is composed of this material, capped by a thin layer of black topsoil.

Loess hill prairies are prominent on many southwest-facing ridges along the Illinois and Mississippi rivers and are often covered with little bluestem, big bluestem, Indian grass and side-oats grama. Common wildflowers found in this prairie are narrow-leafed bluet, sky-blue aster, leadplant, scurf-pea, white and purple prairie clovers, and showy goldenrod.

Prairies in Illinois developed about 8,300 years ago during a prolonged hot, dry era known as the Xerothermic period. Trees, shrubs and other tall plants are occasionally controlled by fires that sweep over grassy prairies. The prairies of McAdam's Peak and the wooded draws provide habitat for the northern fence lizard, sin-lined racerunner, broad-headed skink, black rat snake and others. Spring and fall are terrific times to walk the area looking for migratory raptors and waterfowl activity.

Hunting: Archery and shotgun turkey and deer seasons; 4,000 acres are used for hunting and the equestrian trails are closed during these seasons.

Nearby attractions: Riverboat gambling (Alton Belle, 800-336-SLOT), Army Corps areas, many nearby boat access points, fishing opportunities, hunting and hiking, Sam Vadalabene Bike Trail, Cahhokia Mounds State Historic Site and more. The Raging Rivers Water Park in Grafton, off Illinois 10, is a giant water slide and wave pool park open during the summer and is a terrific high-energy outing for the entire family, call (800) 548-7537.

43 Prophetstown State Park

Land: 53 acres Water: Rock River frontage

From April to November you can smell the fertile farmlands, occasionally hear a balling cow, and enjoy a casual ride along the ribbon of highway that wanders through valleys and rolling ridges toward the little state park call Prophetstown. In Whiteside County, at a big bend of the Rock River, the small state park is actually in the town of Prophetstown, off of Third Street, in a residential neighborhood.

This is the kind of park where you can bring your fishing pole, camp and spend quiet evenings walking about the small town licking an ice cream cone or examining the pastoral neighborhoods lined with neatly clipped lawns and freshly painted houses.

True to the small town appeal are tiny memorials dotting the ridge above the state park along a narrow picnicking and day-use area that commemorates fallen area soldiers. One living memorial, a Douglas fir tree, planted by the Prophetstown Garden Club in 1954, offers a patch of shade, a good view and a living neighbor for a rusty cannon and a bell that further remembers the role of local residents and their heroic efforts during several wars.

Prophetstown was once the site of an Indian village, and derives it name from the Indian prophet, Wa-Bo-Kie-Shiek, which means white cloud, who served as an advisor to the great Chief Blackhawk.

The park was dedicated in 1953.

Information and Activities

Prophetstown State Park
Prophetstown, IL
(815) 537-2926

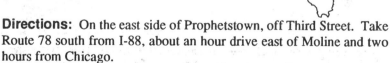

Directions: On the east side of Prophetstown, off Third Street. Take Route 78 south from I-88, about an hour drive east of Moline and two hours from Chicago.

Campground: Use the east entrance to the campground. The narrow roadway runs along agricultural fields, a little stream and ultimately dives into a densely wooded area near the campsites. Vault toilets and a dump station are near the entrance.

The small campground is one medium shaded loop, not very private, with a firewood pile and near a foot bridge that connects to the boat launch and day-use area. Sites 1 and 2, 29-44 have a distant view of the river. There is a nature trail near Coon Creek. There is no swimming. Electrical outlets are available.

Sites are all large. Sites 25-30 are grass pads and can accommodate large RVs. Not all sites have picnic tables.

Emergency numbers include: fire and ambulance, 537-2124; police 537-

2386; County sherriff, 1-772-4044; ranger, 1-772-2659.

Boating: The normally slow-moving Rock River is about 120 yards wide at this bend. There is a one-lane gravel surfaced launch at the foot of the park near plenty of parking and a turn around area.

The public boat launch is provided through the cooperation of the Illinois Conservation Department and is financed by a marine fuel tax.

Fishing: Here are the fishing regulations for the Rock River in this area: smallmouth bass, 6 limit, 12-inch size; largemouth, 6 limit, 12-inch size; walleye, 6 limit, 12 inch size; northern pike, 3 limit, 24-inch minimum size. These rules are enforced from the Rock River at the Illinois state line to the Mississippi River. There are considerable shoreline fishing opportunities at the park.

Other species include large- and smallmouth bass, walleye, sauger, crappies, bluegill, carp and channel cat, in the Rock River. You can also fish in tiny Coon Creek.

Day-use areas: Although there is a small campground, this park is mostly used as a day-use site offering many picnicking sites, shoreline fishing, shady retreats and closeness to a small town. The park is not a destination park, but for a weekend family gathering, the park could work well. It's safe for kids, and the open spaces could accommodate impromptu softball games.

44   *Pyramid State Park*

Land: 2,528 acres   Water: 20 lakes, 350-acres

Named after a large coal mine that once operated in the area, Pyramid State Park has more than 20 lakes varying in size from a tiny .1 acre pond—some call it a puddle—to a 24-acre lake. The typically clear waters of the lakes and their isolated locations—many can only be reached by foot—afford an opportunity for fishermen to get away from the crowds and enjoy some very good fishing in a unique environment.

Historians disagree and accounts vary, but many experts say that the first modern-era discovery of coal in the United States was in Jolliet and Marquette in La Salle County. Of course, Native Americans have long used coal and their byproducts, notably the Pueblo for their pottery-making. Strip-mining, or open cut mining as we know it today, was developed in the early 1800s. In those days muscled teams of horses pulled a shallow scoop that removed the top layer of soil and rock, and miners followed along the crop line with picks, shovels and wheelbarrows. As they trenched, they found more coal, but the problem of handling overlying soil, rock and shale caused large hills to be made of the tailings.

In 1962, the Illinois strip-mine reclamation law became effective. One of the most common methods of reclaiming these lands was to plant trees, and when possible, develop recreation facilities. Pyramid State Park is an example of reclamation and the state's efforts to reestablish woodlands, various habitats, hunting and public recreation.

Pyramid State Park is a outdoorsman's park. The many lakes offer almost endless places to explore with rod and reel, while hunters can enjoy a special handgun deer season at the park. Each fall the campsites fill up with hunters, when the trails are closed to hikers for some excellent hunting. Wild turkeys were introduced in the early 1990s.

This is not a fancy park. It doesn't have food concessions, lodge, rental boats or great natural beauty. But it is a great park for the sportsman in the family.

Information and Activities

Pyramid State Park
R.R. 1, P.O. Box 290
Pinckneyville, IL 62274
(618) 357-2574

Directions: Off Illinois 127, west of Du Quoin. Six miles south of Pinckeyville off I-127, then two miles west.

Information: The park closes at 10 p.m. You may self register for camping at the office and park maps are available at the park office.

Campground: Walk-in camping sites are abundant in the park, and the horse trail includes a rustic camping area near a group of small lakes. Most of the camping sites (Class C & D) have grass pads and picnic tables, but no electricity. Water is available at the south end of the park, near the office. Huron Lake is the youth camping area; and advance registration by groups is required.

Sites 14-18 are at the Pyramid Trailhead (a two-mile moderately difficult trail). Site 19 is secluded with big raspberry bush growing at its edge. In sites 1-6, which is part of the horse camping area, there are hitching posts and shade for the equine.

Sites 1-3 have a small fishing access site to stumpy Boulder lake. The north access area also has camping sites on the lakes. Near Clear and Cottonwood lakes, sites 22 and 23 are right on the lake with immediate lake access. Other camping sites in this area are small with grass pads and along the side of a narrow gravel road. Camping sites at Plum Lake offer some pull-though, as well as sites that are right on the lakeshore. There are no showers at the park.

Emergency numbers: ambulance and fire, 911; sheriff, 357-5212; state police, 542-2171. There is a pay phone at the park office.

Boating: Ten hp maximum. There are four small boat launches for aluminum craft, gravel parking lots and not much else. The launching ramps are narrow.

Fishing: The walk-in lakes do not have much fishing pressure and offer anglers a chance to try crickets for bluegills and rubber worms for bass. The lake bottoms are often rocky and the water clear. Some pretty good sized bluegills and largemouths are taken in the spring. Some of the tiny "lakes," which are little more than pools, produce only small panfish. Some anglers like to wade these lakes using a flyrod and light line to catch them during May and early June.

Small spinner baits, according to the district wildlife biologist, can also be productive. Many of the lakes at the north end of the park have small fishing docks and shoreside parking.

Hiking: Pyramid State Park features more than 16 miles of hiking and bridle trails, most of which are easy to moderate in difficulty. Most trails are loops and all will take you by small ponds, along wetlands, and near

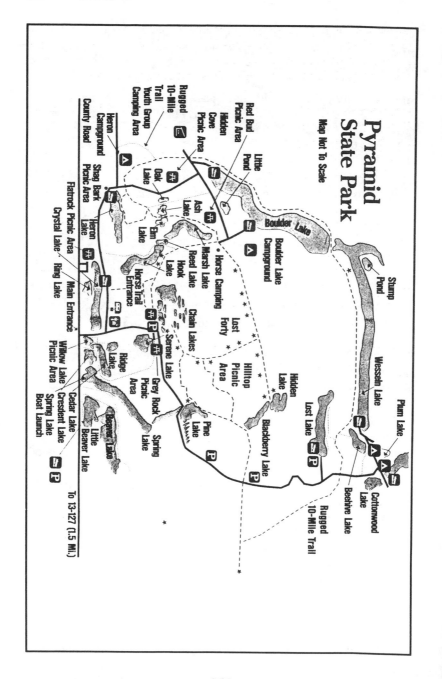

Pyramid State Park

Map Not To Scale

wooded areas as they regenerate and cover mine spoils. The 10-mile perimeter trail circles the park boundary, and is rugged and often used by equestrians. A small park map is available that depicts the trail system. The park is closed to horseback riding and cycling Oct. 15 - April 15.

Day-use areas: The park has a variety of day-use areas that have picnic tables, but generally the day-use area is for fishing and hunting activity. Children, however, would like fishing in the small bodies of water. Bring your insect repellent, you'll enjoy the vistas and hike more in this often-wet park. The Shagbark Picnic and Dogwood Picnic areas are popular with local visitors.

Hunting: Pistol deer season (mid-January), dove fields, fox and gray squirrel, woodcock, trapping for beaver and other opportunities are available. The park is set-up for hunter camping and many food plots with alfalfa and wheat are annually planted to enhance wildlife habitat, quality reproduction and stable populations of game species. There are 2,150 huntable acres. Fox, beaver, raccoon, badger and opossum abound in the area.

A 3-D archery range is also operated by the park and offers 15 targets. Call the site superintendent for additional information.

45   *Railsplitter State Park*

Land: 751 acres Water: Salt Creek

Horseshoes, catfishing and picnics are the themes of the day-use-only Railsplitter State Park, just south of Lincoln. Secluded picnicking sites, great chances to see native wildlife, and a tiny meandering stream are the features in this small park that wraps itself around an Illinois Department of Corrections facility.

Railsplitter State Park
R.R. 3
Lincoln, IL 62656
(217) 735-2424

Directions: The park office is off of Rt. 66, south of Lincoln about two miles, in Logan County. At the entrance you can go to the south or north day-use areas.

Information: The park office is open by chance, and the park is open 7 a.m. - 9 p.m. Keep dogs on a leash.

Campground: None.

Fishing: Salt Creek runs along the east boundary of the park. A small hiking trails traces the creek and offers shoreline anglers plenty of shady places to fish for catfish with liver, or try for large and smallmouth bass, bluegill, bullheads, carp and some crappie. One local catfisherman says the mid-summer is the best time of the year to catch "eating"-sized catfish.

Boating: Canoeing only is allowed on the Salt Creek. A tiny cartop boat launch is located at the north end of the park.

Hiking: Two trails are maintained by the park, a short jogging loop at the first parking lot and a four-mile multi-looped trail that travels along the narrow Salt Creek. The trail passes a small picnic area, crosses a bridge and makes a loop back to the bridge. The park is a mixed deciduous forested area. Birding is quite good and wildlife viewing is excellent due to low hunting pressure and light usage of the park.

Day-use areas: The entire park is a day-use area. Drinking water, tidy shelters, outdoor stoves and toilets are nestled among the oaks, walnuts, sycamores, ash, hickory and hackberry trees. Watch for wood thrushes; there are many to be seen along the roadways and in the forest understory.

Nearby attractions: Lincoln and Logan County attractions include many museums, restored buildings, Lincoln sites, Heritage In-Flight Museum, Lincoln College Museum, Stephen Douglas Site and more.

46 Ramsey Lake State Park

Land: 1,880 acres   Water: 47 acre lake

Many campers enjoy quiet camping and more and more cyclists are discovering the park as a great stopover point as they tour central Illinois. Once known as the "Old Fox Chase Grounds," Ramsey Lake State Park was popular for many fox and coon hunters to try their skills and test their howling hounds. For many years huge hunting and dog trial meets were conducted each September near the big springs at the northwest corner of the park.

The area has the appearance of a county fairgrounds with a dance pavilion, merry-go-round, amusement rides, display tents and hundreds of gawking spectators. When the big spring failed, the event fizzled, and the property began its evolution to a state park. In 1947, the state of Illinois purchased 815 acres of this lake for a lake site, and about 1,000 acres were later acquired.

Hunting, fishing and camping are the most popular activities at the park. If you are looking for a well-managed, developed park that is typically quiet and lightly used, bring your bluegill jigs and try Ramsey Lake this season.

Information and Activities

Ramsey Lake State Park
P.O. Box 97
Ramsey, IL 62080
(618) 423-2215

Information: The park office is near the park entrance and opens daily at 8 a.m. Knowledgeable and experienced staff can assist with any questions about camping, hunting or fishing in the park.

Directions: One mile northwest of Rt. 51 in Fayette County.

Campground: Sites 1-30 in the White Oak Campground (Class A, 92 sites), are reservable for a $5 non-refundable fee. These sites are very nice, complete with dry, timber-lined pads. Several camping clubs, excellent sites and busy holiday weekends make it a good idea to reserve a spot in advance during early summer.

Sites 31-41 and 86-91 are the most popular camping sites largely because they are near the bathhouse in the second loop. Sites 48, 49, 52-54 have a partial view of the lake. Near site 58 there is a walkway to the dam for campers and anglers. Sites 72, 73, 83 and 84 are nice sites close to the shower house.

Most of the sites are large enough for big RV rigs and shady.

The Hickory Grove (Class C, 65 sites) area is non-electric, with grass pads and unmarked camping areas. The group and overflow camping areas have 24 electric sites.

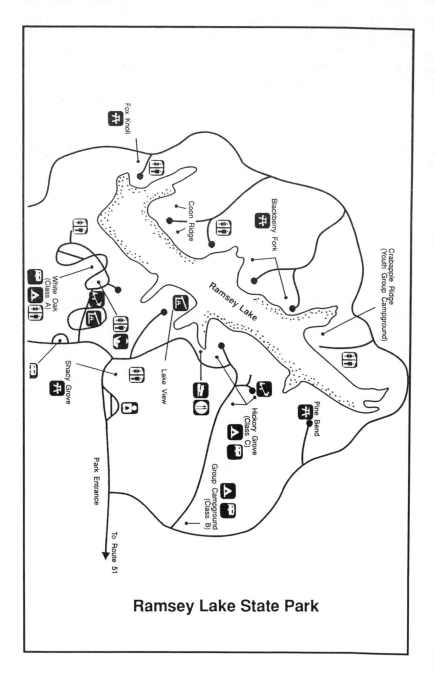

Ramsey Lake State Park

Emergency numbers: ambulance, 1-283-1231; fire, 1-423-2341; sheriff, 1-283-2141; state police, 1-217-536-6161; conservation office, 423-2718.

Boating: A one-lane boat ramp is on a shallow cover next to the bait and food concession store on the east side of the quiet lake. Gasoline motors are not allowed on the lake. The concession stand rents electric trolling motors by the hour and day and sells propane.

Fishing: The concession stand is open weekdays 8 a.m. - 6 p.m. and weekends 6:30 a.m. - 8 p.m. The shopkeeper is a knowledgeable angler who knows the waters and stocks the correct terminal tackle and live bait for lake conditions. Rowboats are rented at the clean, well-lighted store that also serves coffee bright and early each morning. The average depth of the lake is 8-10-feet, with some deeper holes and shoreline structures.

The lake is considered excellent for bluegill. "When the bluegill are hitting, anglers go nuts!" says the concession operator. Crickets, small jigs, minnows, just about anything will work when the gills are on the bite. Dry flys also attract the bluegills. Illinois fishery biologists have repeatedly said the small lake is the best bluegill body of water in the state!

Bass anglers also find good success on the lake, with many tournament hopefuls practicing for contests and throwing all types of buzz baits and crank baits along the structures and shorelines.

In many ways the lake is too fertile. Algae control has been an ongoing problem and aerators are being considered along with other methods to ensure future fishing action.

Hiking: Horses, snowmobiles (the southernmost snowmobile trail in the state), and hikers can share the 13-mile trail at the north end of the park, one mile north of the park entrance. A small rustic horse camp is along the easy trail that wanders through a mixed deciduous woodland, along some broken fields, and near some interesting flora and edges. Unmarked fire lands and the small one-mile hiking trail in the park are often used by visitors for easy hikes along the gently rolling terrain of the park.

Day-use areas: Many picnic areas are conveniently located around the park and they include the Foxknoll, Coon Ridge, Crabapple Ridge Youth Camping Area, Blackberry Fork and others. The Lake View picnic area is on a small land projection into the lake and has a great view of the water.

Hunting: The hunting area has steeply rolling topography which becomes gently rolling uplands. Crop fields and food plots have been planted for winter food and cover, with bushy thickets and draws providing preferred hunting areas. Mature stands of oaks/hickory provide for excellent squirrel hunting. There's squirrel, dove, turkey, archery deer, quail, raccoon, fox, coyote, rabbit and woodcock all in season. Squirrel hunting begins Aug. 1 of each year. Call the site superintendent for additional information.

Nearby attractions: Vandalia has a campground; Ramsey Golf Course.

47   *Red Hills State Park*

Land: 948 acres Water: 40 acres

U.S. Route 50 bisects Red Hills State Park, with the campground, lake facilities and primary day-use areas to the south of the highway and the most rustic and remote day-use areas to the north. The park is punctuated by a 98-foot tower and lighted cross rising from an open area atop wooded Red Hill.

This is the highest point between St. Louis and Cincinnati and the open-air tabernacle (known as "little tabernacle") at the base of the thin cross was financed and constructed by area residents in cooperation with an interdenominational council and is frequently used for worship services. In fact, large Easter Sunday services have been led at the lighted cross annually since 1943. In 1958, neon lights were installed on the 32-foot-wide cross. The cross is located off the north entrance to the rolling state park.

Also at the park is Veteran's Point, a one-quarter acre parcel of land that honors ex-servicemen and women of all wars and provides a quality place for their gatherings.

Red Hills is also an important historical crossroads. By the western edge is the first land in Illinois ceded by the Indians to the United States government. The borderline runs through the park from the southwest to the northeast, and was set by a treaty made in 1795 at Greenville, Ohio, by General Anthony Wayne and the Native Americans, whereby they relinquished all claim to the land northwest of the Ohio River and east of a specific line. Also intersecting the park boundary was the Cahokia Trace which runs east and west U.S. 50 and is visible from the east park entrance. Commonly known as the "Trace Road," it connected Vincennes and St. Louis and for years was the principal route to the West.

A satellite area of the park, the 400-acre Chauncey Marsh Nature Preserve, contains the best remaining example of what is known as a Wabash border march ecosystem—dry and wet prairie, lush bottomland forest and thriving riverside communities.

From ice fishing and skating in the wintertime to the gold and crimsons of autumn, visitors will find soothing breezes, picnicking, camping, hiking and fishing at the sprawling state park.

Information and Activities

Red Hills State Park
R. R. 2, P.O. Box 252A
Summer, IL 62466
(618) 936-2469

Directions: Lawrence County between Olney and Lawrenceville on U.S. Route 50. The office is open 8 a.m. - 4 p.m. weekdays.

Campground: The Class A campground has been upgraded recently and these are about 120 shady sites. Many campers like to nestle near the shower building, while others prefer sites along the lake. All camping sites are relatively flat with fire grills, gravel pads and picnic tables. The campground is filled only on holiday weekends.

The small Class D tent camping area, called the Raccoon Ridge Campground, is on the east side of the lake near the entrance and features some really nice locations on the lake. If you are a tent camper you will enjoy the shady area with lake access and plenty of opportunity to fish and pull your small boat up next to the camping area and the sunsets over the lake. Quiet hours in the campground are 7 p.m. - 7 a.m.

The Lakeside Loop is sites 1-39; sites 40-120 are called the Shady Oak Loop.

Site 1 is hard-surfaced and reserved for disabled campers. All of the sites in the loop from 1-39 are dry, very shady by oak trees, wooded and have gravel pads. This small loop is ideal for medium-sized RV rigs. Site 22 is a pull-through and has 240-volt service and the best site in the park for really big camping rigs.

Sites 85-90 have an excellent view of the placid lake. At site 92 there is a huge poison ivy vine snaking its way up a tree. Poison ivy always has a hairy looking vine that is typically gray and can easily reach a diameter of three inches. There is a lake access in the Shady Oaks Loop.

Campers with a large RV rigs will love sites 77 and 78. Site 94 is perched atop a ridge that faces a deep wooded ravine and is fairly private. Site 105 has a hard-surfaced pad.

Firewood is often available from the campground host.

When staying in the campground or visiting the park, plan a meal at the Trace Inn (618-936-2351), a 45-seat restaurant that has been remodeled above the bait shop. The restaurant offers a good view of the lake and anglers in the distance bobbing in little boats— and excellent homestyle meals. The restaurant is open Tuesday-Saturday, 11 a.m. - 9 p.m., and Sundays, 11 a.m. - 8 p.m.

Emergency numbers: sheriff, 1-943-5766; state police, (217) 536-6161;

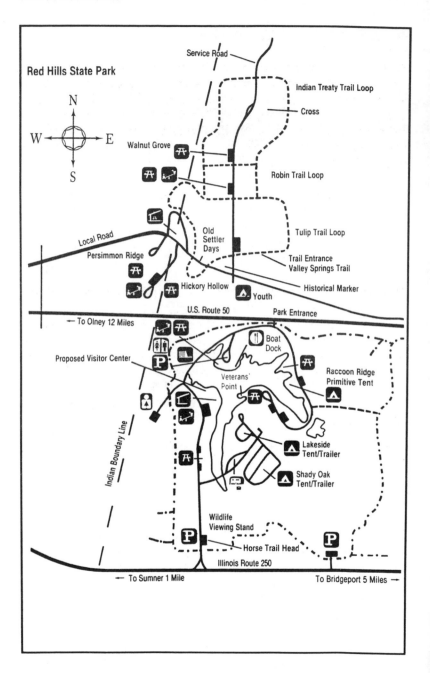

Red Hills State Park

fire, 936-2317; ambulance, 943-1911.

Boating: Gasoline motors are not permitted on the 40-acre lake, but you may use electric motors to wander the shoreline or seeking out structures and fishing holes. The small one-lane concrete ramp is rarely busy in front of the small concession/restaurant where limited grocery, craft shop and fishing supplies are offered. Small boats and paddle boats can be rented at the concession stand. There are some benches and day-use amenities near the small boat launch.

Fishing: The tree-lined Red Hills lake has three miles of shoreline and can reach a depth of about 20 feet. Fishing is good to fair during the spring and summer, before the water temperature climbs in June. Reasonable populations of bluegill can be taken from shore, especially in the evening and near small structures using crickets.

Crappie and sunfish will hit live bait and small spinners. Largemouth bass can be taken from the lake, but locals say they are finicky. They often take buzz baits in the spring, then are attracted only by rubber worms or by accident during much of the summer. Staff reports some very good sized bass taken from the lake each season. Catfish angling in the lower arm with stink baits is a staple for local fishing enthusiasts.

There is a 15-inch minimum size limit on largemouth bass, and you may take six catfish daily.

Hiking: An equestrian trail on the south side of the park is open as soil conditions permit and is shared with hikers. The three-mile loop that is generally flat and easy loosely circles the lake and passes many day-use locations on the east side of the park.

Trails in the north section of the park are moderately difficult and secluded with trailheads at day-use areas. Indian Treaty Trail, Robin Loop and Tulip Trail are in this less-used part of the unit and feature rolling hills, chances to see songbirds in the understory and edges along the trails that combine mixed deciduous woodlots and small open spaces. Biking is encouraged on the roads, but not on the trails.

Day-use areas: In the south section of the park, playground areas and picnic tables are scattered around the lake. All offer a water view, nearby toilets, grills, trash barrels and open spaces for informal games. Areas north of Route 50 also have picnic tables and a shelter house. There are two shelter houses in the park. Kids will enjoy one of the six playgrounds, shoreline fishing, a wildlife viewing area, and maybe a glimpse of a horse and rider using the limited equestrian trails. Basketball players can do some slam dunking at the court near the main entrance.

Nature: Nearby Olney has a population of white squirrels. Red-headed woodpeckers are common in the park. Hellbender aquatic salamanders are sometimes seen in this region along streams and rivers. The adults are gray, yellow and olive, and can reach 12 inches in length. If you see a hellbender, please report your sighting to the Endangered Species Board at (217) 785-8687.

Hunting: Woodcock, squirrel, dove, quail and rabbit are hunted in season. Archery deer is also permitted in the park. There is a check station, but call the site superintendent for details. There are 725 huntable acres in the park—204 open acres, 565 timbered acres and 139 brushy acres.

The high oak/hickory wooded areas and deep ravines to the north are the most often hunted sections. Food plots and small grain strips are planted near wooded areas in both the north and south sections of the park.

48   *Rock Cut State Park*

Land: 3,092 acres   Water: two lakes, 162 and 50 acres

Gently nestled amid lush rolling farmlands, Rock Cut State Park, in Winnebago County, is the place where westward bound wagons fjorded the mighty Rock River toward open plains and grassy prairielands on a journey that crossed a hostile country. But before all of that, the Mascouten and Miami-speaking Native American tribes congregated in the region after the Iroquois drove them from the southern end of Lake Michigan.

The Winnebago ranged southward from Wisconsin to the Rock River valley from about 1740-1840, while the river's upper reaches were on the periphery of the Fox and Sauk territory from about 1765 to 1833. By 1800, the Potawatomi, Ottawa and Chippewa nations extended their range into the area. But they ceded their lands to the United States 32 years later, following the bloody Black Hawk War.

Scots, Canadians, New Yorkers and New Englanders began settling the area near the park in the mid-1800s, clearing the lands and quickly taking advantage of the rich soils, rivers and natural resources of the Rock River corridor.

Today, the dammed waters of Pierce Lake cover much of the old railroad bed within the park, although portions of the railroad grade are visible along Willow Creek below the spillway. Blasting by railroad crews during the 1859 construction left lasting impressions in the park; in fact, their vigorous rock cutting gave the area its name.

Information and Activities

Rock Cut State Park
7318 Harlem Road
Caledonia, IL 61011
(815) 885-3311

Directions: Two hours west of Chicago, east of Rockford off U.S. Route 173.

Campground: Rock Cut takes advance registration for about 30 campsites in the Buckthorn camping area. Reservation may be made by mail or in person at the park office. There is a $5 non-refundable fee. The concession phone is (815) 885-3722 and you can call 911 for any emergency.

The unit manages 212 electric and 60 non-electric sites and Class B sites in five loops. Each campsite has a picnic table and steel camp stove where fires are allowed (firewood is available at the concession at the main boat launch). In the first small loop, Prairie View, sites 500-521 have gravel pads and one handicapped site. Sites 514, 516 and 518 are the nicest sites at the end of the loop. All of the spots can hold small recreational vehicles. There are many young trees, but there is adequate shade through the loop if you choose your camping site wisely.

The park staff recommends the gently rolling White Oak loop, which includes sites 400-441 and is next to the Buckthorn area. White Oak is wooded and has several 50-amp sites, a recycling station, and many well-separated and private sites. Sites 411, 412 and 416 are quite private, while site 417 is private and large enough for big recreational rigs.

In the reservable Buckthorn area, which is shady and well-spaced, camping sites 311, 313, 315, 317, are evenly shaded and private. The Plum Grove area has very open, unshaded sites, especially along the north part of the loop. All handicapped sites are hard-surfaced in all of the loops. Sites 100-116 are shady in the Plum Grove section which is tightly packed and not very private. There is a phone at the centrally located shower building.

Hickory Hill is a tent camping area on a peninsula with great water views. There is access to the lake for shoreline fishing, as well as, picnic areas and high ground for dry and breezy camping. This non-electric Class B area is a good choice if you enjoy tent camping.

Rock Cut operates one rent-a-camp that can accommodate eight people and comes with cots, electricity and more. Call ahead for details. Rent-a-camps are a great way to try camping. Rock Cut is a popular campground and often fills up early Fridays and on all holiday weekends. A small horse camp has no marked sites and it's best to call ahead about availability to this area off Hart Road.

Boating: There is a one-lane launch at the campground and a bigger two-lane launch with a concession operation (open 6 a.m. - sunset, seven days) that rents rowboats, paddle boats and canoes. It also sells bait, snacks and firewood along the shores of Pierce Lake. There is a 10 hp engine limit on the lake. About 60 cars and trailers can find parking here. There are also picnic tables at the modern launch ramp area for those of you who enjoy watching people struggle launching boats and enjoy tall fish tales.

Fishing: Named for Rep. William Pierce, the 162-acre lake has four miles of shoreline, much of it fishable. It reaches 25 feet and offers fair to good fishery for stocked species, especially during the early season. The lake attracts muskie anglers who use jumbo minnow, huge jerk baits

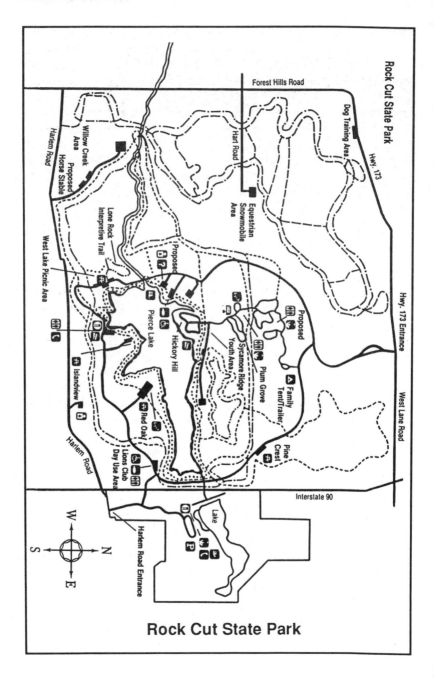

Rock Cut State Park

Campers with large RVs like the shady and wide sites.

and troll the middle of the lake along whatever structure they can find. The 46-foot dam offers some action for panfish, which locals use crickets and red worms to attract. Volunteers have placed seven fish cribs, mostly at the west end of the lake where bass, northern pike and panfish congregate. A number of shallow coves offers habitat and points that boat fishermen can explore, casting to the edges using jerk baits and spinners.

You may keep one muskie per day if it's 36 inches or longer; three northern pike, 24-inch minimum; one 14-inch or larger bass daily; six per day of 14-inch minimum walleye; six catfish daily; 25 crappies daily; and 5 bluegill daily. Attendants at Walsh Concession at the launch have all the details and keep track of what's "on the bite."

There is a fishing pier for the disabled that is also great for younger anglers trying their luck in the narrow lake.

Beach/swimming: You may not swim at Pierce Lake, but you can whoop it up in the waters at small Roland Olson Lake, a 50-acre managed body of water designed for swimming in the eastern part of the park. It is not within walking distance from the main park area. The lake's swimming area is open 11 a.m. - 7 p.m., Memorial Day through Labor Day; no lifeguards are on duty. The sandy beach is about 200-yards long. Amenities include concrete-block changing building, concession trailer, paddle boats, limited fishing opportunity and day-use areas.

Hiking: The easy to moderate hiking trail that circumnavigates the four-mile shoreline of Pierce Lake is a terrific half-day outing. It takes you along the water's edge, through wooded areas, and by other trailheads and spurs that are described on a map available at the park office. From the main trail you can access another six miles or more of trails that are also skied and used by equestrians that reach toward the outer boundaries of the park. The actual equestrian trail is nearly 15 miles long, and during the winter season more than 13 of these miles are open to snowmobilers. Even dog sledders occasionally bring out their teams and enjoy the trail system. The trails are wide, dry, well-maintained and marked. The trail system at Rock Cut is very good, and campers could spend several days exploring all of the areas.

Day-use areas: Children will enjoy a visit to the dam where rushing waters tempt them and parents will feel the cool breezes. The park roadway which circles the park offers a number of scenic turnouts and places to picnic. The Lions Club operates a handicapped-only day-use and picnic area. There are two reservable shelters, and five picnic areas and two playgrounds operated by the park.

The Island View picnic area is on a small bluff above the lake and features a scenic view, shelter, concrete block vault toilet, picnic tables and a clean, nice place for a small family outing. This is the nicest picnic area in the park. A dog training area, off Highway 173, and a number of prairie restoration areas also dot the rolling terrain. Many visitors use the roadways for casual walks, passing by lake views, heavily wooded areas, open spaces and playground equipment that is scattered about the unit.

Winter: Activities include an annual winter festival, ice skating, ice fishing, snowmobiling when there is a four-inch base, and lots of cross-country skiing on self-groomed trails.

Nearby attractions: Rockford Speedway, Atwood Homestead and Forest Preserve, major malls, urban amenities. There are 31 forest preserves with more than 5,050 acres in Winnebago County. Many have day-use areas, ball fields, nature preserves and even golf courses. Call (815) 877-6100 for a map or information.

49 Rock Island Trail State Park

26-mile-long trail

Have you ever wandered along an unused stretch of railroad track, dreaming about far-off places and long-ago times? Did you stop to look at marvelous old bridges, tiny depots that once bustled with travelers, strong trestles, or tree-lined lengths of trails that are like a tunnel? Perhaps you imagined bicycling or walking from town to town along the right of way without the fear of rumbling freight trains, and walking along the bumpy ballast and ties.

Abandoned railroad rights of way do more than simply stir the imagination; rail corridors are being more and more often used for recreation, human-powered transportation and preservation of surrounding natural areas. That's the case for the Rock Island Trail, a 26-mile linear rail-to-trail from Alta, in Peoria County, to Toulon, in Stark County. The long state park offers many natural and architectural attractions in a tree-canopied corridor that is only 50 to 100 feet wide.

In the late 19th century, the United States embarked upon the greatest railroad building spree in history. Immense tracts of land were given by federal and state governments, huge railroad empires were assembled and the genius of American technology broke through barriers of space and time. By 1916, the nation had the largest railroad system in the world with more than 250,000 miles of track. Even the tiniest towns were connected by ribbons of steel, and large cities were virtually cross-crossed by rail tracks.

In 1867 the Peoria and Rock Island Railroad Company was granted a charter to construct a rail system between Peoria and Rock Island. Construction took a couple of years. In 1871 regularly-scheduled passenger trains began running. For more than 40 years, passenger and freight trains rumbled through the small towns of Alta, Dunlap, Princeville, Stark, Wyoming and Toulon.

By 1915, here and across much of the country, the railroad business was buffeted by the rise of auto, truck, bus and airplane transportation. Railroad companies merged, consolidated their routes and, occasionally, went out of business. By the late 1950s rail traffic virtually ceased on the Rock Island line.

Peoria's Forest Park Foundation acquired the abandoned tracks in 1965, and donated the linear stretch of property to the Department of Conservation four years later for future development. The state, using great patience, foresight and planning, methodically overcame obstacles to the development of the rail-to-trail, ultimately agreeing in 1986 to a plan that would include fencing off certain adjacent landowners' properties, the state installed signage, replaced and repaired culverts, trimmed trees, and performed general maintenance.

The trail was completed in 1989 and is open for 26 miles of hiking, biking and skiing. Hats off to the state of Illinois for this initial rail-to-trail project and the future of other similar projects. If you would like more information about the national rails-to-trails movement, contact the Rails-to-Trails Conservancy, Suite 300, 1400 Sixteenth Street NW, Washington, D.C. 20036, (202) 797-5400.

Information and Activities

Rock Island Trail State Park
P. O. Box 64
Wyoming, IL 61491
(309) 695-2228

The Rock Island Trail is a generally easy walking (or riding or skiing) linear pathway that is very well marked with directional signs and mile markers. Long sections of the trail, between Dunlap, Princeville and Wyoming, are laid down with crushed and compacted limestone. Those planning on completing the entire trail will need to leave a vehicle at one end of the trail or segment, or have somebody pick them up at a predetermined location.

Beginning in Alta (the trailhead, marker board and parking lot are one mile from Route 6) walkers travel through a delightful tunnel of trees for about two miles, where they see the beginnings of the Kickapoo Creek Recreation Area that offers primitive camping, water, toilets and scattered picnic tables. Past Kickapoo Creek, hikers have a beautiful view of the creek bed and surroundings before entering the edge of Dunlap. Next come uneven passages between farmlands and some wooded tracts. Along the trail, follow bike signs when you are in towns.

The trail proceeds through the center of Princeville off the railroad bed, but on the north edge of town follow the signs back onto the converted railroad bed. You are about halfway to Toulon at this point.

Continuing north to the outskirts of Wyoming, trekkers pass the old Chicago, Burlington and Quincy Railroad Depot, a small wooden depot with double doors and a gabled roof. From here the trail goes through town and there are places to rest or find a snack. Again follow the biking signs at the north end of town to re-discover the old rail bed.

The best stretch of the hike is between Toulon and Wyoming offering rural scenes and pretty vistas over the north branch of the Spoon River. A wooded bridge here is a great place for photos and refreshments, with only about four miles remaining to the parking lots on the edge of Toulon.

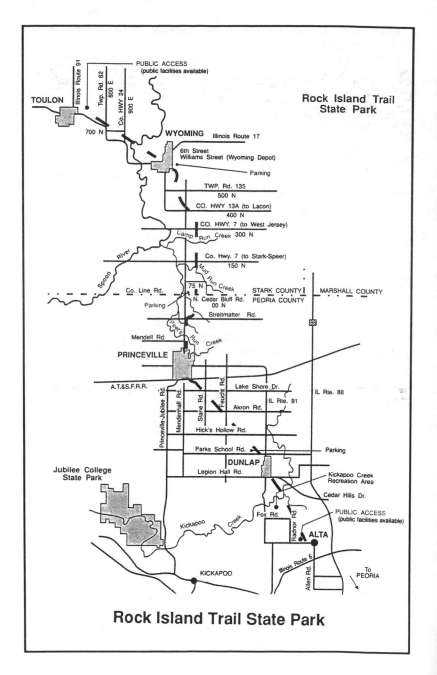

Rock Island Trail
State Park

Rock Island Trail State Park

50   *Sam Parr State Park*

Land: 1,103 acres   Water: 183-acre lake

Like much of Illinois, the early inhabitants of this area were Native Americans, who for more than 1,000 years fished from the rich Embarrass River bottomlands and hunted in nearby woodlands, including what is now Sam Parr State Park in Jasper County. Today, about 100 Piankashaw Indians, who gave up nearly one million acres to the United States government in 1812, live in the county.

It wasn't until the 1950s that area residents began lobbying for the area to become a state park.

Sam Parr, a vocal and ardent conservationist and Fisheries Division administrator, took up the issue and in 1960, 62 acres of land were acquired by the Department of Conservation and the Jasper County Conservation Area. Since, additional property acquisitions have brought the total acreage to 1,103, including the 183-acre tree-lined lake. After Sam's death in 1966, the General Assembly changed the name of the area to Sam Parr State Park. The park was formally dedicated on May 12, 1972.

Segments of the park have been developed using the Pitt-Robinson Act of 1937, which earmarks funds for wildlife management using revenues derived from hunting and fishing licenses and taxes on sporting goods. The fund is often used for habitat improvements, hunting and fishing access, and other projects geared toward public use and wildlife management.

Information and Activities

Sam Parr State Park
R.R. #5 P.O. Box 220
Newton, IL 62448
(618) 783-2661

Directions: Three miles northeast of Newton, at the intersection of Illinois Routes 130 and 33 in the extreme northeastern corner of Jasper County.

Information: The park office is at the end of the first road to the right after entering the park. There is an information board in front of the office, and the office is open weekdays, 8 p.m. - 4 p.m.

Campground: Sam Parr has some of the finest tent sites in the system, and as tent camping increases in popularity, the sites will get heavy use. The Persimmon Point Class D tent camping area is on the west side of the lake near the White Oak Picnic Area, the second drive to the right of Route 33, north of the park office.

The area has a separate parking lot. The sites are scattered under a canopy of large trees with all sites having a view of the lake, picnic tables and fire pit. The tent sites are not marked, but they do lay themselves out under shade and near the lake. The entire 3-4 acre area is mowed and some tent campers simply park their small boats along the shoreline or at a set of two small wooden piers and fish the lake from dawn to dusk.

One warning about the drinking fountain near the 25-car parking lot at the tent camping area. It shoots water about 25 feet and will soak your entire head, neck and back if you aren't careful. Always turn on a fountain before sticking your head over it to drink.

The trailer camping area is one of the most private and widely spaced in the entire state parks system, offering sites that are separated by a wall of vegetation. It's as if each site is carved out of the adjoining woodland. If you like camping in early June, choose site 12, where there are some huge raspberry bushes that provides an endless supply of juicy berries. Get them early, before the kids and birds do!

Sites 12, 14 and 16 have a through-the-woods view of the lakes. The sites are intimate, and not very big; folks with trailers larger than 28 feet might need to scout the lots for sites long enough to accommodate their rigs. Site 22 is directly across from the vault toilets and water. This may be the best trailer campground in the system. Checkout is 3 p.m. and quiet time is from 10 p.m. to 7 a.m.

Boating: Across the street from the tent camping area are the two-lane boat launch and temporary docking area. Two small launches are managed by the unit, boat motor size is limited to 10 hp. Pontoon boats and other slow-moving pleasure craft are abundant on the waters during the warm summer months. The gravel parking surface can handle 50 or more vehicles and trails.

Fishing: Narrow Sam Parr Lake has 9.5 miles of shoreline, two main branches, and a maximum depth of about 25 feet. The lake is heavily fished and considered a fair to good largemouth bass and panfish fishery. Channel catfish are also abundant. Most local anglers use various cutbaits, liver and cheeseballs in the warm waters. The Jasper Co. Bass Club has placed about 15 Christmas trees as structures in the lake. Fishermen should bring their small boats, and camp in the nice tent camping area. There is a fishing map available.

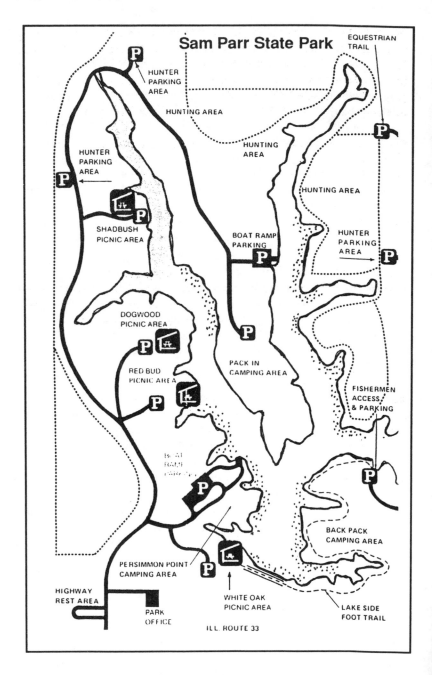

Sam Parr State Park

EQUESTRIAN TRAIL

P HUNTER PARKING AREA

HUNTING AREA

HUNTING AREA

HUNTING AREA

HUNTER PARKING AREA

P

SHADBUSH PICNIC AREA

BOAT RAMP PARKING

HUNTER PARKING AREA

DOGWOOD PICNIC AREA

PACK IN CAMPING AREA

RED BUD PICNIC AREA

FISHERMEN ACCESS & PARKING

BOAT RAMP

BACK PACK CAMPING AREA

PERSIMMON POINT CAMPING AREA

HIGHWAY REST AREA

PARK OFFICE

WHITE OAK PICNIC AREA

LAKE SIDE FOOT TRAIL

ILL. ROUTE 33

Hiking: As with many state parks in this region, the entire park is neatly manicured and trails are well marked and regularly used. The Lakeside Hiking Path at the south end of the park crosses a small dam and leads east to the fishermen's access. A short equestrian trail at the north end of the park is also hikable. Many walkers also use the park's roadways for evening strolls.

Day-use areas: All of the picnic areas are easily accessible from the park road, with most of the lakeside picnicking sites along the west side of the lake. All of the picnic areas are well shaded with picnic tables, vault toilets, water and grills. Many of the picnic sites are a short distance to the lake, offering privacy and a great view of the impoundment. At some points along the lake there are high banks that you can scramble down to the lake to fish, relax or just explore.

Nature: There are a number of open spaces that are managed and planted to aid wildlife by providing food, water and cover. There are two wetland areas that can be viewed from the main park road which look like good birding and wildlife viewing spots, especially during the spring and evening times.

Hunting: Hunting at Sam Parr is popular and considered very good. Check with the site superintendent for upland game species hunting dates. Squirrel, dove, woodcock, rabbit and archery deer are also hunted.

Winter: Ice skating and ice fishing, with some sledding are encouraged as weather permits.

Nearby attractions: The Newton water tower, Jasper Co. Prairie Chicken Sanctuary and Newton Wildlife Area are nearby. Oil wells and farm fields coexist, as you depart the park you'll notice many small one-armed oil wells pumping away amid the lush crops of the area.

51   *Sangchris State Park*

Land: 1,414 acres   Water: 2,162 acres

Sangchris Lake is one of the top largemouth bass angling lakes in the state, and with considerable improvements to the state park, anglers, boaters and family vacationers can enjoy a relaxing weekend or longer. The unit is just 15 minutes from Springfield and all of the area's Lincoln-related attractions.

Designated as a State Fishing Preserve in 1972, the 120 miles of lake shoreline and 2,162 surface acres include a warm-water discharge from a Commonwealth Edison power plant at the south end of the lake, numerous brush cribs made of 600 Christmas trees in 7-12 foot depths, pallet cribs, dropoffs and even a striped bass spawn stripping station near the warm-water discharge.

Sangchris Lake produces an astounding 43 pounds of bass per acre, averaging 12-13 inches, with many 6-10 pounders taken annually. According to local experts, the spring bass fishing is the best, with dozens of five-plus pound fish taken daily. Bluegill average seven inches, channel catfish average 16 inches, and crappies are protected by a 9-inch minimum and a 25-fish possession daily limit.

Over the years the state has aggressively stocked the lake with striped bass, white and black crappie, threadfin shad and channel cats. A good stocking program, enforced limits and underwater improvements continue to make Sangchris Lake one of the best sport fisheries in the state.

Information and Activities

Sangchris Lake State Park
R.R. 1, P.O. Box 58
Rochester, IL 62563
(217) 498-9208

Directions: About 10 miles southeast of Springfield, from Route 29, take Route 104 west to Bulpitt, and proceed north to the park by following directional signs. No swimming is allowed at the lake.

Campground: Traditionally the three-looped Class B campground has closed during the winter season, and reopened in April. The little brown campground office has lots of brochures and maps, and can provide complete information about the area. There are group camping and a horse staging area behind the office.

The Deer Run Campground has Class B electrical sites and is gently rolling and about 75 percent shaded. Each site has gravel pads and tables, fire grills and nearby access to water and toilets. Sites on the east end of the campground are fairly open, but by choosing your site carefully in this area, you can find a level, shady site for the weekend. This camping area is rarely filled on weekends or holidays. There is a tent camping spur in this campground also. Site 25 is the best site in this loop. The outside perimeter of these loops back up against trees and shrubs. Sites 1-40 are about 60 percent shady. Sites 30-32 are good for medium sized trailers.

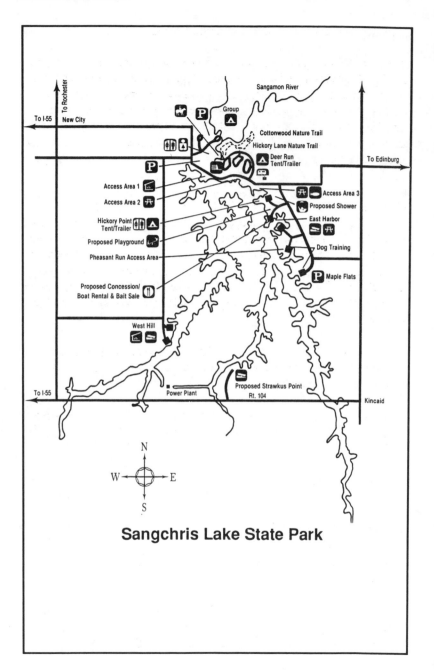

Sangamon River

To Rochester

To I-55   New City

Group

Cottonwood Nature Trail

Hickory Lane Nature Trail

To Edinburg

Deer Run
Tent/Trailer

Access Area 1

Access Area 2

Access Area 3

Proposed Shower

Hickory Point
Tent/Trailer

East Harbor

Proposed Playground

Dog Training

Pheasant Run Access Area

Maple Flats

Proposed Concession/
Boat Rental & Bait Sale

West Hill

To I-55

Power Plant

Proposed Strawkus Point
Rt. 104

Kincaid

N
W — E
S

Sangchris Lake State Park

Sites 37 and 42 are excellent for larger RV rigs.

The newer Hickory Point Camping Area is a neighbor to the two-lane East Harbor Boat Ramp and day-use area. This camping area has had major renovations in the recent past and is one of the better camping areas in this part of the state. A modern shower building, good water views, new parking areas, upgraded pads and electrical services will greet the RV traveler or fisherman. Plenty of handicapped sites, new lighting and updated design are a welcome improvement to this fine fishing lake state park.

Good sites on the water include 5-16, with site 14 right at the point on the water. You can pull your boat up and camp at these sites. Site 16 is terrific, with 17 and 18 right on the water and all sites complete with picnic tables, gravel pads and grills. Many campers believe site 19 is the best spot in the park; I agree. Site 20-22 are shaded by a giant oak, one of the biggest you will see! Camping sites 23 and 24 are on a small cove where you pull your boat right up to your camping site, unload the day's catch, and cook dinner.

Sites 26-28 and 32 are also near the water, near the playground and restrooms. In summary, this is a great camping area. Come early, get a water-side site, and stay long.

Emergency numbers: most police and other emergencies can be handled by a call to 911, or Christian County police, 824-4961; hospital, 788-3030.

Boating: There are four excellent boat ramps to the lake, and one two-lane ramp at the state park. Motors are restricted to 25 hp or less.

Fishing: The most fun bait shop in the area is North Dock Bait and Tackle, which has complete local knowledge of the lake, and out back you can take an airplane ride. Fishing maps are available at most area tackle shops.

Sangchris Lake has many wooden fishing piers in day-use areas that are great for youngsters and adults. The best piers are near the dam, with many local anglers in the evening seeking frying pan-sized crappies.

Waterfront camping sites.

The maximum depth of the lake is 38 feet near the dam that was built in 1964. The bottom of the lake is mostly clay, with heavy siltation in the upper arms. Some roadways and building foundations still exist, with many stumps and standing timber offering excellent underwater structure.

Local experts suggest that anglers look for water of 65 degrees. Water clarity dictates how deep to fish. The upper end of the creek arms and East Arm are most turbid, so concentrate on depths of 5-7 feet. The clearest fishing waters are in the middle of the West Arm. The best fishing depths to try here are 15-20 feet. In the spring, head for the northern end of the lake for the biggest bass.

In most places around the lake, the shoreline has a thick underwater weed crop of coontail and brittle naiad and can be productive after dark using topwater baits. During daylight hours try flipping rubber worms and jig n' pigs along some type of underwater wood or other structures (timber, stumps, stick ups, etc.). Jigging along the bottom is also productive if the water isn't too warm.

The best bass-holding areas are old submerged ponds and levees. Before building the lake there were more than 20 ponds in the creek arms. The levees can be seen on your locator/depth graph, and are 2-4-foot tall humps with deep water on either side.

Try the hot water discharge area in the early spring and late fall for striped bass and white bass. Hot Ditch and the northern end of the West Arm are also good during ths time. The Hot Ditch is especially good for striped bass from late fall to early spring. From May to October, try for striped bass in the area north of the county line and in 12-15 feet of water. For white bass, find the shad schools (look for sea gulls feeding) and pitch at them with jigs and small spoons. For crappies, find the brush cribs, say the locals. If you are staying in the park, you'll find consistently good striper action off Striper Point in 38 feet of water near the north end of the park.

Creel limits: Largemouth bass, one fish greater than or equal to 15-inches in length, and two fish less 15-inches in length; crappies, 9-inch minimum, 25 daily; and striped and white bass, no creel limit for fish under 17 inches; fish longer than 17 inches, you may keep three daily.

Hiking: Sangchris has three miles of hiking trails, which, if you are quiet and lucky, will take you near some of the white-tailed deer that live in the area. A small population of nearly white deer live in the habitats around the lake. They aren't albino, but a genetic variation of common whitetails that arc unique to the area. The park also maintains an 11-mile snowmobile trail and a five-mile horse trail.

Day-use areas: Dog training and archery areas are available. Most of the day-use amenities are carefully scattered along the northeast shoreline of the lake and include picnicking areas, tables, toilets, grills, water and plenty of parking.

Hunting: Waterfowl, dove, deer and upland game are hunted on the tract. Contact the park office for rules and regulations.

52   *Shabbona State Park*

Land: 1,546 acres Water: Lake Shabbona, 318 acres

The shady campground is nice. The ample day-use areas are clean and inviting. The walking trails are gentle, and orange water tower marks the nearby city of Shabbona. But the most impressive and important reason visitors flock to Shabbona (pronounced SHA ba naw) is the quality fishing. From trophy muskie to walleye, Shabbona Lake offers plenty of leisurely shoreline fishing sites or a busy boat launch that is your gateway to some fine bass, bluegill or big muskie fishing.

Once home to tribes of Native Americans, the park was named for Chief Shabbona. Pioneer settlements began dotting the area by 1830. The rich soils, mild winters and abundant waterways help fuel the areas growth as the land was cleared and farm fields began to blanket the region.

The state of Illinois began master planning the area in 1965 when it decided to create a lake and recreation area to support water-based activities. In 1978 more than 1,500 acres were acquired and put under development. Chief Shabbona would not recognize the area today.

In the early 1970s the area that was to be the lake was cleared of trees and shoreline modifications began that would eventually provide earthen fishing piers and underwater fish habitat. By mid-1975 the 3,000-foot earth dam with concrete spillway was finished and a terrific fishing lake was born. Most of the day-use facilities were constructed in 1976, with a major concession area and boat launch with boat rental facility project completed in 1995.

Information & Activities

Shabbona State Park
Route 1, P.O. Box 120
Shabbona, IL 60550
(815) 824-2106

Directions: Just south of the village of Shabbona, on Route 30 about 10 miles west of Hinckley, or 20 miles west of Aurora on Route 30. The Chief Shabbona Forest Preserve is on the east side of the lake.

Information: The camp office, up the first driveway inside the park entrance, is open Monday-Friday, 8 a.m. - 4 p.m. The park is open 6 a.m. - 7 p.m. The park office is at the southern end of the main park road near the Shabbona Grove Picnic Area.

Campground: 50 Class A sites with electricity, a dump station, and shower building with flush toilets are on the northwest side of the lake just inside the main gate. There are 100 Class B sites (showers and vehicle access only). All camping facilities are handicapped accessible. The campground is open year round, but the showers are turned off during the winter, and occasionally road conditions prohibit access in the early spring.

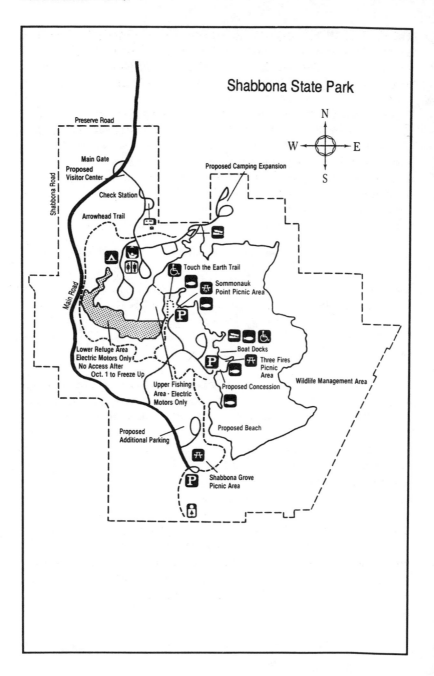

Shabbona State Park

Reservations are not accepted at Shabbona Lake and the campground does fill up on holidays and summer weekends. Weekdays campers can usually choose their own sites. There is a dump station near the camp check station on the left as you enter the shady campground. The Arrowhead hiking trail circles the area.

The first camping loop, 1-60, is called Teal Bay. The camp host is parked on site 1 and ready to help visitors with their questions and needs. Most sites are shady except for sites 55-58, which are open breezy and cool. All campsites have a picnic table and fire ring near the gravel parking pad and there is a vault toilet near site 10. The sites in this loop are suitable for small RVs or tents, although skilled big rig drivers could park in this area. Sites 21-23 are very shady and have a view of the lake, which is about 100 yards away. There are two vault toilets and drinking fountains in the Teal Bay loop.

Sites 101-150 make up Canvas Back Cove, where a small one-lane boat launch is maintained for campers and sites are slightly more spread out and shady. All pads are gravel. Sites 135-138 are less shady, but sites 134 and 135 have a partial lake view. At the end of the loop is the boat launch. Nearby are six swings and other playground equipment, and a picnic area. Site 121 has an excellent view of the lake, but little shade. Sites 111-129 also have water views and light shade. Sites 112-114 are the most popular sites in the loop. A nice bathhouse, phone and trash dumpster are in this Class A loop.

You can stay up to 14 nights in a 30-day period. Firewood gathering is restricted to downed deadwood. Alcohol is prohibited. The campground is clean and there is a fact sheet available that details rules and helpful information.

Boating: Small boats are offered for rent at the main launch and all boat traffic is restricted to motor sizes of 10 hp or less. The 18-acre upper fishing area of the lake is a strict no-wake area where only electric trolling motors or rowing are permitted. Sailboats must not exceed 14 feet. The entire lake is no wake. All boats must be off the lake by 10 p.m. and secured to the dock for the evening.

There are actually four areas designated on the lake: the main lake area is 151 acres; sailing area has 134 acres; upper fishing area, 15 acres and the refuge area 18 acres.

Fishing: There is a terrible disease that some fishermen catch—some say that's all they ever catch—and it's called "muskie fever," a passion for angling for these top-of-the-food chain predator fish that are said to be the best fighters in the fishing world. With a mouth full of teeth and raw power, muskie can slam a jerk bait and inhale a huge minnow in a heartbeat. You might not even see the hit, all you will hear is your reel whining and screaming for mercy. That's the addiction: power, quickness, and size. Forty-inch muskie are often taken at the lake. There's no cure for this disease once you've fought one of these jawed sticks of dynamite.

Because the lake was planned and built by man, plenty of fish holding structures have insured ample natural reproduction and plenty of places to flip a lure, dangle a rubber worm, or troll a crankbait. There are 46 fish cribs, six large brush piles, five earthen piers, two sets of underwater building foundations, a large rock pile, a submerged roadbed with a bridge and natural vegetation. For lake maps and expert advice, try Ken's or Big Jim's Bait (815) 824-2415 shops in the village, or consider a muskie guide. Call Roger at (815) 756-9027.

The lake can reach depths of 40 feet along the old stream channel. Hot spots include the Indian Creek area (concentrate on the creek channel); standing trees in the north end of the lake; the spillway; at submerged brush piles, trees and bridge (obtain a lake map at area bait shops); and dropoffs directly east of the boat launch.

Catch and size limits: largemouth bass: one per day, 14-inch minimum; walleye: six per day, 14-inch minimum; bluegill: 10 per day; channel catfish: six per day; crappie 10 per day. Remember to register your muskie. Reporting forms are available at the park office and at the concession.

Hiking: Nearly five miles of hiking and cross-country skiing trails meander through the park, including a self-guided opportunity. Check with the office for a map, trail conditions and developments. There are seven miles of snowmobile trails. The Arrowhead Trail, which is easy hiking, is four miles long and passes through a mixed deciduous wooded area, fields and open spaces.

Day-use areas: There is no parking on the roadway heading back into the unit, but there is great opportunity to slowly drive the route and look for wildlife or select a picnic site. A number of vistas look off toward the lake and edge areas, where you might spot a deer or other wildlife.

At the end of the park road is a day-use area with scattered picnic tables, vault toilets, grills and a lake overview. A fishing pier/shelter and plenty of shoreline fishing are available at the boat launch. Also in this open area is a redwood bench dedicated to "Big Jim" Drury, a longtime police officer, bait shop owner and supporter of the park's development. There is also a marker honoring Senator Dennis Collins, of the Illinois General Assembly for his more than 40 years of service. The park is like that— personal, appreciative and clean.

There are many picnic tables and lots of parking. The boulder-lined shoreline gives way to flat open areas that allow for a safe area that children could fish or play near.

Hard-surfaced walkways help disabled visitors access toilets, especially designed fishing pier, picnic shelters, sanitary facilities and telephone. Swimming is prohibited and pets must be under control at all times. Groups of 25 or more must register for picnic shelters; otherwise,it's first come, first served.

Nearby attractions: Woodhaven Lakes condo camping, DeKalb is 30 miles away, and Lake Michigan is within a two-hour drive.

53 Siloam Springs State Park

Land: 3,323 acres Water: Crab Apple Lake, 58 acre

Densely wooded, hilly, improved, and underused—these are terrific reasons to visit the rugged and pleasant park named after the "medicinal waters" of the springs that run strong after each rainfall. Siloam Spring State Park was originally part of the military tract of western Illinois (lands set aside to be given to combat veterans), and the area was acquired in 1852 by George Meyer for his service in the Black Hawk and Mexican wars. When he died at age 102, legend has it that the spring waters of the site offered a life-giving or prolonging medicinal effect.

Shortly after George's death, Qunicy Burgesser, a businessman and stock dealer, began marketing the "curative" waters. He touted that the spring waters could cure almost any ailment, even drunkenness and drug addition. In 1884, he erected a couple of springhouses, a bathing house and the Siloam Forest Home Hotel, which became a fashionable resort for many years. You can still see remains of the hotel and springhouses while driving through the park.

Burgesser, a super salesman, bottled water from the No. 2 spring and sold it for decades in the region, even as far off as Kansas City.

In 1935, the Siloam Springs Recreation Club purchased the site, restoring it to provide local recreation opportunities. Some years later citizens of Brown and Adams counties raised funds to match a state grant and in 1940 work began to improve the park and start it on its way to becoming a state park. In the mid-1950s an earthen dam was constructed, and the park was dedicated in 1958. Today, ongoing renovations keep the park attractive and user friendly, but not as popular as it should be.

Information and Activities

Siloam Springs State Park
R.R. 1, P.O. Box 204
Clayton, IL 62324
(217) 894-6205

Directions: South of Kellerville, six miles north of Illinois 104, 25 miles east of Quincey and 52 miles west of Jacksonville. Directional signs are poor.

Information: Open 6 a.m. - 10 p.m. daily, the park office is open weekends and is the first left upon entering the main park entrance. No swimming or wading are allowed.

Campground: Up a small hill is the Hickory Hill camping. Take the first road to your right upon entering the park at the main entrance. Recent renovations and upgrades have improved the shady 80-site, Class A area.

The 150 Class B camping sites (Pine Grove and Oak Ridge) features scattered shade, level, picnic tables and fire blocks. Some of the sites are near the lake. All campers can use the showers at Siloam Springs.

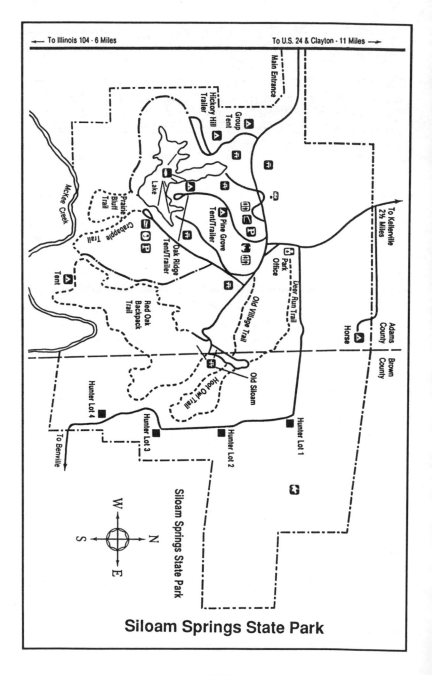

Siloam Springs State Park

The horse camp is on the Adams and Brown county line, north of the park. Horses are not allowed on the hiking trails.

Fishing: The small tree-lined lake offers 5.7 miles of shoreline and a maximum depth of 35 feet in places. The average depth is about 15 feet. The lake is occasionally stocked with largemouth bass, bluegill, redear, crappie, channel catfish and carp. Traditional fishing techniques work on the under-fished lake. Try angling from one of the six fishing piers. Kids will love the piers.

Creel limits: Largemouth bass, daily limit of six, all bass between 12-inches to 15-inches must be returned; trout (trout stamp required), five daily; catfish, five daily. Floating tub fishing is allowed with permission only.

Boating: Electric motors only are allowed. A newer two-lane launching ramp is next to the concession stand that offers rowboat rentals, food items, bait and other supplies. A dockway along the front of the concession stand is a pleasant place to watch waterfowl and watercraft cruise the lake. There is room for about 20 cars and trailers in the lot at the boat ramp.

There is also a small car-top boat launching area at the lake.

Hiking: There are about 12 miles of trails scattered about the park, with the Backpack Trail (at about three miles out you'll reach a small camping area; a permit is required to camp in the area) the longest. The Backpack Trail is four miles long and takes you on a southwesterly trail that includes slopes and creek crossing, creek views, and by a stone house, and is considered moderately difficult. The Hoot Owl Trail is north of the Backpack Trail. The Prairie Bluff trail offers a popular and easy one-mile walk for park guests after buying a cold can of pop at the nearby food stand.

The nicest trail is Crabapple Creek Trail, which wanders past tiny McKee Creek and some large boulders.

Day-use areas: You can actually stand on the Brown and Adams county line at a little suspension bridge near the large day-use area that

Deer Run trailhead.

has picnicking amenities. The little road that wanders throughout the park is a one-lane roadway that takes you through convenient day-use areas, by a number of trailheads, over bridges, and near points of interest. The pleasant mini-driving tour will give you a view of the main park area, up and down some hills, and around many little areas. From the road you can choose a trail to hike, open spaces to play in, or a picnic sites for the family outing. Ice fishing and cross-country skiing are popular activities in the winter.

There are about five reservable picnic shelters. The main shelter, a concrete block, and roofed-in area, also has a green and brown playground adjacent to it, making it a large and attractive place for family outings.

Hunting: Contact the site superintendent for details.

Nearby attractions: Griggsville, home of the purple martin towers.

54   Silver Springs State Park

**Land: 1,314 acres   Water: One mile of Fox River frontage;
Loon Lake, 16 acres; Beaver Lake, 6 acres**

Gently rolling farmlands are occasionally punctuated by broad wooden round barns and giant tube-like farm elevators that bulge with cereal grain as you drive Route 47 off of roaring Interstate 80. You'll see dairy cattle grazing and generally lounging about with full udders and dirty noses, tanned farmers atop equipment, and a quiet rural lifestyle that makes many Chicago-area dwellers envious.

As you enter the wooded park along a ridgeline, you'll soon drive down a steep grade to the shoreline of kidney-shaped Loon Lake, which is stocked with rainbow trout twice a year. A salmon stamp is required if you decide to try your luck at the tree-lined lake or along the one-mile of the gently flowing Fox River.

If not, most day-use visitors begin their adventure at the park office, a renovated farmhouse which stands in the shadow of a silo south of Loon Lake along Fox Road and has a number of native animal mounts displayed in the front room. Here park staff have maps, a self-guided nature trail brochure, hunting and fishing information and much more. They can also direct you to the park's namesake, Silver Springs, a tiny spring at the northeastern corner of the property along Fox Ridge Nature Trail. The trailhead is just north of the park office, at the East Entrance.

The shallow spring joins the river and has abundant water cress plants growing along its meandering length. Some park visitors sneak a taste of the lush little plants during the spring season when the leaves are young and succulent. The entire trail is about two miles long and worth a hike to this small, cool and pleasant area.

Information & Activities

Silver Springs State Park
13608 Fox Road
Yorkville, IL 60560
(708) 533-6297

Directions: Five miles west of Yorkville off Illinois 47, two miles south of Plano. Take Fox Road east from 47 in the city of Yorkville. The park is on the south side of the Fox River, one hour or so east of Chicago.

Information: Open year-around, the park office is on the north side of Fox Road, five miles west of Yorkville. It open Monday-Friday, 8 a.m. - 4 p.m. The park is open 7 a.m. to sunset weekdays. Plano is only two miles away and offers fast food restaurants, antique shops and other amenities.

Campground: The 13-site primitive Cedar Ridge Campground is on the west side of Fox River Road, about one mile from the canoe rental. The rustic campground requires a short walk in, there are no vehicles permitted in the area, but the walk is worth the effort. The heavily wooded

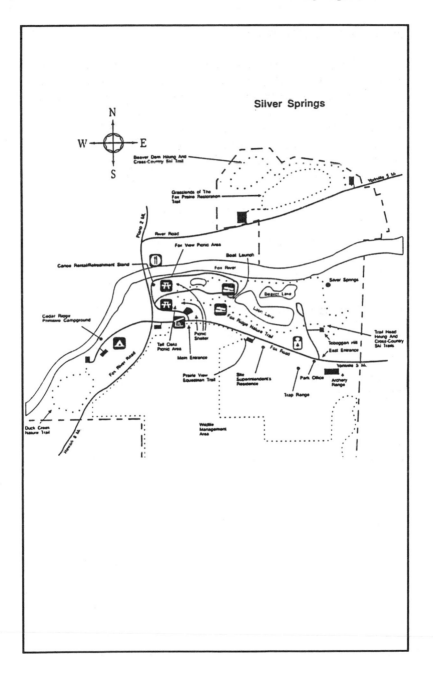

site along the Fox River usually has sites available on weekends. This is a rustic, primitive campground with no showers or electricity. Vault toilets are handicapped accessible. You can self-register, and pre-registered groups of 100-125 can be accommodated at the campground.

Boating: You can rent a canoe for a quiet paddle about Loon Lake and Beaver Lake or try the 100-yard-wide Fox River, where placid shallows and tree-lined shores can be explored from a waterway perspective. The canoe rental concession is open during the summer on weekends. There are two boat launches in the park one on Look Lake, and a one-lane launch offering access to the Fox River where you may operate unlimited horsepower boats. Late in the season water levels can be quite low in some locations along the Fox River. Gasoline motors are prohibited on the two park lakes.

Fishing: Loon Lake is stocked with rainbow twice annually and there is a five fish daily limit. A salmon stamp is required. The trout program is managed by a regional fish biologist stationed at the park. Locals use corn or mini marshmallows, small spoons, small spinners and Velveeta Cheese as bait. In the two small lakes at the park, you might catch channel catfish, small and largemouth bass, crappies and bluegills.

River fishermen can try the Fox, which can produce good walleye catches up river from the park in the spring. Tiny jigs (1/8-ounce) tipped with a minnow, fished on the bottom with a light touch, can produce good result. In the river shallows rough fish can be caught in spring, summer and fall. The Fox can also yield small and largemouth bass, northern pike, occasional musky, catfish and panfish.

There are many shoreline fishing locations along the winding asphalt road that traces around Loon Lake and along the Fox River, bass must be 15-inches to keep; six catfish daily is the limit. They ask that you do not return bluegill and crappies of five inches or less to the lake. One small pond has been stocked with grass carp. They are fun to watch as they hungrily gulp at the surface and snack on watery vegetation. There are three benches and a fire pit here for day-users.

Hiking: You can bring your horse for a scenic ride along a six-mile bridle trail that takes you along a wetland, a small rearing pond, and the old

Burlington Railroad tracks. The trail is in a wildlife management area and is open except during the hunting season.

The park also has a terrific self-guided trail that features water and its role in nature and our lives. There is a small booklet available at the park office which includes a bird list and 13 descriptions that match numbered posts along the 1.5-mile trail. The booklet has a map and details pond life, decomposing cycle, nature's engineers, Silver Springs, the Fox River, wetlands, facts about winter and much more. This is a well prepared and researched self-guided trail and booklet. More parks should have this feature.

Duck Creek Trail near the campground, with Beaver Dam Hiking and Cross-Country Skiing Trail on the north side of the river near the region which is being managed as a prairie restoration area that also has a short trail with access from River Road.

There are many scenic areas along the Fox River and throughout the park that have picnic tables, charcoal grills, water and vault toilets. The rolling terrain, mature trees overhead and privacy make Silver Springs a good day-use park that is near metro Chicago. Urban children will have fun at this rural park, especially if parents spend some time talking about rural life, the importance of farming and man's role in the natural world. Groups of 25 or more must register to use the picnic shelters. No swimming is allowed at the park.

One of the nicest day-use areas is at Loon Lake. A picnic site with a handicapped accessible toilet is near the trailhead to Silver Springs. There are three picnic shelters in the park, horseshoe pits, small timber-type playground equipment and 13 vault toilets.

Hunting: The park staff believes that its best feature and biggest attraction is good hunting and proximity to Chicago. There is an archery deer hunt, good upland game opportunities, turkey, duck and goose, a trap range, dog training site, and dove hunting. Contact the park for additional details on seasons, rules and regulations.

Winter: Cross-country skiing, a sledding hill, ice skating and a four-mile snowmobile trail are offered.

55   South Shore State Park

Water: Lake Carlyle

Situated along the shore of Lake Carlyle, near the Saddle Dam, just east of the city of Carlyle, is the underdeveloped South Shore State Park, a sister park to the beautiful Hazlet State Park on the west shore of the lake.

South Shore is primarily a day-use park, offering several picnicking places like the Blue Bell Picnic Area, Pine Grove Picnic Area, Lakeshore Picnic Area and the Crappie and Cove Picnic Area, where shoreline anglers or day-users can spend a leisurely day along the busy lake.

South Shore State Park
c/o Hazlet State Park
Carlyle, Ill 62231
(618) 594-3015

Directions: North of Huey off Route 50, east of Carlyle, the park is virtually an extension of Hazlet State Park and is under the same management.

Campground: Hickory Hollow is a Class D campground at the north end of the park. It offers sparse gravel pads and shady, little used camping sites. Sites 2, 5, 7, 9, 10, 11, 12 and 13 all have lake views and are dry and shady. Site 11 has the best view, while site 12 is large. Sites 19-23 are shady and somewhat private. All of the camping sites have picnic tables and fire pits, with vault toilets.

Boating: The four-lane launch is lightly used, but the parking lot is huge. A small picnic shelter is near the boat launch.

Additional information about fishing and boating, lake conditions and more is detailed in the Hazlet State Park section.

56 Spitler Woods State NaturalArea

Land: 202 acres Water: Squirrel Creek

There are few natural areas or parks in the state that can claim they are almost exactly the way they were 200 years ago. Few natural areas escaped the lumberman's ax or the farmer's plow. Fewer yet have historically prohibited hunting, and even fewer have been preserved for nature study and passive use.

Spitler Woods, eight miles southeast of Decatur and a half mile east of Mt. Zion off Route 121, was named for Ida B. Spitler, who donated much of the land to the state in 1937 for the purpose of preserving for posterity this lush area of shaded ravines and towering trees, while allowing some active day-use areas adjacent to the preserve.

Information and Activities

Spitler Woods State Natural Area
705 Spitler Park Drive
Mt. Zion, IL 62549
(217) 864-3121

Spitler Woods is a nature preserve with about a 35-acre day-use area on the northwest side of the property. The day-use area is mowed and has many picnic areas convenient to parking lots. These areas are equipped with tables and fire blocks, nearby toilets, drinking water and various game courts that include horseshoe pits, volleyball and playground apparatus for youngsters. Limited group camping is by registration only.

Broad expanses of east central Illinois were once densely covered with deciduous forests. When the area that comprises Spitler Woods was originally surveyed in April 1821, it was described as "gently rolling woods composed mainly of oak, hickory, walnut and maple trees." The understory was abundant with many wildflower species that include violets, jack-in-the-pulpit, dutchman's breeches, Solomon's seal, blue bells and wood anemone. Thick groves of sassafras trees offered a crisp herbal tea used by settlers in the area.

Ida Spitler was one of the original nature preservationists, loving the rolling forest enough to protect the site from the farming and lumbering that destroyed surrounding lands for many miles. Consequently, the woods retained lots of varieties of trees and shrubs native to central Illinois and has continued to be an excellent area to observe wildlife and undisturbed flora. This entire area is now a dedicated nature area containing a terrific, and rare, stand of climax timber growths in the entire state. Because of the value of this truly natural area, visitors should exercise extra care along the two trails. Do not pick anything, stay on the trails, and nothing should be removed from the site.

The Red Oak Trail (half a mile) is designed to be handicapped accessible and makes a loop that includes an area sometimes called the Ramble Trail. Squirrel Creek Trail (two miles) is a moderately difficult trail with a few steep grades. An exercise trail is also maintained at the park.

57 Starved Rock State Park

Land: 2,462 acres   Water: 4 miles on the Illinois River

Your visit to Starved Rock State Park should begin a couple of miles east of the park at the terrific Illinois Waterway Visitor Center, operated by the U.S. Corps of Engineers. Not only can you watch the operation of the lock and dam, learn more about the history of the Illinois Waterway at close range, you can see the 125-foot sandstone butte, Starved Rock, the huge outcropping that the park is named after.

The Waterway Visitor Center is open seven days a week and features an indoor and outdoor observation area, hands-on exhibits, a slide show, and main exhibit area and auditorium that is accessible to the disabled. The center also helps to interpret the history of the waterway, especially as it relates to the Heritage Corridor. My favorite exhibit at the visitor center is an actual pilothouse from the towboat John M. Warner, which sank in the 1980s and is restored and open for your imagination. You can step inside, grip the wheel, move some controls, and pretend you're the ship's captain. Well, at least, that's what I did. Toot. Toot.

The Illinois River cuts deeply through gently rolling farmlands, following a course that was largely carved by glacial melt that eroded the land and left deep canyons and scenic bluffs. In geological terms, the Starved Rock region is young, only 10,000-14,000 years old. From 60-foot waterfalls and rock ledge overhangs to the gentle flow of the Illinois River, the area is both rugged and tame, developed and wild.

But not as wild as it once was.

The name Starved Rock comes from the legend that the Illini tribe was forced to take refuge on a high rock overlooking the river. The enemy Potawatomi tribe had only to surround the towering rock until the defenders eventually starved to death. Today it's hard to starve to death in the area. I personally fought off starvation at the lodge's dining room and then later at the concession stand—it was a tough battle.

Information and Activities

Starved Rock State Park
P. O. Box 116
Utica, IL 61373
(815) 667-4726

Directions: South bank of the Illinois River, from I-80 take Route 178 south to the entrance. The park is about six miles east of LaSalle Matthiessen and Buffalo Rock state parks.

Information: The park has a 15-minute taped information system that can be reached by calling the above telephone number. The best place for park information is the new visitor center, which is generally open weekends May-October. The 7,000-square-foot center features interpretive displays, sales counter, park information and skilled staff. The park office is also open 8 a.m. - 4 p.m. on weekdays.

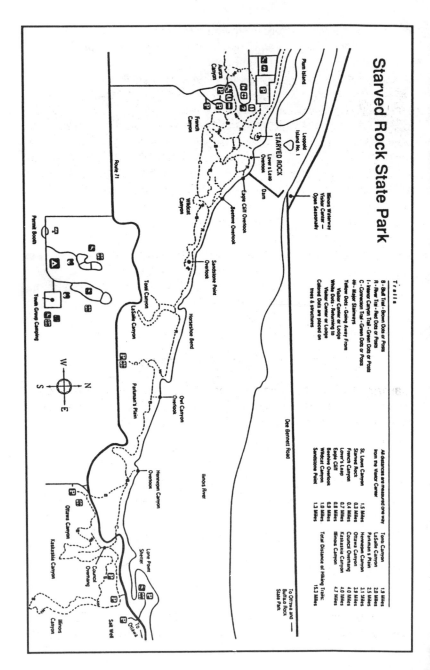

Starved Rock State Park

View of Starved Rock from I & M Canal Interpretive Center.

Campground: The campground is south of the main park off of Route 71, about two miles from the lodge. It consists of two main loops and a youth group camping area and is nestled into the rolling lightly wooded terrain.

More than one million visitors annually come to Starved Rock State Park. Many camp in the popular campground. The campground is full on all summer weekends, and reservations are taken by mail for sites 59-133 in the east loop. There are total of 133 Class A sites with water, electricity and showers. Permits may be obtained at the park or camp office.

Watch for the jumbo speed bumps and remember that quiet hours are 10 p.m. to 7 a.m.

Sites 59-65 are large and open for big rigs; 66-68 and 129-133 can also accommodate large motorhomes or trailers. Site 69-97 are shady with picnic table and grill, and close to newer drinking fountains and other upgraded campground amenities.

In the no reservation sites, most pads are gravel, and open. All sites have electrical hooks and picnic tables. The best sites in this fairly open area are 32-35, which have shade and are near vault toilets.

Emergency numbers: state police (815) 224-1150; park office 667-4726; fire 667-4221. A telephone is at the camp office. Get your camping permit at the booth that is open 4 p.m.-10 p.m. Friday-Saturday; park office weekends 9 a.m.- 4 p.m.; and at campsites weekdays 5 p.m. -10 p.m. Firewood is available from vendors outside the park. The gates are locked at 11 p.m. One tent is allowed per site.

The reservation loop, sites 59-133 is much preferred with more shade and privacy. Both loops have showers and flush toilets near the entrances, and there are three set of vault toilets in each area, as well as dump stations and garbage drops.

Lodge and Conference Center: There is still strong flavor of the rugged but pleasing design elements that mark the projects constructed by the Civilian Conservation Corps in the 1930s. From the huge timbers and cedar shingles to the lofty rock fireplace, the lodge is refurbished, elegant, warm and peaceful.

A new lobby links the indoor pools, children's pool, whirlpool, saunas and outdoor patio with the restaurant.

The lodge has 72 luxury hotel rooms, nine newly renovated pioneer cabins, and two deluxe cabins that are near the pool.

The log and rock lodge still has the original Great Room that is tastefully furnished with decorative rugs and art that frames the massive stone fireplace that occupies the center of the large room. The restaurant is open sevens days a week and can accommodate group banquets of 250 people. The lodge is heavily used for conferences and has many break-out meeting rooms, complete A/V equipment and hospitable service. Meetings don't seem like meetings here! For more information about the lodge, call (815) 667-4211 or write.

The gift shop is open 10 a.m. - 5 p.m. The lodge also features two hospitality rooms, two outdoor pavilions, the Back Door Lounge, satellite TV, handicapped accessible rooms and facilities, and meeting planning services. There is an ATM at the lodge.

Boating: There are five lanes at the main boat launch at the west end of the park with direct access to the Illinois River, near Plum Island. An additional launch is proposed for future development. Boats are not allowed within 600 feet of the dam and at no time should you wade or swim. There are especially strong undertows in portions of the river. Canoes can be rented at the launch from Memorial Day to Labor Day.

Fishing: Shoreline anglers have miles of opportunity along the Illinois River. Rough fish are the typical catch. In the spring walleyes can are taken near the dam, while white bass, sauger, crappies and rough fish are taken during the rest of the year. The overall water quality and ultimately fishing are dramatically improving in the Illinois River. There are guiding services and four bait shops in nearby communities.

Hiking: The 15 miles of moderate to difficult hiking trails along the towering bluffs and rocky canyons of Starved Rock State Park are well-marked and open year-round. Due to the sometimes difficult terrain of the trails, extreme caution is advised. Hikers must be off the trails by dark.

Metal maps are located at all trail access points, intersections and points of interest to keep you oriented. There are colored dots along the trail that correspond to colors on the maps, and letter symbols on the trail brochure to further assist you. Yellow dots indicate that you are walking away from the lodge or visitor centers, while white dots indicate you are returning. Maps and trail information are available at the visitor center and the park office.

St. Louis Canyon: The waterfall at the head of St. Louis Canyon (1.5 miles) is more than 60 feet high and in the winter is a spectacular icefall. This is a "box canyon," having only one way in and out. This canyon has one level that has been cut out by the water through a weak area in the rock, called a fault.

La Salle and Tonti canyons: Along the trails that wander through these

The lodge and environs are some of the finest in the state.

canyons are the same flora and fauna that early settlers saw as they explored the area. La Salle (1.5 miles) is the larger of the two canyons and is east of Tonti (1.9 miles), which meanders off to the west and is a single-level canyon like St. Louis. The multi-level of La Salle reflects the different types of erosion that is occurring.

The Illinois, Sac and Kaskaskia are also multi-level canyons. The often slippery trail at the bottom of the Tonti canyon flood runs along a streambed and can floor after rains. This trail system is lightly used and away from the more heavily used portions of the park, which makes it a better location to observe wildlife or take a solitary hike. Rock climbing and repelling are prohibited.

Other trails include: Starved Rock (.3 mile), French Canyon (.4 mile), Lover's Leap (.7 mile), Beehive Overlook (.9 mile), Wildcat Canyon (1 mile), Sandstone Point (1.3 mile), Parkmans Plain (2.5 miles), Hennepin Canyon (3.1 miles), Ottawa Canyon (3.9 miles), Council Overhang (4 miles), Kaskaskia Canyon 4 miles) and Illinois Canyon (4.7 miles).

There are also many less demanding trails along the river that offer excellent scenic vistas.

Day-use areas: Many developed picnicking areas are available with tables, vault toilets and drinking water. The visitor center, which is a wonderful facility with interpretive displays, historical information and other learning opportunities, features plenty of information about the day-use areas, trail system, camping, open spaces and so on. There is no beach; swimming and wading are prohibited.

Horse rental: West on I-71, on weekends during the spring and summer, (815) 667-3026. There are 11 miles of bridle trails and an equestrian campground along Route 71 in the far western portion of the park.

Nature: From rolling fertile farmlands to waterfalls or icefalls, rivers and streams, sandstone overhangs, box canyons, wondrous wildflowers and bluffs, Starved Rock has a complex, fragile and marvelous set of ecosystems to explore.

210 species of birds have been identified in the area during the past 20 years and there is a birding checklist available at the visitor centers. Birders or wildlife enthusiasts will revel in the 15 miles of diverse trails that pass by wetlands, near 18 canyons, along vertical walls, near open fields, along the popular River Trail, or atop sandy bluffs. About 175 wildflowers have been identified on the site. There is a wildflower list that details blossoming seasons. Photographers should talk with staff about low impact practices. There is also a tree locator map/educational brochure available. The map details trees near the lodge.

There is some type of naturalist programming just about daily; check with the visitor center for details on hikes and interpretive programs.

Hunting: There are two public hunting areas. For waterfowl and doves in sunflowers during special seasons. Call ahead for details.

Special events: Winter Wilderness Weekend, Cross-County Ski Weekends, Fall Color Weekend, Montreal Canoe Weekend, guided hike from the visitor center twice daily on weekends.

Nearby attractions: La Salle Historical Society Museum, Wild Bill Hickok State Memorial and Peru Mall.

58 Stephen A. Forbes State Park

Land: 3,099 acres   Water: 585-acre lake

Stephen Forbes State Park is a getaway park, not fancy, not high-energy, not a busy destination park, but a rolling grove with a very good campground, very good fishing, great quarter-pound hot dogs, and shady peaceful walking trails and quiet roadways that connect pleasant day-use areas.

Campers even seem to walk quietly at the park as they watch the activities at the shoreline, boat ramp, fishermen's creels, softball and volleyball areas, and the Rocky Point swimming beach, which is fenced in, but not lifeguarded. Fishing from the shore is encouraged, and so are sitting under a tree in the summer sun and sometimes eating too much at the picnic tables.

The park was originally only 20 acres with a tiny two-acre pond. Today the large park has more than 3000 acres, with 1,150 acres in forests of oak and hickory which surround the calm waters of the main lake. The lake was completed in 1963 and name for famed biologist Stephen Alfred Forbes, who was world renowned and author of more than 400 scientific publications which are still used extensively in the study of aquatic biology, ornithology, ichthyology and ecology.

Information and Activities

Steven A. Forbes State Park
6924 Omega Road
Kinmundy, IL 62854
(618) 547-3381

Information: Office hours are 7:30 a.m. - 3:30 p.m. weekdays; the park closes at 10 p.m.

Directions: In Marion County, the park is 15 miles northeast of Salem. From Route 50 take Omega Road north to the park entrance. From I-57, take exit 127 and go east through Kinmundy for five miles to the park entrance. The park office is the first road to the left once inside the park gate.

Campground: Over a wooden plank bridge you'll hear your RV clanking as you approach the Oakridge Campground that offers travelers and vacationers a respite from the hectic world on 113 Class A sites, 10 walk-in tent camping sites, and several non-electric sites in the main camping area. There are two rent-a-camps that are reservable and offer novice campers a chance to camp overnight without buying lots of expensive equipment. The shower building has parking for three cars, and all of the Class A sites have gravel pads, picnic tables and fire grills.

Unlike many state campgrounds, Forbes' sites are well-spaced, often buffered by vegetation. In some cases there are 30 yards between camping sites. The 95 percent shady campground offers a chance to pull your boat up near your camping site, making this park's camping facilities popular with serious fishermen from throughout the region.

Forbes' camping area has a few pull-through sites. Sites with a water view include 24, 25, 26, 27 and 28. The most popular camping sites are 81-84 and 113-116 due to their proximity to the boat dock. Other fine camping sites include 114 and 115 at the end of a loop; they are good for two families to claim for a weekend. Sites 82-84 are smaller, but very private and near a stairway down to the lakeshore, where some campers park their boat. 68 and 69 join each other. Handicapped sites are 59 and 61. Sites 35-38 are great for big RV rigs. At site 27 there is a pathway that connects campers to the concession stand.

There is a boat pull-up area at site 27. The campground is open year-round, but the showers are closed in late fall.

Fishing: The tree-lined lake has about 18 miles of shoreline and contains a few good-sized muskie, while the tiny Boston Pond has some trout in its waters. The main lake also has a good to very good fishery for channel catfish and bluegill. Some largemouth, striped bass, and crappies are also taken. There are slot limits; check with the park office regarding fishing regulations on the lake. A handicapped fishing pier is near the boat ramp on the main lake.

Local anglers favor small orange or yellow lead-headed jigs tipped with minnows for crappies, while channel cats respond to liver baits on the bottom.

The concession stand has fishing equipment, gasoline, and bait, rowboat rentals and food.

The Natural History Survey Experimental Fish Lab operates on the lake. Office hours vary.

Boating: Boating is popular on the lake with many pontoon boats docking at the overnight and seasonal moorings near the main launching ramp. There is no horsepower limit on the lake, but there are a number of "no wake" zones.

Hiking: The 2.7-mile Oakridge Trailhead is at the campground near the shower house on the north end of the lake and offers moderately difficult travel as you meander along the hilly lakeshore. It will take about an hour

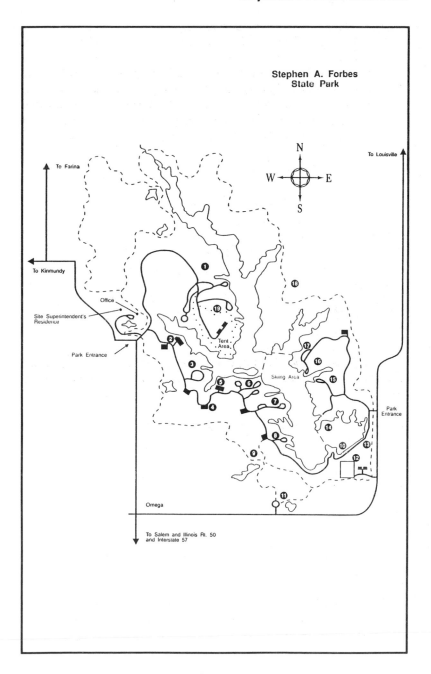

Stephen A. Forbes
State Park

to hike the pathway that offers some nice views of the lake, docks, fishermen in boats, and day-use areas. There are some benches along the trail.

Three small trails are maintained by the unit: Marlow Pond (.5 mile) travels along a stream and crosses a small bridge; Henneman Trail (.3 mile) takes walkers by an 1800s cemetery; Phillips Creek Trail is on the east side of the park and offers access to the lake.

Bridle trails: The 24-site Forbes Equestrian Camp off of Brubaker Road, one mile east of Omega, connects riders to more than 15 miles of horse trails that circle the lake, offering panorama views and flatland travel. Hardy hikers are also welcome to use the long trail.

Day-use areas: The park's beach is about 60 yards wide with picnic tables, a boat dock and fencing. There is a small fee to visit the beach, which is open Memorial Day - Labor Day.

The park is very popular with day-users who enjoy the many lake-view shady turnouts. Choose from Lookout Point, Stage Coach Trail, Black Oak, Sassafras, White Oak Whippoorwill or Circle Drive day-use areas near the lake. Circle Drive has game fields, picnic tables and vault toilets. Many of the picnic shelters can be reserved in advance; call the office for details and costs.

Hunting: Turkey and deer; call the site superintendent for details on regulations and seasons. The campground host has fed up to 39 wild turkeys at a time and spots deer in the park daily!

59 William G. Stratton State Park

c/o Gebhard Woods
Morris, IL
(815) 942-0796

The park is open 7:30 a.m. to 10 p.m. daily. Swimming and wading are prohibited. The is an urban state park in Morris, under the I-47 iron bridge. There are no camping or hiking trails at the park.

Between the Illinois River and the I & M Canal, Stratton State Park is a tiny, but busy, day-use park that is known for Jet Skiing, pleasure boating, water skiing, and fishing. The river is 200 yards wide along this section, typically flat, and heavily used by boaters and springtime anglers.

Stratton is the only state park with a designated personal watercraft (Jet

Ski) launching ramp. The tiny craft frolic in the river, shooting a rooster-tail toward the sky on just about any summer day. Virtually all ages have embraced the revving motorcycles of the water, zooming about in every direction, doing stunts, small jumps, and looking like they are part of a beer commercial. They are increasing in popularity. There are several Jet Ski (personal watercraft) supply stores in the area.

For the more traditional recreational boaters, there are four concrete ramps under a huge iron bridge with at least 150 parking spaces nearby. The ramps are busy on the weekends, but boaters seem to get in and out quickly, due to the large amount of room to park and staging lanes in front of the ramp. A convenient wooden floating dock is next to the ramp for temporary mooring while you launch and retrieve your boat.

Riverside benches offer a great—and sometimes shady—view of boat traffic, while picnic tables, a small concession stand and toilets provide for a nice, not always quiet site for a picnic.

The I & M Canal trail travels through the park. Fishermen also come to the area, primarily in the spring and fall for fishing in the Illinois River.

Local anglers often launch at Stratton and head north to the confluence of the Illinois River, where the Des Plaines and Kankakee rivers join near Dresden Island Dam. A variety of habitat, including side channels, small islands and slough, offer fair to good large- and smallmouth bass action.

Largemouth are most often taken from the main channel border near weed cover, brush, stumps, willows and fallen trees. Spinners tipped with minnows, jigs and plastic worms of bright color are often used by local experts. Once the water temperature reaches 75 degrees, the action slows for both large- and smallmouth. During the summer, try early morning and evening near the dam and along points with deep water dropoffs.

Walleye catches are increasing in this section of the Illinois River. Most anglers drift fish, using jigs and minnows on the bottom, near structures. Spring trolling can also produce good walleye catches. Catfish are also taken in the area using typical stink baits. Try fishing the nearby canal also. It's especially good for small rough fish and youth fishing from the shoreline.

60   *Volo Bog State Park*

Land: 870 acres   Bog: 47.5 acres

Volo Bog is the only quaking bog in Illinois that exhibits all stages of zonal plant succession (many different types of plants), including an open water center.

Raised or quaking bogs such as Volo are common in northern Midwest, but very rare as far south as Illinois. Most bogs form in poorly drained basins where glacial lakes gradually became covered by a floating mat of vegetation and usually develop acidic soils. Volo Bog consists of two kettle-holes occupying approximately 50 acres. The deeper kettle was approximately 50 feet deep and still has open water in the center, but the small kettle has filled in with decomposing plant material and peat.

The original lake at Volo was poorly drained with steep banks and open water in the center of the bowl-shaped basin that trapped falling leaves and other debris. Today, a terrific narrow boardwalk takes visitors across the bog, through many plant communities, to the center of open water, then back to the barn-like visitor center.

One interesting fact is that the half-mile interpretive boardwalk has actually sunk three times over the years due to the nature of the wetland, fluctuating water levels and peat soils. Even today, when you walk the trail, you'll notice that your weight will cause the ground to sway and the wooden trail surface to push down below the water level in some spots.

Prior to the construction of the more permanent wooden trail system, visitors often brought their own boards and laid them end to end as they walked or just jumped from hummock to hummock.

The bog was first documented by W. G. Waterman of Northwestern Illinois University in 1921. In 1958, backed by a $40,000 donation, the Illinois Chapter of the Nature Conservancy purchased the natural area. By the mid-1960s land development threatened the bog and a "Save the Bog" campaign was formed by local residents, which led to dedication as an Illinois nature preserve.

The preserve is a sanctuary for native vegetation and wildlife, and is maintained in its natural conditions so that future generations can see the Illinois landscape as it appeared to the pioneers.

This living example of our natural heritage is also valuable for scientific study in ecology, geology, soil science and nature history. It provides habitat for rare plants and animals.

Visitors are clearly welcome, but please help perpetuate the area by not disturbing or removing anything. All natural features are protected by law.

Additional acreage has been purchased, wonderful boardwalks installed, and an excellent learning center offers a variety of natural history programs.

Volo Bog was dedicated as an Illinois nature preserve in 1970.

Volo Bog Interpretive Trail.

Information and Activities

Volo Bog State Park
28478 W. Brandenburg Road
Indleside, IL 60041
(815) 344-1294

Directions: 90 minutes northwest of Chicago, in Lake County.

Information: The visitor center, a converted barn with a towering silo, is open Sunday - Thursday, 9 a.m. - 3 p.m. The park is open 8 a.m. - 8 p.m. daily. The interpretive center offers a variety of quality environmental education programming year-round; reservations are required for many programs. The Tamarack Gift Shop is operated in the visitor center.

Friends of the Volo Bog, a support group, can be reached at (815) 344-1294, or request a membership form by writing The Friends of the Volo Bog, 28478 W. Brandenburg Road, Ingleside, IL 60041.

Campground: none.

Boating: none.

Fishing: none.

Hiking: Bog interpretive tours are offered on Saturdays and Sundays at 11 a.m. and 1 p.m.

The three-mile Tamarack View Trail, next to the trailhead for the Volo Bog Interpretive Trail, is designed for hiking and skiing (six-inch base required) and tracks through mixed wooded areas, varied wetlands, fields and prairies, and along some of the higher elevations in the park. The trail offers a good view of the bog.

The half-mile Volo Bog Interpretive Trail is one of the most interesting and finest interpretive trails in the state park system. It has a narrow wooden boardwalk that features and clearly explains the natural history of bogs and the plant succession process that forms them.

Pick up a brochure that has clear explanations of 14 marked stations along the winding bog trail. You'll learn about the giant hunk of ice that fell off the glacier 15,000 years ago to form the little lake that is now transforming into a bog.

As you begin your walk and enter the marsh/sedge meadow, it's fun to remember that you are walking where a lake existed about 1,000 years ago. Although the ground appears dry, it is really quite the opposite. The type of plants in this zone (willow, jewelweed, wild cucumber, nightshade, and others) actually require lots of moisture, but cannot tolerate as much water as marsh plants.

You will learn about and pass by highly acidic areas, where only certain types of plants survive, called marsh moats. From the "trembling leaves" of aspen to shrubs and the tamarack evergreen that loses it leaves, the bog is a wonderful place. Visitors to the bog will learn about the natural death of a lake and birth of a forest, water cycles and the filtration factor of wetlands, birds (there's a birding list on the self-guided brochure) and lots of information about wildflowers, even edible ones. The hike will take an hour, or, like me, you might end up spending more than two hours along the terrific floating boardwalk examining the bog and its unique communities of plants, insects and animals.

Nature: Each season brings its own beauty to Volo Bog, and seasonal visits allows nature lovers a chance to see the bog and its wide variety of flora and fauna as they change.

In the spring, fern fiddleheads reveal their beautiful fronds and bog buckbean and leatherleaf bloom. Wading birds, passing waterfowl and migratory songbirds stop by for a visit. Summer at the bog brings orchids, and delicate pine and rose pogonia, sandhill cranes staking the wetlands, and many mammals busy raising young. Fall, the golden time, is painted in tones of yellows and crimson with the gold needles of tamarack trees and the deep red leaves of sumac contrasted by deep green sphagnum moss. Winter is the time to track animals, identify trees, ski and look for crossbills as they crack open the tamarack cones and visit the wildlife viewing station.

Visitor center: I saw no information about the converted barn which

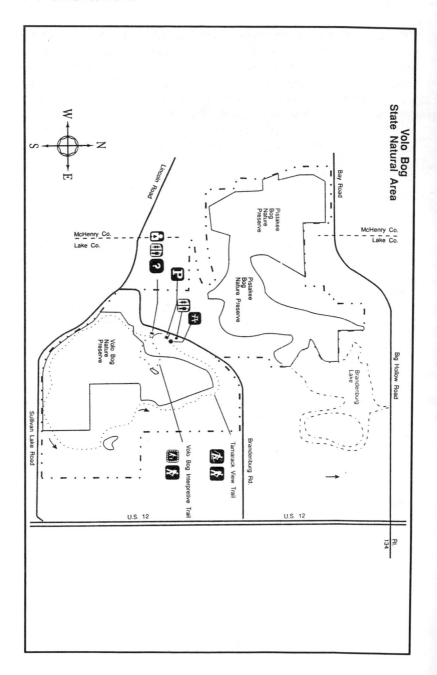

is now a wonderful interpretive center, but I did learn plenty about the area's intriguing natural history. The huge barn has two main levels and is filled with interpretive displays and information. The center has displays about the native plants, a water logged world display, bats, live animal displays, observation honeybee hive, spotting scopes, touch table with skulls and pieces of natural materials, many brochures and educational fact sheets, wetlands plants of the bog, ferns of the bog, information about cinnamon fern, royal fern, marsh fern and sensitivity fern, and the geological history of the area and the state.

Upstairs in the visitor center is a fine diorama that depicts the wetlands and exhibits various animal mounts and plant species. Examples include a great blue heron, arrowhead, red-winged blackbird, sensitivity fern, pitcher plant, greenback heron, belted kingfisher, kestrel hawk and much more. The display was a donation of the Northrop Corp. There are also a reference library and computers in the part of the building with rough saw lumber wall paneling.

Maybe the most interesting fact to read about is the well-preserved corpse that was found in peat by construction crews when they were building the docking trail to the lake.

Day-use areas: Illuminated by solar-powered lights (funded by the Illinois Department of Energy), the gravel parking lot is adjacent to a small day-use area that is defined by a split-rail fence and offers a number of picnic tables, trash barrels and toilets. There are no cooking grills at the day-use area.

61 Wayne Fitzgerrell State Park

Land: 3,300 acres   Water: Rend Lake, 19,000 acres

You can tune your AM radio to 530 and receive information about the entire Rend Lake area—or you can just drive around, and at every turn discover new places to explore. From the radio you'll learn about what's going on in the 21,000 acres of public lands that cradle the huge lake. From golf to fishing, boating and swimming to the terrific, modern Rend Lake Resort, campers and visitors will find shopping, hunting, day-use areas, bait shops, restaurants, a dam, huge marina, boat rentals, beach, stable, game courts, trap range and lots more in the high-energy area.

Wayne Fitzgerrell State Park is part of all this action, and a focal point where campers, resort guests, anglers and all types of visitors can enjoy or, use as a starting point, for trips into the surrounding recreation areas.

You can start your visit to the area at the Rend Lake Visitor Center or the state park office; both have lots of information on the wide variety of facilities and attractions in the region.

One of the things that is most impressive about the park is its clear, clean and professional signage directing visitors to the many amenities of the park. The level of maintenance is also excellent for such a large and highly used park. Visitors will find three shower houses, equestrian trails, smooth roadways, and tightly clipped grass in the public areas. It's easy to see why this is a destination campground for Airstream and other RV clubs with its upgraded electrical system, wide access roads and modern facilities.

Fitzgerrell State Park is home to southern Illinois' biggest outdoor playground, a paradise for all types of outdoor enthusiasts. Each year it seems more and more activities are added to the area's menu of things to do and see.

Visitors can watch nationally known field trials for dogs, sleek sailboats, a Boatel (a marina motel), excellent dining at the resort named Windows, swimming pool at the resort, hiking, skiing, sport fishing, open spaces and much more. The park and its environs has it all for the outdoor lover.

Information and Activities

Wayne Fitzgerrell State Park/Rend Lake
R.R. 1 P.O. Box 73
Whittington, IL 62897
(618) 629-2320

Information: Office hours are weekdays, 7:30 a.m. - 3:00 p.m.; staff on the weekends works in the park and on security patrol.

Directions: In Franklin/Jefferson counties, six miles north of Benton, on Illinois Route 154. It's a 1.5-hour drive from St. Louis and six hours from Chicago via I-57.

Campground: Wayne Fitzgerrell State Park operates 250 Class A and 40 primitive camping sites. There are no pull-through sites, and each of the camping areas is located on five peninsulas with three shower houses in the Class A areas. The recently updated Class A areas are modern, clean and updated. Sites at the points of the peninsulas are heavily used and very nice places to spend a few days. The campground is filled on all holiday weekends, although there are usually many fine sites on other summer weekends.

The campground is open year-round, but the shower buildings are closed during the winter. Campers with big rigs can request 50 amp sites; no reservations are accepted. The U.S. Army Corps of Engineers operated Gun Creek Recreation Area takes camping reservation at (618) 629-2338. The Rend Lake Management Office/Corps of Engineers, (618) 724-2493.

This is one of the best modern campgrounds in the state park system. Sites are well separated and usually shady; they have packed gravel pads, updated electricity outlets and often room to park your boat right at the camping site. There are more water view sites in this park than any other state park.

Here are some of the most used and best camping sites in the first loop: In loop 1-31 there is only light shade, with sites 8 and 9 being the exceptions. Sites 15 and 16 are at the end of the loop, near the water and shady.

At the end of loop 32-62 (Hickman's Point) there is a little one-lane boat ramp, and across the way is a view of the resort and lodge complex. Campers in this area will enjoy a great view, busy swallows that dip and dive and dart for insects, and shady and breezy camping sites. The best sites in this loop are 36, 42, 44 (great water view), 45, 47 (near restrooms) and 58. There is a hard-surfaced handicapped accessible site in this loop.

In the Lakeview loop, sites 63-107, you'll find slightly wider lots, open, and all sites back up against a wood line. The best sites in this loop are: 74-85 have a great view of the lake, 85 is very shady, 77-82 are on the point next to the lake and site 79 is at the tip of the point and breezy.

In loop 108 -173, a ball field and modern play equipment greet you near

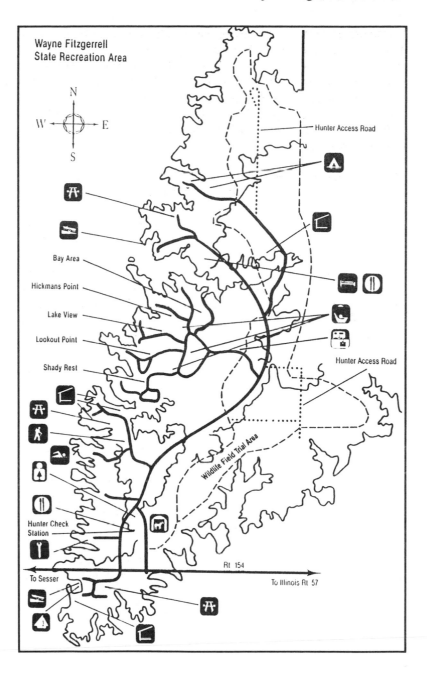

Wayne Fitzgerrell
State Recreation Area

N
W — E
S

Hunter Access Road

Bay Area

Hickmans Point

Lake View

Lookout Point

Shady Rest

Hunter Access Road

Wildlife Field Trial Area

Hunter Check
Station

Rt 154

To Sesser

To Illinois Rt 57

the entrance. One-foot diameter trees offer light shading and the sites are a bit smaller than the Lakeview Loop. Site 165 is very nice, while 114 and 121-130 are on the point with a wonderful view and access to the lake. The nicest site in the loop is 128. 132 is very private. 126 is at the point of the peninsula with almost no shade.

At the Shadyrest loop, sites 174-250, there is a shower house nearby, two handicapped sites, and large site for big RVs. The campground host at this loop is at site 179. Site 181 is hady and tree covered, as are 188-212. Sites 202-204 are probably the best sites in this loop; many maple and ash trees provide a great canopy of shade. If you like more open sites, try 213-230.

The primitive camping area is at the north end of the park. The access road bisects open managed spaces and follows a lush farm field, getting slightly narrower as you draw closer to the tent camping area. The horseshoe-shaped primitive camping area is also on its own peninsula offering shade, picnic tables, fire grills and shoreline access. Tent sites are designated, but there's plenty of room for about 40 tents spread out under the canopy of trees and along the lake's edge. You can pick your own site; most areas are dry and level.

Emergency numbers: Franklin County sheriff, (618) 438-4841; Jefferson County sheriff, 242-2141; state police, 542-2171; ambulance and fire, 724-2432.

Resort: Rend Lake Resort offers first-class waterside rooms, a swimming pool, tennis court, gift shop, Boatel (marina motel), fine dining at the Windows Restaurant with outside seating and banquet facilities, 27 holes of golf only 10 minutes away, handicapped accessible rooms, fireplaces in some rooms, courtesy docks, pontoon and paddle boat rentals, outdoor balconies, panoramic views and the finest staff anywhere.

Warm and friendly, John Reilly's staff offers excellent hospitality and expert service for groups, conferences and family guests in the modern resort. From fishing boat rental to fishing, upland and waterfowl hunting and golf packages, the resort can customize all types of recreational programs. Kids will love the elevated cabins and swimming pool.

Windows Restaurant.

Repeat customers, delighted with the resort, keep it booked solid most of the year. You must call well in advance—it's well worth the planning and time—at (800) 633-3341.

Boating: Recreational boating and Jet Skis are big at the lake. The park offers five two-lane concrete ramps, and one single-lane ramp at the campground. There are about 25 launching ramps around the perimeter of the lake and there is no horsepower limit on the lake waters. Rend Lake Resort rents boats. The Rend Lake Marina at (618) 724-7651 also rents boats and offers complete marina supplies.

Fishing: An Army Corps of Engineers project, Rend Lake, the second largest inland impoundment in the state, was filled with water from the Big Muddy River in 1971 and today features beaches, pleasure boating, sailing, and, of course, very good fishing. The lake was formed by constructing a two-mile compacted earth dam across the river about three miles northwest of Benton. The lake's water level is controlled by a 435-foot concrete spillway. The lake provides water, flood protection, downstream water quality and recreation.

Serious anglers should obtain a copy of the Rend Lake Fishing Guide, a 24-page booklet produced by the Illinois Department of Conservations,

Division of Fish and Wildlife Resources that has detailed maps, information on access points, fish species, natural history, and other related information.

The booklet even has a section named "You and Your Fishing Trip" that details solid information on trip planning, practice sessions, fishing tips, warnings about the weather, courtesy, and talking with your bait shop clerk.

The most popular sport fishes in Rend Lake are black and white crappie, white bass, largemouth bass, bluegill, black and yellow perch and channel catfish. Other species occasionally caught by anglers are green and longear sunfish, carp, bowfin, freshwater drum, warmouth and yellow bass. White bass, not normally found in southern Illinois, were stocked many years ago and are now offer an excellent summer and fall opportunity.

Anglers should try fishing in the spillway and auxiliary channel below the dam. More than 24 species have been caught in this area, with crappies, bullheads, carp, drum and bluegill being the most frequently caught.

Crappie fishing is best during spring and fall, and is good through the ice. In the summer try catching them in their deep haunts. Use small hooks, No. 2-6, with minnows or other small live bait. A quill bobber or a spinner blade with an 1/8 ounce weight six inches above the lure also works well. Tightlining, using all of the above except the bobber, is popular, along with a light jigging action with a maribou jig or plastic beetle. Shoreline anglers can try the rip-rap causeways or spillway areas. Let your bait drift in these areas, teasing the crappies out from the cover. In clear water try a tiny spinner near structures, like pillars, steep banks, stickups and so on. Hand-size eaters are taken during most of the year. Try some lantern crappie fishing at the lake; you'll be surprised how well you'll do!

Largemouth bass, the "king" of sportfishing at Rend Lake, attracts tournament anglers and pilots who own huge tackle boxes and fancy electronics, cruising much of the lake's surface. Bass angling on the lake is best from early April to mid-June and again in early September to mid-October, when the water temperature is between 55 and 75 degrees. The best spots to fish in the spring or fall are shorelines, rock riprap, or shallow, brushy or weedy areas that are used either for spawning or protective cover.

When the water reaches 80 degrees move your efforts to deeper waters or cooler waters along step banks, in river or creek channels, or old pond beds and spring seeps that have cover. Plastic worms, deep diving plugs and spinner baits work during this time of the year. Fish will move morning and evening to shallow waters for feeding.

Ounce for ounce, bluegills offer the fastest action on any lake. At Rend Lake, the scrappy fighter is easy to catch on fly or ultra-light tackle, and make fine eating when fried over the camp stove or fire. The best bluegill fishing is from May through mid-June when they are on spawning beds, typically in two to five feet of water. Once you have located these areas, crickets, grubs, redworms, small minnows, or grasshoppers will start the action.

After spawning time, bluegills dispense to the shady cover of stickups, floating logs, undercut banks and rock riprap to spend the summer and early fall. Summer evenings are a great time to use your fly rod to cast for fish coming to the surface feeding on emerging insects. If you don't like the fly rod, try casting a light spinner or a wet fly with bobber. Through the ice, waxworms are productive.

Channel catfish are the most popular species with local anglers, and many visiting anglers to the region. First stocked in 1974, channel cats have increased annually. The fish run from early May until mid-October. Peaks of good fishing occur whenever there's a rise in pool level, especially in the shallower bays influenced by the tributary stream. Channel catfish spawn in June and early July when the water temperature reaches about 75 degrees. After the eggs are laid, the males protect the young until they break into schools at about two inches in size.

Channel cats typically feed at night, but they can be caught in murky water or in holes during the daylight hours. As usual, stink baits, any bait that gives off a strong smell such as cheese, blood, soured fish, clam or liver, can work on jumbo cats. Pole and line fishermen will do well in the river and creek channels, or bay and shoreline areas where there are mud and sand bottoms. Slip sinkers and crayfish, minnows, worms, shrimp, liver, sour clams and leeches will often attract the attention of hungry channel catfish.

Channel catfish taken from Rend Lake waters are considered excellent eating when fried crisp and served with barbecued beans, salad and ice cold beer.

White bass were planted in the lake in 1971 and have become a popular sport fish. Early spawning is a good time to try riprap areas along the dam and Route 183. After spawning, during late May and early June, the fish can be caught in the shallow flats during the early morning and late evening hours. Any bright colored spinner or spoon can catch their attention. Try off the dam, I-57, Marcum Beach, Sandusky Creek Bay and around the islands.

Hiking: Nine miles of horseback riding trails are sometimes chewed up and difficult to walk. Only one hiking trail is inside the state park, and it is a flat 1.5-mile trek through a mixed deciduous wooded area. A more interesting hiking trail is the Blackberry Trail, at Sandusky Recreation Area, south of the state park. The easy trail has a brochure available from the visitors center that offers brief identification and interpretive information.

Day-use areas: There are two public beaches on the south side of the federal area, call (618) 724-2493, and one beach at the park. There are three reservable picnic shelters, and one jumbo shelter at the resort. About 100 picnic tables are scattered throughout the park.

The nearby Rend Lake Visitor Center offers a number of natural history and environmental science programs each summer. Call (618) 435-2765.

Special notes: Regional and national dog trails test the speed, training and endurance of fine hunting dogs. Some of the finest dogs and trainers in the nation come to the area annually. Watching these events is fun for the entire family.

Nearby attractions: Southern Illinois Arts and Craft Market, Mitchell Art Museum, Jent Factory Outlet Mall, Factory Stores of America and Petticoat Corner, a country Western dance hall.

62 Weinberg-King State Park

Land: 772 acres   Water: 3.8-acre pond

There are more small wooded areas than farmlands in the gently rolling terrain surrounding the very rural, lightly used Weinberg-King State Park in Schuyler County. In 1969, Gertrude K. Allen, deeded lands to the state in a brief informal ceremony which comprises 500 acres of the park's current holdings.

The land gift commemorated her parents, the late Frederick M. and Fredericka Weinberg-King, and her three brothers. The state Legislature honored the kind action of the 85-year-old benefactor by officially naming the area Weinberg-King State Park.

The lands were valued at $250,000 and maintained as a permanent pasture. A poultry farm and later a "turkey house" was operated and later removed to make way for the main park entrance. The natural rolling terrain and steep hillsides feature many mature trees that include tall locust, osage orange, and many species of wildflowers.

Information and Activities

Weinberg-King State Park
P.O Box 203
Augusta, IL 62311
(217) 392-2345

Directions: Three miles east of Augusta on Illinois Route 100.

Camping: Both tent/trailers (Class C) and horse camping are on the first road to the left upon entering the park, past the tiny pond that is dotted with wood duck nesting boxes, a half-dozen picnic tables and a small fishing pier. All campers need to obtain a camping permit from the park ranger, whose office is in a low brown-colored building that is open by chance. The small staff is often in the park working. The campground has a nice view of the wooded valley, but is in other ways mostly open and lightly shaded. The six-acre tent camping area is sparse and lightly used, but there are basic amenities that include water, picnic table, dump station, litter barrels, shelters and fire pits.

Fishing: William Creek contain bluegills, bullhead, channel catfish and smallmouth bass for bank anglers.

Hiking: Horseback riding trails, 15 miles in wooded and field areas, are closed during hunting season. The Blackberry Run Trail is at the end of the eastern day-use area near the wildlife viewing area.

Day-use areas: Each picnic shelter is at a dead end, and is as private as you can get in a state park. The light use of the park makes this an excellent choice for family outings. All of these private day-use or picnicking areas have small playground equipment, toilets and water.

Hunting: Upland game hunting is considered excellent, the spring turkey season is popular.

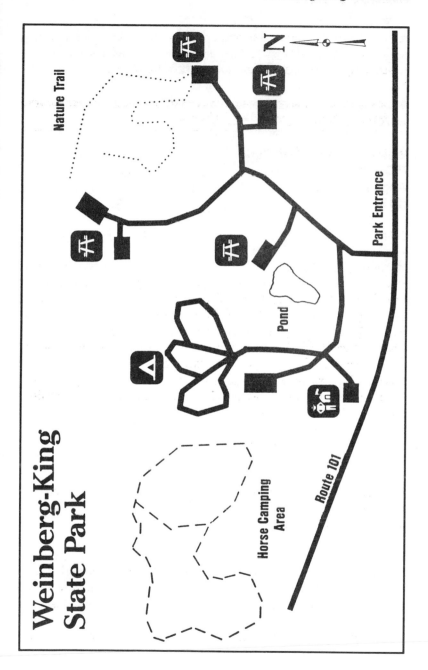

63 Weldon Spring State Park

Land: 370 acres   Water: 29.4-acre lake

The two tiny springs that gurgle and flow down a narrow concrete raceway are under a canopy of mature trees in a cheery setting that frames the view of the lake and modern concession stand, boating and anglers tipping their rods up and down in the distance. Weldon Spring, which has a 135-year tradition of providing relaxing enjoyment to its visitors, is one of the best family-oriented state parks in the system.

Why? History, year-round activities, seven miles of terrific trails, a fine campground, horseshoe courts like you've never seen before, great food at the concession stand, fishing, boating, and my favorite, the one-room Union School Interpretive Center.

After growing up in a family with many teachers, a couple of whom spent more than half of their careers teaching in a one-room school house, I found the Union School Interpretive Center the highlight of the park. The white clapboard school was built in 1865 and once stood in a grove of oak trees two miles north of Chestnut, Illinois, where it served the students of Aetna Township, in Logan County until it was closed in the mid-1940s. The building was donated to the Weldon Spring Foundation by the family of George Bunn, and has been lovingly restored. It is now used as an outdoor education center for area youth and visitors to the park.

The citizens of DeWitt County have donated funds, services, time and materials to move the structure and get it open for business. The center is staffed by volunteers and operated by a cooperative effort of the park and Friends of the Union School. Summer interns ususally staff the center during the summer, while volunteers keep the center open on most Sunday afternoons, 2-4 p.m.

Inside the school house is a restored classroom, complete with learning material, wooden teacher's desk, fire stove, clock, old books and slates, and row upon row of classroom-style seats. In small rooms off the classroom are natural history displays that include native animal mounts, hands-on learning centers, maps and other interpretive displays that explain the park history and natural areas in the unit. An impressive snowy owl is near other natural materials that include nests (including a hummingbird nest the size of a walnut), furs, horns, plants and many other interpretive items.

Outside of the school is a very nice prairie area with plant specimens and interpretive planting beds, eastern bluebird nesting boxes, and a short trail through the restored grasslands.

Information and Activities

Weldon Springs State Park
R.R. 2, P. O. Box 87
Clinton, IL 62727
(217) 935-2644

Directions: Three miles southeast of Clinton, in DeWitt County.

Information: The park office is open daily, November to March, 10:30 a.m. - noon and 12:30 p.m. - 3:30 p.m; April to October, 8:30 a.m. - noon and 12:30 p.m. to 4 p.m. The office is near the entrance and has a well-stocked brochure rack. They also sell nifty Weldon Springs T-shirts.

For information about neighboring Clinton Lake Recreation Area, a high-energy, developed area for boating, fishing in the 4,900-acre lake, swimming at the 1,000-foot beach, hiking, camping at 300 Class B sites, and many fine day-use areas, call (217) 935-8722.

Campground: There are 78 camping sites in the traditional campground that has a newer shower building. Nearby group camping for up to 300 is available in the Black Locust area. Youth camping is possible at Long Point by advanced registration. The entire campground will strike you as the perfect family campground. By the way, watch out for the "little ones" riding all sizes of bikes and Big Wheels along the hard-surfaced campground lane.

Site 61 is a great camping site for the disabled, with a valley view, hard-surfaced pad and near the toilets. A few years ago *Family Circle Magazine* named Weldon Springs campground one of the 10 best, and it's easy to see why. Plenty of shade, rolling terrain, privacy and quality grounds maintenance is obvious.

Sites 14 and 16 have a nearby trailhead that connects to the outdoor amphitheater. All sites in the 20s, 30s and 40s are shady and perfect for a weekend getaway.

Maybe the finest loop in the campground is sites 61-70 with shade, privacy and areas where you can park your boat trailer. Sites 71 and 73 have a slight view of the lake through the thick understory. Camping sites in the center of the campground are delightfully shady by lovely sycamore trees and other mature giants. Most any size RV rig can fit into this area with room to spare.

The Lakeview concession stand is open Tuesday - Sunday, 7 a.m. - 7 p.m., with snacks, full meals, bait, supplies, volleyball equipment, paddle/john boat rental, ice and firewood. The chicken sandwiches and ice cream are great!

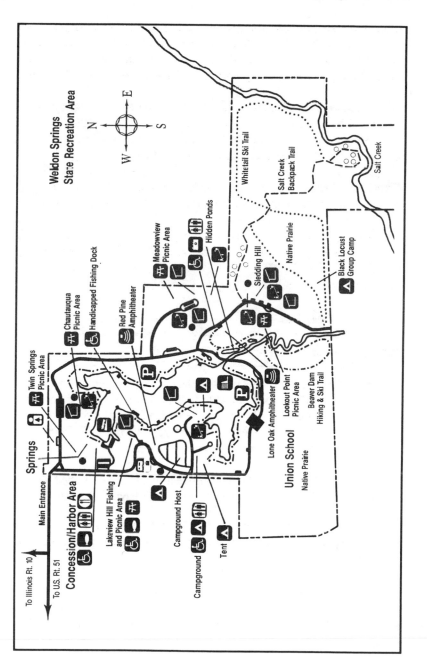

Weldon Spring State Park

Weldon Springs
State Recreation Area

Chautauqua Picnic Area

Handicapped Fishing Dock

Red Pine Amphitheater

Meadowview Picnic Area

Hidden Ponds

Whitetail Ski Trail

Salt Creek Backpack Trail

Salt Creek

Sledding Hill

Native Prairie

Black Locust Group Camp

Twin Springs Picnic Area

Springs

Main Entrance

To Illinois Rt. 10

To U.S. Rt. 51

Concession/Harbor Area

Lakeview Hill Fishing and Picnic Area

Campground Host

Campground

Tent

Lone Oak Amphitheater

Lookout Point Picnic Area

Union School

Native Prairie

Beaver Dam Hiking & Ski Trail

335

Union School outdoor education center.

Emergency information: If you should hear a steady siren for two to five minutes, you should tune your radio to 1340 AM or 102.9 FM. Emergency numbers: ambulance, 935-4444; fire, 935-3159; sheriff, 935-3196; state police, (815) 844-3131. In case of drowning, call 935-9596. Phones are at the boat dock, park office and concession area.

Boating: The one-lane boat ramp below the little arched bridge connects the day-use area to Lakeside Trail. Boats are restricted to electric motors.

Fishing: Black bullhead, carp, brown bullhead, golden shiner, crappies, channel catfish, largemouth bass, redear sunfish and bluegill are commonly taken. There are six fishing docks around the lake, many of the docks are handicapped accessible.

Local experts say some of the best fishing in the tiny lake is near the point by the youth camping area at the southwest end of the lake. Generally,

The spring-fed lake is calm and popular with families.

fishing is fair, with evening shoreline fishing a wonderful chance for youngsters to catch small panfish.

The lake, built in 1900 and enlarged in 1930, is spring-fed and can reach maximum depths of 28 feet, with an average depth of about 10 feet, and 1.9 miles of mostly tree-lined shore.

Creel limits: largemouth bass, 14-inch minimum, six per day; channel catfish, six per day; trot lines and bank poles are prohibited. Please do not discard bait minnow or fishing line into the lake.

Hiking: Near the boat ramp is the two-mile Lakeside Self-Guided Nature Trail that circles the lake over moderate terrain. The trail passes 29 marked posts that accompany a self-guided brochure available at the office or the concession stand. The trail will take more than two hours if you stop and read the brochure at each labeled station. You will likely see indications of beavers working the shorelines, black walnuts and thick

337

red cedar, the dam and spillway, a bald cypress tree, a ravine of sycamore and lush vegetation, and a grove of oaks and springs.

Day-use areas: Hard-surfaced trails and many horseshoe and volleyball courts are available. A sign in front of the lake near the central day-use area says, "It takes 12 years for a cigarette butt to decompose. We appreciate your cooperation in placing cigarette butts in the containers provided, not on the ground."

A performance stage is near the springs at the front of the park. There are eight large picnic areas, six with shelters. Most day-use areas have tables, cooking grills, water hydrants, toilets and lots of parking and open space. One day-use area has a volleyball court or you can install portable volleyball equipment available at the concession stand.

Nature: Visit Union School and pick up a birder's checklist to learn about prairie flora and much more.

Nearby attractions: Clinton Lake Recreation Area; the Homestead, a mid-Victorian mansion--call (217) 935-6066 for tour information; "Leave the Concrete Behind" is the marketing tagline used by the DeWitt County Tourism Council. Call them for information at (217) 935-3364.

64 White Pines Forest State Park

Land: 385 acres   Water: creeks

In the spring wildflowers bloom madly; in the summer hikers take to the paradise-like walks of whispering pines; in the fall the limestone bluffs flush with splashes of crimson and gold; and in the winter, when a soft blanket of snow covers the park, a white peacefulness washes the terrain.

The 385-acre unit offers seven marked trails of varying difficulty, most of which are less than a mile in length and wander on the east side of Pine Creek. Razor Back Trail takes you atop the bluff on the park's south side. Picnicking, pine trees, four camping areas, fishing Pine Creek—becomes a lost memory until you enter the lovely dinner theater and lodge complex. The theater is a terrific compliment to the towering pines and soft songs of flickering birds, offering the best of civilization, live entertainment and fine spirits nestled under a canopy of trees next to tiny log cabins that are almost always occupied by urban warriors on vacation.

Built by the Civilian Conservation Corps in the 1930s, White Pines Inn has recently undergone extensive but historically sensitive restoration that kept the flavor of the lodge and skillfully blended updating the accommodation with its historic setting.

White Pines Forest State Park is one of the most developed in the system, located in the heart of the Rock River Valley. The park rests along the boundary of the old Chicago-Iowa Trail, which was once the principal route for east and west travel across the northern part of the state. The moss-covered cliffs, strung with vines, frames the interesting concrete fords that span the creeks in two places, allowing visitors to actually drive through the flowing stream.

This is the first time I have seen concrete fords I could drive through that connect day-use areas of the park and campground. On my first visit to the park, on a quiet very warm July weekday, I couldn't help stopping my car right in the middle of the 30-foot-wide ford, open my car door, step out of the car and immediately fall on my face—emerging soaked from head to toe in the cold waters. It seems I forget that the green plant material growing on the concrete just under the surface of the five-inch-deep water is slipprier than spit on marble. Use caution, but do dip your feet in the cold creek waters.

Information and Activities

White Pines Forest State Park
6712 West Pines Road
Mt. Morris, IL 61054
(815) 946-3717

Directions: About two hours west of Chicago, near Mt Morris, take I-64 to Mt. Morris and follow the signs.

Campground: The terrain is gently rolling, wooded and mostly shaded. It offers four campgrounds where you can choose your own site. Many

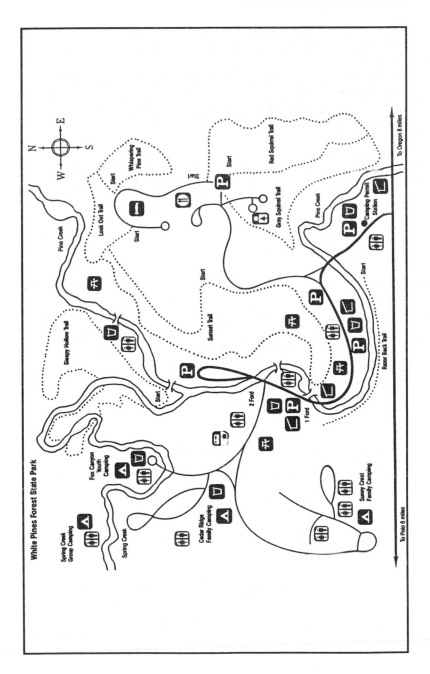

pines have been planted in the campground and there are sites with overlooks to agricultural lands and along towering groves of white pines. There are 107 Class C sites. High water can close the campground in the spring or after heavy rains.

On the route to the southern campground is a large day-use area offering access to a creek. The bluffs and sheer rock walls are a backdrop to the quiet areas scattered and separated along the roadway.

Be sure to check your brakes after crossing the ford that you must cross to enter the rolling campground. There is a seasonal camp store.

Sites 83-90 back up against a thin grove of white pine. If you like a view check out sites 101, 103 and 104; open sites 50-61 have grass pads. Camping under the pines can provide shade without blocking all of the breezes. After the early part of the season, small droplets of pine sap usually stop.

Sites 23 and 24 are on a point that overlooks a tranquil crop field. Sites 35-48 are along the grove of pines. There is firewood sold at the concession stand near the lodge.

Cabins: The park features 25 one-room guest cabins and 12 with adjoining rooms. Each cabin sleeps four people and includes its own bathroom and shower, one double bed and two twin beds. The "Sweetheart" cabin offers a canopy waterbed. All cabins are air-conditioned and heated, and have telephones and television. The traditional-looking cabins are neat, clean, modern and open year-round. The cabins are behind the inn with a a shady courtyard separating them. Nearby are sand volleyball and horseshoe courts. The cabins are almost always full on weekends; they are about 75 percent occupied Monday-Thursday.

Inn: The lodge is built of huge timbers and features a historic lounge with a giant stone fireplace and gift shop that offers countrycrafts made by local artisans. Entertainment at the lodge includes the dinner theatre, which runs much of the year, and a piano bar for evening relaxation. The dinner theater features chorus shows, one-man plays, comedy plays, revues, roaring '20s, murder mystery dinners, skits, and many professional productions. Phone (815) 946-3817 for information and cabin

The park operates a dinner theater, historic lodge, guest cottages, gift shop and lounge.

reservations. Closed during January and February.

Emergency numbers: 911; sheriff (non emergency) (815) 732-2136; state police, 625-0151; hospital, 288-5531; towing, 946-3921. There is a phone at the camp office and pop office.

Boating: There is no boating on the small creeks that run along the bases of the rock-faced bluffs.

Fishing: The smallmouth bass fishery in the two creeks is being restored, and rainbow trout are planted each spring to compliment catfish and bluegill. About 20,000 smallmouth bass are planted on a regular basis. Local anglers keep it simple, using nightcrawlers and tiny spinners. Bluegill action is good when they are on the beds in the spring. Bait is sold at the concession stand. The Pine Creek is 16 miles long, with some crappie and sunfish taken at various locations. The maximum depth of the creek is 12 feet.

Hiking: There are seven trails of varying difficulty, six of which are less than a mile long. All of the trails are loops that start and end in the same place. Gray Squirrel Trail (7/8 mile) and Red Squirrel Trail (5/8 mile) are rolling gentle trails near the inn. The Sleepy Hollow Trail (1.4 miles) is difficult and takes you by Fox Canyon, at the youth campground area and crosses Spring Creek in four places.

Whispering Pines is a three-quarter-mile self-guided trail with 13-marked posts that match a brochure that offers descriptions of natural history features, tree identification, wild berries, examples of habitats and much more. The trail is near the inn on the northeast corner of the unit.

Day-use areas: There are plenty of places for picnicking and family outings. Four picnic shelters are maintained, with two of them reservable. Playground equipment is located along Pine Creek Drive and in other scattered areas. There are brochures and information at the camp office.

Near the campground entrance is a tree identification area (arboretum) that features single specimens of species of trees that are found in the area. The trees are well separated and labeled, and there is a handy White Pines Forest State Park Tree Identification Guide available at the main office. Trees in this area include black cherry, bitternut hickory, black oak, shagbark hickory, walnut and mulberry. There's about 25 species featured. Across the road are a ball diamond and lots of open spaces. The bluffs and rock walls along the creeks act as a stage for picnicking areas and peaceful open spaces along the roadway. Climbing in the park is not allowed.

Nature: There is a significant effort to replant white pine throughout the park, and there is one area with some very old white pine stands. I saw many common flickers along the creek, swallows, and terrific wildflower displays. Use the self-guided nature trail for a nature tour. Sleepy Hollow Trail is an excellent natural area and takes about 1.5 hours to hike.

Winter: Cross-county skiing and sledding.

Nearby attractions: White Pines Deer Park (kid's zoo), White Pines Riding Stable, John Deere Historic Site in Grand Detour. Go-kart track with miniature golf attraction on Pine Road, near the deer park.

65   *Wolf Creek State Park*

Land: 2,000 acres   Water: Lake Shelbyville, 11,000 acres

Wolf Creek and Eagle Creek state parks face each other across the central portion of Lake Shelbyville, providing the perfect setting for outdoor recreation and relaxation. For details about fishing, the lake and region, see the section on neighboring Eagle Creek State Park.

In central Illinois, just minutes from Decatur and Champaign, the state park is adjacent to thousands of acres of carefully designed and maintained facilities operated by the Corps of Engineers for camping, boating, windsurfing, fishing, horseback riding, swimming, hunting, hiking and camping. Aside from the amenities and activities at the state park is a terrific side trip to the Lake Shelbyville Fish and Wildlife Management Area. It has nearly 6,000 acres of mixed habitats, places for great canoeing, fishing in ponds or two rivers, nature study, hikes, six boat launches, and hunting.

You can stop at the park office or the Corps' Visitor Center and pick up a Lake Shelbyville map that provides detail about recreation facilities, directions and ideas for things to do in the area. The region has many small communities that feature tourist attractions, shopping, great dining, and lodging. Many campers at Wolf Creek enjoy day trips around the area, or a nearby jaunt to ice cream shops in the evening.

Information and Activities

Wolf Creek State Park
R.R. 1, P.O. Box 99
Windsor, IL 61957
(217) 459-2831

Directions: On the east side of Lake Shelbyville, eight miles northwest of Windsor.

Information: Park is open 6 a.m. - 10 p.m., except for campers and boaters.

Campground: Wolf Creek allows advanced registration by mail or in person for the Lick Creek (140 sites) camping area for a $5 non-refundable fee. For more information, call (217) 756-8260. From April - October, call (217) 459-2831. Rent-a-camps are also operated at the park.

There are 304 Class A camping sites with restrooms and showers, electricity and picnic tables and 78 Class C sites, and two family tent camping areas. There are also group and equestrian camping areas.

Campground hosts are available for information. They agreed that sites in Owl Circle are the most popular with the camping public.

Site 16 is shady and fairly private in Owl Circle, while 36-55 in the Bent Oak area are compact. 44, 46 and 48 are shady. Site 51 is good for a small

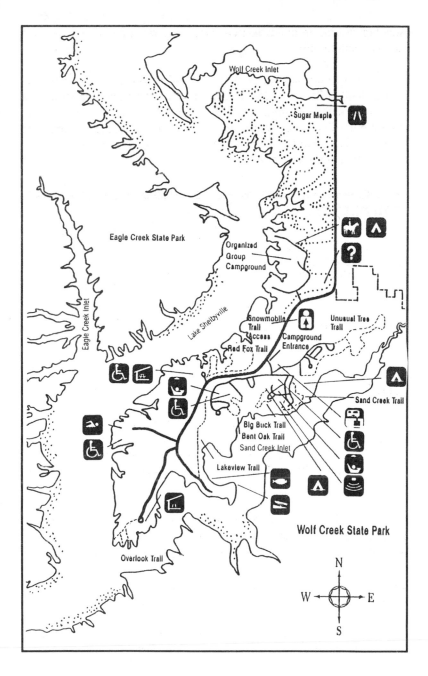

Wolf Creek Inlet

Sugar Maple

Eagle Creek State Park

Organized Group Campground

Eagle Creek Inlet

Lake Shelbyville

Snowmobile Trail Access

Campground Entrance

Unusual Tree Trail

Red Fox Trail

Sand Creek Trail

Big Buck Trail

Bent Oak Trail

Sand Creek Inlet

Lakeview Trail

Wolf Creek State Park

Overlook Trail

N
W — E
S

The campground is large and shady and campground hosts are on-duty.

RV unit. The Bent Spoke Trail is at the end of this loop. On both sides of the Bent Oak area the rear of each camping site is backed up against a wood line.

Off of Red Fox Lane, the main campground road, is site 65 that backs into a small wooded area. Most of sites 61-90 are very open, with 80 and 82 hard-surfaced for disabled campers. All of the sites in all of the loops have picnic tables, fire boxes and nearby water. The showers are near sites 81 and 82.

At the southern most loop (sites 92-141), there are rent-a-camps at sites 129 and 130. Sites 105 and 106 are excellent private sites set under mature trees and likely to be quiet. Frankly, this entire loop, 100-141, is shady and nice. Even the 78-site overflow area is well-maintained and good for weekend outings.

Sand Creek, which on the map looks a little like the ears of Mickey

The old Quigley Cemetery has some interesting headstones.

Mouse, is small but popular. There are no trees for shade in the center where the playground and shower are located. The little loop from 211-230 is shady and level. Site 225 are probably the most private in this loop. The Fisherman's Circle loop is near the amphitheater. The entire loop is pleasant and a good choice, especially if you like to play on the nearby horseshoe court.

One of the best sites in the campground is site 306.

The walk-in tent camping areas are at the end of this loop across from site 125. Sites A-H are busy, shady, private and dry.

The horse and group camping areas are near Quigley Cemetery, which overlooks the lake. The horse camping is among the best in the system, with lots of shade, private camping sites, mature trees, excellent trails (Timberline Trail, 15 miles) and hitching posts at virtually every camping site. The campground is often busy with organized riding groups. Sites are plenty large enough to back your big gooseneck trailers into.

Emergency numbers: sheriff, 774-3941; state police, 1-867-2211; ambulance, 459-2311; rescue squad, 1-774-3433; fire, 459-2300.

Boating: Good to excellent fishing keeps the huge four-lane boat launch busy on weekends and overflowing on holidays. Nearly 200 cars can be packed into the ramp parking lot. There are plenty of day-use amenities, including a fish cleaning station, in the ramp area. There are boat rental and other marina supplies in the area.

Fishing: There's great fishing in the lake. Check the information in the fishing section for Eagle Creek State Park.

Hiking: Wolf Creek offers seven hiking trails, a 16-mile snowmobile trail, and a 15-mile equestrian system of trails at the north end of the park.

The Red Fox Trail is a 2.5-mile hike beginning at the Red Fox picnic area. It explores a heavily wooded area that leads to several scenic overlooks on the lake. There are three loops.

Overlook Trail, .75-mile hike begins at the end of the overlook drive. It has three forks that lead to views of the lake.

Unusual Tree Trail is a 1.75-mile trail with two main entrances and two loops. *Sand Creek Trail* is a 3.4-mile trail that begins in the Sand Creek camping area and ends up by the amphitheater at Fisherman's Circle.

Big Buck Trail is a moderate half-mile trail also at Sand Creek. It offers a loop that leads to the lake. *Bent Oak Trail* is a moderately difficult one-mile walk departing from the Lick Creek Campground that leads hikers through ravines.

Day-use areas: Beach hours are 10 a.m. - 8 p.m. It is located at the end of the road just before Lookout Trail. There is a small fee levied at the dark-colored, sandy, 100-yards-wide beach. Changing houses, play equipment and six picnic tables are at the small swimming area. There is no lifeguard on duty.

South of the beach, at the southern tip of the park, is the overlook day-use area with a reservable picnic shelter, about 15 tables, water, toilets and open spaces.

About the author

Bill Bailey is one of America's foremost experts on outdoor recreation, environmental education and public information. He is the author of 15 books including *Ohio State Parks, Kentucky State Parks, Thrill Sports, New York State Parks* and *Penn. State Parks* guidebooks. Bill is a former executive director of a large environmental eduction center; chief naturalist; communications consultant; publisher and senior public administrator. He lives with his wife and two sons in Saginaw, Michigan.